Contents

KU-494-148

The world around us

Acknowledgements

Joy Godwin wrote two new units for the Second Edition: Unit 64, *Mobile devices*, and Unit 70, *Academic writing*. The publishers would like to thank Joy for her contribution to this edition.

The authors and publishers acknowledge the following sources of copyright material and are grateful for the permissions granted. While every effort has been made, it has not always been possible to identify the sources of all the material used, or to trace all copyright holders. If any omissions are brought to our notice, we will be happy to include the appropriate acknowledgements on reprinting and in the next update to the digital edition, as applicable.

Key: BL = Below Left, BR = Below Right, CR = Centre Right, CL = Centre Left, TL = Top Left, TR = Top Right.

Photographs

All the photographs are sourced from Getty Images.

p. 9: John P Kelly/The Image Bank; p. 13: beyhanyazar/iStock; p. 14 (photo 1): Tom Merton/OJO Images; p. 14 (photo 2): Bruce Forster/The Images Bank; p. 14 (photo 3): Westend61; p. 26 (TR): Alex Wilson/DigitalVision; p. 26 (CR): John Short/Perspectives; p. 26 (BR): Matt Cardy/Stringer; p. 35: Adisorn Sutthiwanich/EyeEm; p. 37 (TL): Sam Diephuis/Blend Images; p. 37 (CL): ronniechua/iStock; p. 37 (BL) & p. 120: Hero Images; p. 37 (TR): Hill Street Studios/Blend Images; p. 37 (CR): Alistair Berg/DigitalVision; p. 37 (BR): Richard Drury/Stone; p. 38: Radius Images; p. 41: Rob Stothard/Stringer; p. 50: Yuri_Arcurs/DigitalVision; p. 51: Images Etc Ltd/Photographer's Choice RF; p. 53 (photo 1): Allan Baxter/Photolibrary; p. 53 (photo 2): KenWiedemann/iStock; p. 53 (photo 3): Richard Nebesky/Lonely Planet Images; p. 53 (photo 4): Zoonar RF/Zoonar/Getty Images Plus; p. 53 (photo 5): Trinette Reed/Blend table; p. 55: FOXYPEAM/Moment Open; p. 56: Daly and Newton/OJO Images; p. 57 (TL): Image Source; p. 57 (TR): Claver Carroll/Photolibrary; p. 60: Zubin Shroff/Stone; p. 63 (photo 1): Auscape/UIG/Universal Images Group; p. 63 (photo 2): Mark de Leeuw; p. 63 (photo 3): Jose Luis Pelaez/The Image Bank; p. 63 (photo 4): lissart/iStock/Getty Images Plus; p. 63 (photo 5): David Malan/Photographer's Choice; p. 63 (photo 6): Mike Kemp/Blend Images; p. 64: gpointstudio/iStock; p. 65 (photo 1): Cbpictures/Westend61; p. 65 (photo 2): Flying Colours Ltd/DigitalVision; p. 65 (photo 3): eyjafjallajokull/iStock; p. 66: Hoxton/Martin Barraud; p. 67: bowdenimages/iStock; p. 68 (CL): Ray Kachatorian/The Image Bank; p. 68 (BL): phbcz/iStock; p. 68 (CR): Antenna; p. 70: inhauscreative/iStock/Getty Images Plus; p. 76: vadimguzhva/iStock; p. 79: Nico Kai/The Image Bank; p. 81: Roberto Machado Noa/LightRocket; p. 84: David Lees/DigitalVision; p. 85 (TL) & (CL): Juanmonino/E+; p. 85 (TR): John Rensten/Photographer's Choice; p. 85 (CR): Tooga/The Image Bank; p. 85 (BL): visualspace/iStock; p. 87: Commercial Eye/The Image Bank; p. 88: Peter Dazeley/Photographer's Choice; p. 90: Wavebreakmedia Ltd/Getty Images Plus; p. 92 (TL): asiseeit/E+; p. 92 (BR): sturti/Vetta; p. 95: Claudia Burlotti/Stone; p. 102: Jetta Productions/Blend Images; p. 104 (TR): EmirMemedovski/E+; p. 104 (BR): Kevin C Moore/Cultura; p. 104 (CR): PeopleImages/DigitalVision; p. 108: Amos Morgan/Photodisc; p. 119 (photo 1): Bernhard Lang/The Image Bank; p. 119 (photo 2): Michal Venera/Photolibrary; p. 119 (photo 3): Vasily Pindyurin; p. 126: Ken Redding/Corbis; p. 128 (TR): Carl Court; p. 128 (BR): romrodinka/iStock; p. 132 (iphone): ET-ARTWORKS/iStock/Getty Images Plus; p. 132 (tablet): Maciej Frolow/Photographer's Choice; p. 132 (netbook): Angelika-Angelika/iStock/Getty Images Plus; p. 133: drbimages/E+; p. 136: 123ducu/iStock; p. 140: DEA/W. BUSS; p. 145: Paul Bradbury/Caiaimage.

Illustrations

Ludmila (KJA Artists), Katie Mac (NB Illustration), Gavin Reece (New Division) and Miguel Diaz Rivas (Advocate Art).

Cambridge Dictionaries

Cambridge Dictionaries are the world's most widely used dictionaries for learners of English. The dictionaries are available in print and online at dictionary.cambridge.org. Copyright © Cambridge University Press, reproduced with permission.

Using this book

Why was this book written?

It was written to help you improve your knowledge of phrasal verbs in English. Phrasal verbs are verbs which have a main verb and a particle which, together, create one meaning (e.g. a plane *takes off* from the airport; an adult *looks after* a child). You will come across a great many phrasal verbs when you listen to and read English, and so it is important that you learn about their meanings and about how they are used. You can use this book either with a teacher or for self-study.

There are more than 5,000 phrasal verbs and related noun and adjective forms in use in English. This book focuses just on those phrasal verbs which you need to know for everyday spoken and written communication in English, and it aims to provide the information and practice which will help you understand and use them correctly.

How were the phrasal verbs in the book selected?

The approximately 1,000 phrasal verbs and related noun and adjective forms which are presented in this book were mainly selected from those identified as significant by the CANCODE corpus of spoken English developed at the University of Nottingham in association with Cambridge University Press, and the Cambridge International Corpus of written and spoken English (now known as the Cambridge English Corpus). You can also find them in the Cambridge Dictionary online by going to the following website: http://dictionary.cambridge.org

How is the book organised?

The book has 70 two-page units. The left-hand page explains the phrasal verbs that are presented in the unit. You will usually find an explanation of the meaning of each phrasal verb, an example of it in use and, where appropriate, any special notes about its usage. The right-hand page checks that you have understood the information on the left-hand page by giving you a series of exercises that practise the material just presented. The exercises pay particular attention to checking understanding of the phrasal verbs and how they are used so that you will be able to use them accurately and appropriately.

The units are organised into different sections:

First we start with important information about phrasal verbs in general (Units 1–5): what they are, how their grammar works and so on. This is an important training section, and we recommend you do these units first.

After the introductory units, there are units on the most common verbs which are used to form phrasal verbs (Units 6–12) and units on the most common particles found in phrasal verbs (Units 13–21).

The rest of the book teaches you the phrasal verbs which are associated with particular concepts (e.g. time), functions (e.g. giving and getting information) and topics (e.g. business, feelings, student life).

The book also has a key to all the exercises so that you can check your answers. At the back of this book, you will find a useful Mini dictionary. This provides clear definitions of all the phrasal verbs and related noun and adjective forms that appear in this book. The Mini dictionary also indicates the unit number where you can find a particular phrasal verb.

How should I use this book?

It is strongly recommended that you work through Units 1–5 first so that you become familiar with the way phrasal verbs operate and with the terminology that is used in the rest of the book. After that, you may work on the units in any order that suits you.

What else do I need in order to work with this book?

You need a notebook or file in which you can write down the phrasal verbs that you study in this book as well as any others that you come across elsewhere.

You also need to have access to a good dictionary. We strongly recommend the *Cambridge Phrasal Verbs Dictionary* as this gives exactly the kind of information that you need to have about phrasal verbs. Your teacher, however, may also be able to recommend other dictionaries that you will find useful.

We hope that this book will help you understand and use new or difficult phrasal verbs that crop up (see Unit 44 Student life: reading and writing) in your reading and listening in English and that, by the time you finish the units, you'll be saying: 'English phrasal verbs? Show me a new one and I'll figure out what it means in seconds!' (see Unit 69 American and Australian phrasal verbs).

1 Phrasal verbs: the basics

A What are phrasal verbs?

Phrasal verbs are verbs that consist of a verb and a particle.

verb	particle	example	meaning
look	**up**	You can **look up** any new words in your dictionary.	You can find the meaning of any new words in your dictionary.
go	**through**	I will **go through** your application form with you.	I will carefully read your application form and discuss it with you to make sure that it is correct.
make	**out**	I just can't **make** Jake **out** at all.	I just can't understand Jake's behaviour.

Particles are small words which you already know as prepositions or adverbs. Here are some of the most common phrasal verb particles:

about (a)round at away back down for in into off on out over through to up

B What do I need to know about phrasal verbs?

First you need to know the meaning of the whole phrasal verb as a unit. The Mini dictionary in this book will help you. For example, **look** means to use your eyes and **up** means the opposite of down, but the phrasal verb **look up** can have several different meanings:

Look the word **up** in the dictionary. [**look up** = search for information in a book/computer]

I'll **look** you **up** next time I'm in London. [**look up** = visit someone you have not seen for a long time]
Things are **looking up**. [**look up** = improve]

Next you need to know the grammar patterns of phrasal verbs, e.g. whether the verb takes an object. The table shows the way the grammar patterns are shown in this book and in many dictionaries. Note that *sth* means 'something'; *sb* means 'someone'.

grammar pattern	comment	example
eat out	the verb is used without an object	We were too tired to cook at home so we decided to **eat out**. [eat in a restaurant] Not: We decided to eat out a-meal.
bring back sth or **bring** sth **back**	the verb must have a non-human object	This photograph **brings back happy memories**. [makes me remember or think about something from the past] Not: This photograph brings back my-sister.
ask out sb or **ask** sb **out**	the verb must have a human object	I'd love to **ask Poppy out**. [invite Poppy to go to a place like a cinema or a restaurant] Not: I'd love to ask my-dog out.
look after sb/sth	the object can be either human or non-human	I'll **look after the baby** while you're cooking. Will you **look after my plants** while I'm away?
ring sb **back**	the object must come before the particle	I'll **ring you back** later. [phone you again] Not: I'll ring back you.
look after sb/sth	the object must come after the particle	Can you **look after the cat** while I'm away? Not: Can you look the dog after while I'm away?
drop off sb/sth or **drop** sb/sth **off**	the object can be before or after the particle	I **dropped off the present** at her house. [delivered/left] I dropped **the present** off at her house.

Exercises

1.1 **Underline the 11 phrasal verbs in these sentences.**

1 I sent off the order last week but the goods haven't turned up yet.
2 I came across an interesting book in the university library and noted down the title.
3 The starter motor was playing up and the car broke down when we stopped at the service station.
4 I brought up this item at the last meeting. It's really time to sort out the problem.
5 I wish he'd stop messing us about! He's put the meeting off three times and now he wants to call it off altogether.

1.2 **Match the 11 phrasal verbs from sentences 1–5 in exercise 1.1 above with their meanings from the box below.**

cause inconvenience		deal with	stop working	find	arrive	mail	cancel
write	postpone		not work properly	mention			

1.3 **Decide which of these sentences contain errors. Explain why they are wrong and suggest a correct answer. Use the table in B to help you.**

1 That song you just sang brings back memories of my days at college.
2 She looked the children after when their mother was in hospital.
3 I promised to ring my brother back. He called earlier when I was busy.
4 We ate out a wonderful dinner last night.
5 It was a beautiful summer evening so I asked the cat out for a drink.

1.4 **Sometimes phrasal verbs are followed by a particular preposition to make three-part verbs. Try to learn these prepositions with the phrasal verbs. Look at these examples of three-part verbs, and then complete the sentences below with a preposition from the box. Use a dictionary or the Mini dictionary at the back of this book if necessary.**

Cambridge Dictionary

dictionary.cambridge.org

EXAMPLES   I'm **looking forward** <u>to</u> the weekend.
                She's been **going out** <u>with</u> him for six months now.

with	against	with	on	with

1 She seems to **look down** .... on .... people who are less intelligent than her.
2 To save money, the company decided to **do away** .... with .... free parking for staff.
3 I **came up** .... against .... a serious problem when I tried to save my work.
4 How can some students **get away** .... with .... doing no work and yet pass the exams?
5 Her son is so horrible. I don't know how she **puts up** .... with .... him.

That's not what I meant when I said, 'Can you drop me off at the beach, please?'!

2 The meaning of phrasal verbs

A The most common verbs

Here are the most common verbs that form part of phrasal verbs:

break	bring	call	come	cut	get	give	go	keep	knock
look	make	pass	pick	pull	put	run	set	take	turn

Units 6–12 deal with a selection of these verbs which form a large number of useful, everyday phrasal verbs.

B Meanings

The basic meanings of the verbs in A refer to concrete actions (e.g. *break* means separate into pieces), but when they are part of phrasal verbs, they often have abstract meanings too. Sometimes the concrete meaning can help you guess the abstract meaning, for example, you can **look back** to wave goodbye to someone as you leave in a car (concrete meaning – look behind you), or you can **look back** on your past life (abstract meaning – remember or recall).

verb	concrete meaning	abstract meaning
give	I **gave** my worksheet **in** at the end of the lesson. [handed it to the teacher]	Her parents finally **gave in** and let her go to the party. [agreed to something they had refused before]
get	She **got on** the bus. [entered]	Leo and Ella don't **get on**. [don't like each other and are not friendly to each other]
come	Would you like to **come round** this evening? [come to my home]	He was unconscious for three hours but **came round** in hospital. [became conscious again]

C Synonyms of phrasal verbs

A phrasal verb can often be replaced by a single verb with more or less the same meaning. The single-verb synonyms are often, but not always, more formal (see Unit 5, section C).

phrasal verb	single-verb synonym
put off	postpone
take off	remove
turn up	arrive

less formal	more formal
Let's **put off** the meeting until Friday.	Let's **postpone** the meeting until Friday.
Please **take off** your shoes when you enter the temple.	Please **remove** your shoes when you enter the temple.
Everyone **turned up** on time for the meeting.	Everyone **arrived** on time for the meeting.

> **Tip**
>
> If you know a single-verb synonym of a phrasal verb, write it in your vocabulary notebook and note whether or not the phrasal verb is more informal.

Exercises

2.1 **Complete these sentences using verbs from the list in A opposite.**

1 The car b.. down on the way to the airport.
2 It took him a long time to g.. over his illness.
3 It isn't easy to learn German but you must k.. on trying.
4 If you'd like a lift to the station tomorrow, I can p.. you up at 9 a.m.
5 Please t.. off your phones. The performance is about to begin.
6 The heavy snow blocked the roads and c.. the farm off completely.

2.2 **In which of the sentences in exercise 2.1 above could you put the particle in a different position?**

2.3 **Decide whether the phrasal verbs in these sentences are concrete or abstract in meaning, by writing C for concrete or A for abstract in the brackets.**

EXAMPLE   He looked up (C) and saw a hot-air balloon in the sky.

1 I would never go against ( ) my parents' wishes.
2 Shall I cut out ( ) this recipe from the food magazine? It looks good and is quick and easy to make.
3 About five miles into our journey the engine cut out ( ) and we broke down ( ) completely. It was over an hour before the rescue service turned up ( ).
4 Do we need to dress up ( ) tonight or is it informal?
5 I shall never really appreciate what people went through ( ) during the war.

2.4 **Replace the underlined verbs in these sentences with phrasal verbs made using the verbs and particles from the boxes below. If necessary, use the Mini dictionary at the end of this book.**

make	chase	brush	leave	fall

up	for	out	aside	out

1 They just <u>ignored</u> my complaints; it made me very angry.
2 I <u>believed</u> his story about having lost all his money. How stupid I was!
3 I couldn't <u>understand</u> what he was saying with all the noise.
4 Could you <u>pursue</u> Emily's report? She promised it last week but I haven't seen it yet.
5 If you are phoning from outside the country, <u>omit</u> the first zero in the city code.

2.5 **Use more formal equivalents from the box instead of the phrasal verbs in these sentences. Write the formal verbs in the correct form.**

decline	issue	organise	cancel	escape

1 The government have put out a statement condemning the recent protests.
2 The union accepted the new pay deal and called off the strike.
3 The number of people not owning a smartphone nowadays has gone down dramatically.
4 There was a disturbance in Blackmoor Prison yesterday and three prisoners got away.
5 Could you see to lunch for our visitors? There will be four of them.

3 Particles in phrasal verbs

This unit looks at the role of particles in phrasal verbs. A particle is either a preposition (e.g. from, to, with) or an adverb (e.g. out, up, about). You can create phrasal verbs by adding different particles to a basic verb.

A What do particles mean?

In some phrasal verbs the particle has a clear basic meaning. Look at the examples of different particles used with the verb *invite*. On the right, you can see what the original speaker probably said.

Jack **invited** me **out**.	Jack	Let's go out together.
Rosie **invited** me **in**.	Rosie	Please come in!
Molly **invited** me **over**.	Molly	Come to our place.
Alex **invited** me **round**.	Alex	Come to my house for dinner or a drink.
James **invited** me **up**.	James	Come upstairs to my flat.
Mia **invited** me **along**.	Mia	Come with us!
Stan **invited** me **back**.	Stan	Come back home with me.

B What other meanings can particles have?

Most particles convey a number of different senses. For example, *over* can have various meanings, including:

a) changing position, e.g. in **fall over** [fall to the ground] or **move over** [change the place where you are sitting or standing to make room for someone else].

b) an idea of thoroughness, e.g. in **read over** [read thoroughly] or **talk over** [discuss something thoroughly before making a decision].

The meanings of particles are looked at in more detail in Units 13–21.

C Where does the particle go?

With verbs that have an object:

• Sometimes the particle has to go *before* the object of the verb,

  e.g. I'm **looking for** my keys (not: I'm looking my keys for).

• Sometimes it must go *after* the object,

  e.g. I **have** a lot of work **on** (not: I have on a lot of work).

• Sometimes the particle may go either *before* or *after* the object,

  e.g. The thunder **woke up** the children *or* The thunder **woke** the children **up**.

Note that if the object is a pronoun (e.g. him, them), then the particle must go *after* it,

e.g. The thunder **woke** them **up** (not: The thunder woke up them).

Exercises

3.1 **Look at section A and then answer the questions about these sentences.**

1 My brothers were going to the cinema and they asked me along.
Did the speaker go to the cinema on her own, with her brothers or do we not know for sure?
2 When I took Ruby a birthday present, she asked me in but I had to get to my lecture.
Did the speaker go into Ruby's house?
3 When I saw George on the balcony, he asked me up.
Who was in a higher position, George or the speaker?
4 When the Richardsons asked me back after the concert I was happy to accept.
Where did the speaker go after the concert?
5 My cousin has asked me to go over to his flat this evening.
What word could replace *over* with no change in meaning?

3.2 **Look at B opposite. Are the phrasal verbs underlined in the sentences below examples of the (a) or the (b) meanings of *over*?**

1 Think it over before you make up your mind what to do next.
2 You may turn over the page now and read the exam questions.
3 It's raining too hard to drive. Pull over to the edge of the road.
4 Look over your answers before the end of the exam.

3.3 **Look at C opposite. Then read these definitions and decide whether the sentences below are correct or incorrect. If necessary, correct them.**

> **have on** has, having, had
>
> **have sth on** to have an arrangement to do something (never in continuous tenses)
>
> **have sb on** to persuade someone that something is true when it is not, usually as a joke
>
> **have on sth** *or* **have sth on** if you have clothes or shoes on, you are wearing them (never in continuous tenses; never passive)

1 I have on three important meetings tomorrow.
2 John has an amazing tie on.
3 Sue was only having on her sisters when she told them she was planning to become a model.
4 I'm having a lot of work on today.
5 I don't believe you! I'm sure you're having me on.
6 Lola was wearing her new jeans this morning and she had on them yesterday.

3.4 **Put the words in the correct order to make sentences.**

1 to / you / for / make room / Can / move / over / your sister?
2 finished / she / over. / Harry / it / to read / When / her essay, / asked / Daisy
3 his house / tomorrow. / Luke / back / me / has invited / to
4 when he / Max / his driving test. / his parents / he'd failed / only having / was / told them / on
5 tomorrow? / What / you / on / do / have
6 the light / in her bedroom, / was / she / at home. / Eva / had / I knew / on / so

4 Nouns and adjectives based on phrasal verbs

A

Nouns made from verb + particle

In English we often create nouns from verbs, e.g. *to invite / an invitation*. In the same way it is sometimes possible to create a noun from a phrasal verb. Look at these examples.

Tom	I got **ripped off** when I phoned that 0877 number [informal: was charged too much]. The call cost five pounds a minute!
Lily	Yes, those numbers are a big **rip-off**.
Grace	Her son **dropped out** of college last year. [gave up his course]
Ed	Mm. There were a lot of **dropouts** that year. I wonder why?
Oliver	Somebody **broke in** last night and stole a computer from the school. [entered by force to steal something]
Isla	Really? That's the second **break-in** this year!

Rules for the use of verb + particle noun forms

- The plural is formed by adding –s to the particle, not the verb, e.g. **break-ins**, **dropouts**, **rip-offs** (not: ~~breaks in~~, ~~dropsout~~, ~~rips-off~~)
  An exception is **goings-on** [strange or amusing events], which is always plural.
  There was a lot of gossip about the **goings-on** at the office party.

- Verb + particle noun forms are sometimes written with a hyphen, e.g. **break-in**, **check-in**, **cover-up**; and sometimes without, e.g. **dropout**, **checkout**, **crackdown**.
  Nouns with *-out* and *-over* are usually written as one word, e.g. **dropout**, **lookout**, **checkout**, **handout**, **changeover**, **leftovers**.
  Nouns with *-in*, *-up* and less common particles usually have a hyphen, e.g. **lie-in**, **mix-up**, **put-down**, **run-through**.

- In pronunciation, the stress is on the verb, not the particle.
  a **BREAK**-in at the office   college **DROP**outs

B

Nouns made from particle + verb

Some phrasal verbs have noun forms where the particle is first. The stress in pronunciation is usually on the particle.

phrasal verb	particle + verb noun	example
set out	outset	I knew from the **outset** that there would be problems. [beginning]
fall down	downfall	The economic crisis caused the **downfall** of the government. [sudden failure or end]
look on	onlooker	Crowds of **onlookers** watched as the police arrested the man. [someone who watches an event but doesn't take part]

C

Adjectives

There are also adjectives which are based on phrasal verbs. Make a note of any you meet.

e.g. a **broken-down** vehicle [vehicle whose engine had stopped working]   a **breakdown** vehicle [vehicle which helps drivers who have broken down]   **blocked-up** drains [drains where the water cannot flow properly]

   English Phrasal Verbs in Use Intermediate

Exercises

4.1 Complete the following table. If a noun form does not exist, write 'none' in the table. Use a dictionary if necessary. Decide whether the noun is written with a hyphen or as one word.

phrasal verb	verb + particle noun
show off	show-off
warm up	
hold on	
hide out	
turn over	
tear down	

4.2 Circle the correct noun form in these sentences. Use a dictionary if necessary.

1 There was a big <u>pile-up / up-pile</u> on the motorway involving five vehicles.
2 The government has announced a series of <u>backcuts / cutbacks</u> in funding for universities in order to save money.
3 When the higher taxes were announced, there was a public <u>outcry / cryout</u>.
4 Several <u>standerbys / bystanders</u> did nothing while the thieves robbed him of his cash.
5 The new drug marks a <u>throughbreak / breakthrough</u> in the treatment of cancer.

4.3 Complete these sentences with adjective forms of phrasal verbs from the box below.

throwaway	outgoing	bygone	getaway	off-putting

1 The robbers abandoned their .... car in a car park near the airport.
2 I find his manner very .... He's so unfriendly.
3 They decided to use .... paper plates and cups for their party.
4 Let's invite Alice – she's very .... and loves parties.
5 The pictures of the steam trains were like something from a .... era.

4.4 Write down the infinitive form of the phrasal verbs from which the adjectives in exercise 4.3 above are formed.

4.5 Match the sentences on the left with a suitable response on the right.

1 I was looking for a way to turn off the air conditioning.	I know, I need to watch my outgoings.
2 Have you heard about the scandal in the office?	Yes, but I don't understand the input.
3 The economy is not doing so well these days.	The on/off switch is in the hall.
4 A database can organise all the information you type into it.	Yes, there's been a downturn.
5 You have to consider how much you spend each month.	Mm, amazing goings-on!

5 Metaphor and register

A Multiple meanings of phrasal verbs

A phrasal verb can have a number of different meanings, e.g.

He **got on** the bus. [entered the bus]

get on

Liam and Toby **get on** really well. [like each other and are friendly]

Shh! I'm trying to **get on** with my work. [continue doing my work]

Often there is no direct connection between the various meanings and you just have to learn each different meaning of the phrasal verb. The best way to do this is by trying to remember a sentence using the phrasal verb.

B Literal and metaphorical meaning

Sometimes the basic meanings of a phrasal verb and the additional meanings are clearly linked. This is because some additional meanings are based on a metaphor or image which has a direct connection with its literal or basic meaning. A metaphor is a way of expressing something by comparing it with something else that has similar characteristics. Here is an example:

LITERAL (BASIC) MEANING

blow up a balloon [inflate or fill with air]

blow up a building [make it explode]

METAPHORICALMEANING

someone **blows up** [suddenly becomes very angry]

Sometimes a phrasal verb exists as a phrasal verb only in the metaphorical meaning, but you can guess what it means from the meaning of the basic verb without the particle. For example:

These statistics look strange. Have we **slipped up** somewhere?

Here **slip up** [make a mistake] clearly comes from **slip** [fall usually because the floor is wet or the ground is icy].

C Register

Another important aspect of phrasal verbs is register. Phrasal verbs are typical of spoken English or informal writing, e.g. letters to friends and articles in popular journalism. There are often one-word equivalents, or synonyms, for use in a more formal spoken or written style. For example: **miss out** a question *or* **omit** a question. See section 2C in Unit 2 for other examples.

As with all English vocabulary, there are some different uses from one geographical area to another. For example, British, American and Australian users of English all talk of **clearing up** a room [putting things away tidily], but only British and Australian speakers would use **tidy up** as a synonym.

See Unit 69 for more examples of how phrasal verbs differ in North America and Australia.

Exercises

5.1 **Match the different meanings a–f of *take in* with the appropriate sentences 1–6 below.**

a) make smaller
b) allow in through a hole
c) deceive
d) give a bed to
e) include
f) understand the meaning or importance

1 Because so many passengers were stranded at the airport, some local families offered to take them in overnight.
2 The news is so shocking – I still can't take it in.
3 The excursion will take in two of the most beautiful castles in the region.
4 Maria has lost weight – she's going to have to take in a lot of her clothes.
5 Alfie was totally dishonest, but he was so charming that I was taken in by him.
6 We'd better return to the shore at once – the boat seems to be taking in water.

5.2 **These pairs of sentences show phrasal verbs which can be used in both literal and metaphorical ways. Explain the two meanings and the connection between them.**

1 a) I **stepped in** a puddle of water and my feet are soaking now.
   b) She **stepped in** to stop the argument from becoming more serious.
2 a) This music is rubbish. I wish you'd **switch off** the radio.
   b) The lecture was so boring that I **switched off**.
3 a) There's a hole in my bag. I think my pen must have **dropped out**.
   b) He **dropped out** of college and became a mechanic.
4 a) We **tied** the boxes **down** on the roof of the car.
   b) Marcos dreams of travelling, but he feels **tied down** by his family and work responsibilities.

5.3 **Use your knowledge of the basic verb in the underlined phrasal verbs as well as the context of the sentence in order to work out the meanings of the phrasal verbs.**

1 What are you <u>driving at</u>? I wish you would say exactly what you mean!
2 The teacher did all she could to <u>drum</u> the vocabulary <u>into</u> her pupils before the exam.
3 The old education system used to <u>cream off</u> the best pupils and teach them in separate schools.
4 The noise of the children playing completely <u>drowned out</u> his speech.

5.4 **Write a one-word formal equivalent for each of the underlined phrasal verbs.**

As the rain didn't <u>let up</u>, the football game was <u>called off</u>. So the team <u>got down to</u> discussing its strategy for the next match instead. We didn't <u>get out of</u> the clubhouse until the cleaners <u>turned up</u> in the evening.

> ## Over to you
>
> If you encounter a phrasal verb that you thought you knew but it does not seem to make sense, use other clues in the context to work out what the meaning might be. It may be quite different from the meaning that you already knew.

6 Come

Come expressing an idea of movement or change of state

phrasal verb	meaning	example
come along	arrive at a place	Not many people bought tickets for the concert in advance, but quite a few **came along** and bought tickets at the door.
come apart	separate into pieces	The antique picture frame just **came apart** in my hands.
come around or **come round**	become conscious again	A nurse was with me when I **came round** after the operation.
come out	disappear or become less strong (of dirt or colour on clothing/material)	Let your shirt soak overnight and the stain will probably **come out**.
come out	become public knowledge after it has been kept secret (of the truth)	If this story **comes out** about the Prime Minister, he'll have to resign.
come out	be given to people (of results or information)	When do your exam results **come out**?
come out	leave after a period in a place (of hospital/prison)	Ava's **coming out** of hospital at the weekend. She's much better now.

Come expressing an idea of happen

I was planning to arrange a surprise holiday for her birthday, but I'm not sure it's going to **come off**. [happen successfully or as planned]

I've had to organise the school fair again this year – I'm not quite sure how that **came about**. [happened, especially something which is not planned]

Oscar   Will you tell your boss about your plans to stand for the local council?

Sophie   Only if the subject **comes up**[1] in conversation. I nearly told him at work this morning, but then something **came up**[2] and we had to deal with it straight away. Mind you, I don't know if a place on the council is going to **come up**[3] for a while yet, so perhaps I'll wait.

[1]   is mentioned or discussed
[2]   happened unexpectedly, usually a problem or difficult situation
[3]   become available

Other meanings of *come*

I am doing a research project for my degree on the psychology of ageing, but I've **come up against**[1] a few problems. I **came across**[2] someone who's done an almost identical study, so I've got to **come to**[3] a decision: do I want to continue with it or not? I guess in the end my decision will **come down to**[4] what my professor recommends.

[1]   encountered or had to deal with (a difficult situation)
[2]   discovered (or met) by chance
[3]   make (a decision about something)
[4]   depend mostly on or be influenced most by

Exercises

6.1 **Complete these sentences with a particle from A opposite.**

1 Do you have any glue? My shoe is coming ....*apart*........ and I want to stick it together.
2 I spilt some tomato juice on the tablecloth. Do you think it will come ....*out*........ if I put it in the washing machine?
3 The last thing I remember was feeling very dizzy. The next thing I knew, I came ....*around*........ in hospital and a doctor was standing by my bed.
4 The government is going to release a report on traffic congestion. I wonder when it's coming ....*out*........ .
5 We were just chatting at the corner when Sam Gore came ....*along*........ with his girlfriend.
6 I hear Adam's operation was successful. When is he coming ....*out*........ of the clinic?
7 Some very shocking facts have come ....*out*........ about government corruption, thanks to an investigation by a national newspaper.

6.2 **Use a phrasal verb from the opposite page to complete these dialogues.**

1
Anna   I lost the report I was writing and had to start all over again

Ben   Really? How did that .... ?

Anna   Oh, it was some computer virus.

2
Arthur   David keeps saying he's going to sail around the world.

Ivan   Huh! Do you think it will ever .... ?

Arthur   Probably not. He's such a dreamer.

3
Louis   We'll let you know what we decide. We'll phone you.

Bella   When do you think you'll .... a decision?

Louis   Probably at the meeting on Friday.

4
Maya   I thought you were coming to the party last night.

Katie   Yes, I was intending to, but right at the last minute something ....

Maya   Oh, I see. Well, you must come next time.

6.3 **Rewrite the underlined words in these emails giving advice, using phrasal verbs with *come*.**

●●●   ✉   Reply   Forward

I know that you are <u>having to deal with</u> a lot of problems at work every day at the moment, but don't worry, they're only temporary, and I've heard that a new job opportunity is going to <u>arise</u>, which could change things completely. Whenever your name <u>is mentioned</u> in conversation, everyone always speaks very highly of you.

●●●   ✉   Reply   Forward

You think you have <u>met someone by pure chance</u> who seems to share the same world view as you, but be careful, I don't think she is what she seems to be. Don't forget that, in the end, true love <u>is mainly about</u> finding someone you can trust.

7　Get

A　Learning phrasal verbs in pairs associated with a context

phrasal verbs	meaning	example
get together (often + **with**)	If two or more people get together, they meet in order to do something or spend time together.	It's nice to **get together with** people you **get on with**.
get on (often + **with**)	If two or more people get on, they like each other and are friendly to each other.	
get on (often + **with**)	continue doing something, especially work	I must **get on with** my work. I **got behind** because I spent too much time online.
get behind (often + **with**)	If you get behind with work or with payments, you have not done as much work or paid as much as you should by a particular time.	
get sth over with	do and complete something difficult or unpleasant that must be done	Let's **get** this **meeting over with**, or else we'll never **get away** before the rush hour and it will take ages to get home.
get away	leave a place or person, often when the situation makes it difficult for you to do so	
can't/couldn't get over sth	be very surprised or shocked that something has happened or that something is true	I **can't get over** how she manages to **get away with** doing so little work. It's obvious to everyone, but the boss never seems to notice.
get away with sth/doing sth	succeed in not being criticised or punished for something wrong that you have done	

B　More phrasal verbs with *get*

Isaac How do you manage to survive without a job?

Holly Oh, I **get by** with a bit of help from my parents. [have just enough money to pay for the things I need, but nothing more]

Lauren The problem is that the regulations don't allow us to use next year's budget.

Juliet Oh, don't worry. We'll **get around/round** it somehow. [find a way of dealing with or avoiding a problem]

Yanis Have you rung the travel agent's yet to confirm our bookings?

Ronan Sorry, I haven't **got around/round to** it yet, but I'll do it after lunch, I promise. [do something that you have intended to do for a long time]

Poll I really think you ought to apologise to you-know-who about you-know-what.

Ivan I'm sorry, I don't know what you're **getting at**. Who? What? [If you ask someone what they are getting at, you are asking them what they mean, usually because they have said something indirectly.]

Ellie Do you think I can **get away with** not using any handouts in my talk? [do something successfully even though it is not the best way of doing it]

Rory Yes, people often just throw them away anyway.

Exercises

7.1 Choose the correct particle to complete these sentences.

1 Why don't you get your homework ....b.......... with so you can enjoy the rest of the evening?
   a) around   b) over   c) by   d) away
2 As soon as Lydia and I met, we knew we were going to get ......c...... well.
   a) round   b) at   c) on   d) up
3 I just can't come out with you tonight as I've got so ......d...... with my work.
   a) up   b) over   c) away   d) behind
4 Why does Sara always get ......b...... with arriving late? It doesn't seem fair.
   a) by   b) away   c) on   d) over
5 I'm going to have to get ......a...... to filling in my tax form soon.
   a) round   b) over   c) away   d) behind
6 I hope you'll be able to get ......a...... from work at a reasonable time tonight.
   a) away   b) behind   c) at   d) over
7 Your mother couldn't get ......d...... the cost of restaurants in London.
   a) up   b) round   c) by   d) over

7.2 Match each question on the left with the most likely response on the right.

1 How do you and Joseph get on?   I manage somehow, though it isn't easy.
2 What exactly are you getting at?   I just wasn't organised enough.
3 How do you get by on a student loan?   Sure, that would be nice.
4 How did you get so behind?   I certainly hope so.
5 When are you going to get round to it?   Let me put it another way for you.
6 Shall we get together this evening?   We're great friends.
7 Will you manage to get away soon?   Soon, I promise.

7.3 Rewrite the underlined parts of these sentences using a phrasal verb from the opposite page. Make any other necessary changes.

1 I've been planning to sort out my files but I haven't <u>found time to do it</u> yet.
2 I <u>can't believe</u> how much money they spent on their New Year's party.
3 Don't try to <u>travel without</u> paying your train fare – an inspector might come on and want to see your ticket.
4 The teachers in the school often <u>meet</u> after work on Fridays in a café near the school.
5 They <u>avoided</u> the problem of offending anyone and just invited all their friends to the wedding.
6 I usually find it quite hard to understand what Professor Mactoft is <u>trying to say</u> in his lectures.
7 I hope <u>no-one will mind if I don't send</u> any Christmas cards this year.
8 Emily has <u>not done nearly as much work on her thesis as she should have done by now</u>.

Over to you

Learning verbs in pairs associated with a particular context can help you remember them. Look again at all the phrasal verbs on the opposite page. Try to make different pairs and write them in sentences putting them in context, as in section A.

8 Go

A Amelia's story

Amelia has been **going through**[1] a difficult time at work, so she decided to cheer herself up by **going in for**[2] a competition. The prize was a luxury holiday in the Caribbean. Amelia has had to **go without**[3] a holiday for several years now, so she really wanted to win. The competition was to write a story beginning 'Suddenly the lights **went out**[4]...'. The problem was that Amelia could not think of an idea for her story.

'How can I **go about**[5] getting a good idea?', she asked me. 'It must be something special so that the judges **go for**[6] my story over all the others.' I suggested she went to the city library to **go through**[7] some books of short stories – she might get some ideas there. So she **went off**[8] to see what she could find.

She soon found some great stories. She read one and then another and she **went on**[9] reading all day. Then she noticed a strange smell and suddenly the lights went out. The library was on fire! Of course, that gave her the idea for her story. I hope she wins.

[1] experiencing an unpleasant or difficult situation
[2] doing or competing in
[3] not have something which you usually have
[4] stopped giving light
[5] start to do or deal with something
[6] choose
[7] examine the contents of something carefully
[8] left a place to go to somewhere else
[9] continued

B Some more phrasal verbs with *go*

phrasal verb	meaning	example
go along with sb/sth	support an idea, or agree with someone's opinion	Whatever you say, Lottie will **go along with** you.
go on	continue to exist or happen	It **went on** raining all day.
go on	happen	There's a police car outside the shop. Do you know what's **going on**?
go through with	do something unpleasant or difficult which you planned or promised to do	I don't want to do the exam now, but I'd better **go through with** it.
go together	if two types of thing or people go together, they are usually found with each other	A bad cough and a sore throat often **go together**.

> **Tip**
>
> Many of the very common English phrasal verbs, for example the ones in Units 6–12, have several different meanings when combined with one particle. There are a few different meanings on this page for *go on* and *go through*; however, there are other possible meanings for both of these verb and particle combinations. Remember this if you meet a phrasal verb in a new or unusual context because it may have quite a different meaning there from one you are more familiar with.

Exercises

8.1 Complete the text below using the correct particles from the phrasal verbs in A opposite.

I was going .... (1) some old letters the other day when I found one from my friend Nancy. After school she had gone .... (2) to train as a doctor and ended up in Africa. She had to go .... (3) years of very hard study before she qualified. Life in Africa was not as comfortable as it was in our hometown, and there were many things she had to go .... (4) which the rest of us think of as necessities in our daily lives. But despite all the hardships, she went .... (5) working and helping people less fortunate than herself. I admire her so much. I wondered how I might go .... (6) making contact with her again, as I have no idea where she is living now.

8.2 Rewrite these sentences using phrasal verbs with *go* so that they keep the same meaning.

1 I'm thinking of competing in the New York Marathon next year.
2 There were some difficult times in my father's life.
3 Unemployment and high crime levels often exist side by side.
4 He decided to undergo the operation even though there were risks.
5 I refused to support their decision to close the youth club.
6 I didn't realise how late it was and I didn't stop studying till after midnight.
7 We had to survive with no hot water for 24 hours while they were repairing the pipes.
8 Do you think I should try the advanced level exam? It might be too difficult.
9 She just left without saying goodbye. I wonder if I offended her?
10 What was happening in the staffroom at lunchtime? I heard someone shouting.

8.3 In these sentences, some of the phrasal verbs from the opposite page are used with new meanings. Choose the correct paraphrase. Use a dictionary if necessary.

1 We had to throw the fish away as it had **gone off**.
   a) Someone had switched off the oven.
   b) The fish had become bad because we kept it too long.
   c) The fish had fallen off the table onto the floor.
2 I wish you wouldn't **go on** about your problems all the time! I have problems too, you know!
   a) I wish you wouldn't think obsessively.
   b) I wish you wouldn't be very secretive.
   c) I wish you wouldn't talk constantly.
3 She's been **going about** her daily activities despite the tragic news.
   a) She's been avoiding her usual activities.
   b) She's been thinking of carrying on with her routine.
   c) She's been carrying on with her routine.
4 Ask her to dance with you. **Go on**!
   a) Continue doing what you're doing.
   b) Step onto the dance floor.
   c) Do it now, don't hesitate.

Cambridge Dictionary
ictionary.cambridge.org

Suddenly the light went out leaving George and Jasmine in complete darkness.

Over to you

The verb *go on* has a noun and an adjective associated with it: *goings-on* (noun) and *ongoing* (adjective). Look in a good dictionary to find out how they are used and make a sentence with each one in your vocabulary notebook.

A Look in a physical sense

The idea of seeing, observing or noticing something is included in many phrasal verbs with *look*.

Tim	Did you manage to read the report?
Ivy	Well, I **looked at** it, but I haven't read it properly. [read it quickly and not very carefully]
Tim	I'd like you to read it if you could. We need to **look at** the conclusions and make some decisions. [examine or consider something carefully in order to make a decision about it]

Amber	How do I get to your village coming from the city?
Noah	When you're on the motorway, **look out** for a sign saying 'Willowsdean'. That's where you turn off. [carefully watch the things around you so that you will notice a particular thing]

The bank robbers had a **lookout** standing at the street corner to warn them if the police came. [noun: a person who is watching for danger]

I wasn't in the demonstration. I was just an **onlooker**. [noun: someone who watches an activity or event without becoming involved in it; from the phrasal verb with the same meaning **look on**]

B Look in an abstract sense

If you …	then you …
look up to sb	respect and admire them
look down on sb/sth	think that someone or something is less important than you, or that something is not good enough quality for you to use
look after sb/sth	take care of someone or something by doing what is needed to keep someone or something well or in good condition
look ahead	think about what will happen in the future and plan for those events
look around/round	try to find something you want (e.g. a job) by asking different people or by looking in different places
look forward to sth/doing sth	feel pleased and excited about something that is going to happen

Exercises

9.1 **Choose the correct answer.**

1 If you are looking around for a new job, you are ...
   a) applying for a new job   b) trying to find a new job
   c) worried about your new job
2 If you look out for someone who is picking you up in their car, you ...
   a) carefully avoid getting hit by their car   b) watch the road and warn them of danger
   c) watch for their car so you will see them when they arrive
3 If you look down on cheap restaurants, you ...
   a) consider them not good enough for you   b) see them from the top windows of your house
   or flat   c) always consider them before going to a more expensive one
4 If you look after someone's cat while they are away, you ...
   a) follow the cat everywhere   b) search for it because it is lost
   c) care for it and give it what it needs
5 If you look up to your English teacher, you ...
   a) stand up when you speak to him or her   b) admire and respect him or her
   c) raise your head because he or she is taller than you

9.2 **Complete these sentences with a suitable particle.**

1 I'm really looking .... to seeing my cousins again next week.
2 She's looking .... for a new English course. She's not very satisfied with the one
   she's following at the moment.
3 She loves looking .... children, so she has decided to train as a nanny.
4 We have to look .... to the time when our son will go to university.
5 The new boss is a terrible snob. She looks .... on most other people.
6 I didn't have time to read the newspaper yesterday. I only looked .... it very quickly.

9.3 **Complete the diagram using words from the opposite page.**

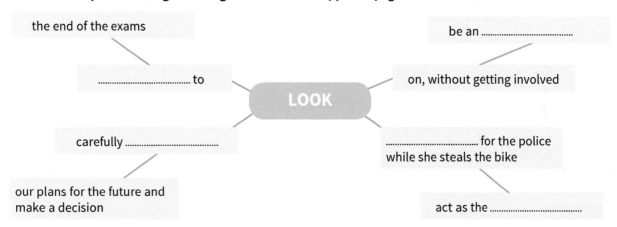

9.4 **Here are some more phrasal verbs based on *look*. Read each sentence and try to guess the meaning of the phrasal verb. Use a dictionary if necessary.**

1 You could **look up** the new words in a dictionary.
2 When I was in Boston on business last week I **looked up** an old friend.
3 After a long recession the economic situation is **looking up**.
4 I **looked over** the report on the way to the meeting.
5 I **looked through** the report and scribbled down a few notes.
6 Detectives are **looking into** the murder.

Cambridge
Dictionary
ictionary.cambridge.org

10 Make

A Make + the particles *for*, *out* and *up*

up something = form the whole of something

for somewhere = go in the direction of

out something/someone = be able to see or hear something or someone with difficulty

up something (or **make** something **up**) = invent something, e.g. a story or a game

MAKE

out someone (or **make** someone **out**) = understand why someone behaves as they do

up something (or **make** something **up**) = say or write something that is not true in order to deceive

out something (or **make** something **out**) = understand something, especially why something has happened

Examples:

Can you **make out** the words of this song?

When we got to the park, the children **made for** the swings while I sat on a bench.

Katie didn't want to go to the concert, so she **made up** an excuse about being ill.

The children loved Uncle Robert because he was so good at **making up** new games.

Over 30% of the university population is **made up** of overseas students.

Notice how **make out** with the following three meanings is usually used with *can* or *could* in a negative sentence and is not usually used in the passive.

I **couldn't make out** a word he was saying.

Jack is behaving very strangely at the moment. I just **can't make** him **out**.

I **can't make out** why my computer won't let me save this document.

You probably already know that the noun *make-up* can mean cosmetics, e.g.

My sister never goes out without **make-up** on, but I only wear it for special occasions.

However, **make-up**, from the verb **make up**, can also mean the combination of things which form something, e.g.

The class has an interesting **make-up**, with students from three continents and 12 different countries.

B Make + two particles

phrasal verb	meaning	example
make up for sth	provide something good in order to make a bad situation better	The wonderful food in the restaurant **made up for** the rather uncomfortable seats.
make it up to sb	do something good for someone who you have done something bad to in the past, or to someone who has done something good for you	I forgot Abigail's birthday yesterday, so I'll have to take her somewhere nice to **make it up to** her.

Exercises

10.1 Read these comments by different people and then answer the questions below by writing the correct name in the box.

> **Theo** I can't make out what she's saying, can you?
>
> **Martha** I just can't make him out at all, can you?
>
> **Lars** I treated her a bit insensitively at the party so I gave her a present to make up for it.
>
> **Logan** I made up a story about losing my wallet, so he paid the bill for me.
>
> **Zara** I loved the trip. The beautiful scenery made up for the awful roads.

1 Who invented something that was not true?

2 Who said something good had made a bad experience less bad?

3 Who has difficulty hearing something?

4 Who wanted to restore a damaged relationship?

5 Who can't understand someone's behaviour?

10.2 Correct the mistakes with the phrasal verbs in these sentences.

1 As soon as we had checked in at the hotel, we made straight at the beach.

2 She made out some story about the bus being late, but I'm sure she just overslept.

3 Why the camera was not working properly could not be made out by anybody.

4 Harry is very good at making over stories for the children; they love his tales.

5 Can you make what that white thing on the horizon is out?

6 The report is made of three sections up.

The make-up of the new cabinet clearly reflected the extreme wing of the party.

> ## Over to you
>
> Use a good dictionary or search the Cambridge University Press dictionary website at http://dictionary.cambridge.org to see how many more phrasal verbs with *make* you can find. Write down three that you particularly want to remember in example sentences.

11 Put

A Put verbs related to physical actions

With all these phrasal verbs the particle can come either before or after the object, e.g. to **put on** a DVD or to **put** a DVD **on**.

I spent yesterday **putting in** a new washing machine. [fixing new equipment or a new system in the correct place]

Could you **put** the air conditioning **on**, please? It's so hot in here. [make a device work by pressing a switch]

I don't think you've seen this DVD. I'll **put** it **on**.

[put something that sounds or pictures are recorded onto into a machine so that you can hear or see the recording]

Would you mind **putting** that light **out**? It's shining directly onto my computer screen. [making a light stop shining by pressing a switch]

I see they're **putting up** a new block of flats near the park. [building a structure]

It poured with rain while we tried to **put** our tent **up**. [open something that is folded or rolled up so that it is ready to use]

B Put verbs and time

| Lucas | Joey, I'm sorry to have to **put** you **off** again, but I'm just too busy to see you today [tell someone you can't see them or do something for them till a later time]. Could we **put** our meeting **back** till next week? [change the date or time of an event so that it happens later than planned] |

| Joey | Sure. We can **put** it **off** until next Monday. [decide or arrange to do something at a later time] |

| Pilot | Ladies and gentlemen, we're now coming in to land at Mexico City. You may want to **put** your watches **forward**; the local time is 8.35 a.m. [make a watch or clock show a later time] |

In Britain, around the last weekend in October, all clocks are **put back** one hour. [make a watch or clock show an earlier time]

C Put verbs and relations with other people

If you ...	then ...
are **put out**	you are annoyed, often because of something that someone has done or said to you
put up with sb/sth	you accept unpleasant behaviour or an unpleasant situation, even though you do not like it
put sb **on to/onto** sth/sb	you tell them about something or someone that could help them, often something or someone they did not know about before

Exercises

11.1 **Correct any mistakes in these sentences. If there are no mistakes, write *correct* at the end of the sentence.**

1 I like sleeping in tents but I don't like putting up them.
2 Put that music on that you downloaded yesterday. I'd like to hear it.
3 We put last week in a new dishwasher. It's wonderful.
4 Will you put on the TV? I want to watch the tennis.
5 That light is too strong. Shall we put out it?

11.2 **Complete the text using particles from the opposite page.**

● ● ●   ✉   Reply   Forward

'I don't know how Harry puts .... (1) with his boss. He works so hard but his boss
even gets him to put the lights .... (2) for him when it starts to get dark, and it's
always Harry who has to put .... (3) new shelves and do other jobs like that. His
boss never thinks twice about putting him .... (4) at short notice when they've
arranged a meeting. I know Harry feels put .... (5), but he never complains.
We should really do what we can to put him .... (6) some better jobs.

11.3 **Rewrite these sentences so that the actions are the *opposite* of the ones underlined. Use phrasal verbs from the opposite page and make any other necessary changes so that the sentences make sense.**

EXAMPLE   Please <u>turn</u> the radio <u>off</u> now. I'm trying to sleep.

Please put the radio on now. There's a programme I'd like to listen to.

1 Could you <u>switch</u> the light <u>on</u> please? I can't see to read.
2 They're <u>pulling down</u> those old buildings near the railway station.
3 The Scouts <u>took</u> their tent <u>down</u> very quickly and loaded it into their bus.
4 Could we possibly <u>bring</u> our meeting <u>forward</u> to 10 o'clock?
5 When we moved into our new house, we decided to <u>remove</u> an old, rather ugly fireplace.
6 Can you <u>turn</u> that music <u>off</u>, please? I can't concentrate on my work.

11.4 **Here are some more phrasal verbs based on *put*. Match the phrasal verbs in the sentences 1–5 with the definitions a–e. Use a dictionary if necessary.**

Cambridge Dictionary

ctionary.cambridge.org

1 Harriet is very good at **putting** her ideas **across**.
2 We are always very careful and **put** the fire **out** after the barbecue.
3 I'm not **putting** that **on**. I'd look ridiculous in it!
4 Charlie has **put up** a poster about the concert. Have you seen it?
5 The plane was due to **put down** in Los Angeles at 3.50 a.m. but was diverted to San Francisco at the last minute.

a) stick or fasten a piece of paper to something, e.g. a wall, so that it can be seen
b) express in such a way that others can understand easily
c) land
d) put a piece of clothing on your body
e) extinguish or stop something burning

12 Take

A   *Take* in a physical sense

If you **take apart** something or **take** something **apart**, you separate it into its different parts.

> Freddie loves **taking** clocks **apart**, but he never manages to put them together again.

If you **take back** something or **take** something **back**, you return it to the person or organisation that you bought or borrowed it from.

> When you go into town to **take back** your books to the college library, could you also **take** these trousers **back** to the shop for me? They're too small.

If you **take aside** somebody or **take** somebody **aside**, you separate someone from a group of people so that you can speak to them privately.

> My boss **took** me **aside** at the Christmas party and told me he was going to give me a promotion in the New Year.

If you **take off**, you suddenly leave a place, without telling anyone where you are going.

> Most people stayed at the party until quite late, but Rose **took off** early for some reason.

B   *Take* in an abstract sense

phrasal verb	meaning	example
take up sth or **take** sth **up**	start doing a particular job or activity	My son has recently **taken up** collecting coins as a hobby.
take off sth or **take** sth **off** (sth)	subtract a particular amount from a total	The shop assistant **took off** ten per cent because the item was damaged.
take away sth or **take** sth **away**	subtract a first number from a second number	If you **take** 11 **away** from 33, you're left with 22.
take back sth or **take** sth **back**	admit that something you said was wrong	I shouldn't have called you lazy – I **take** it **back**.
take in sth or **take** sth **in**	look at something carefully, noticing all the details	He showed us a photo of his house, but I was so tired that I didn't really **take** it **in**.

C   Other senses of *take*

Lucy has started swimming regularly. She has **taken out**[1] a year's membership at a local sports club and has **taken to**[2] going to the swimming pool every lunch hour. She is so **taken up with**[3] her swimming that she wouldn't even **take** me **up on**[4] my offer to buy her lunch in the best restaurant in town. The exercise certainly **takes** it **out of**[5] her – she is too exhausted to go anywhere in the evenings.

[1] subscribed to or registered for something officially
[2] started to do something often
[3] very busy doing something
[4] accept
[5] makes her feel very tired

> **Tip**
>
> Because the most common verbs, e.g. *take*, *get*, *make*, have so many different phrasal verbs with different meanings associated with them, it is useful to group the meanings, as in the sections of this unit. Try to do this for other common verbs and their phrasal verbs as you meet new ones, and try to record an example sentence in your vocabulary notebook to help you remember them.

Exercises

12.1 Each line of this text contains a phrasal verb with *take*, but some of them are used incorrectly. If a line has a correct phrasal verb, tick the box. If the line is incorrect, cross out the incorrect word and write the correct word in the box.

EXAMPLE   The watch was broken so I took it ~~off~~ to the shop.

back

I bought a new jacket but it had a mark on it so I took it back.

The shop assistant took me offside so that other people could be served.

She said that if I was prepared to keep the jacket she would take away

ten per cent. I didn't really take in what she was saying at

first, but once I understood, I decided to take her over on the offer.

12.2 Use a phrasal verb from the opposite page to complete these dialogues.

1
Lewis   I find it very offensive that you called Thomas an idiot.
Hugo   OK, OK. Sorry, I shouldn't have said it. I ....

2
Matt   Megan seems really keen on her tennis these days.
Clare   Yes, she's really .... it. She's so .... with it that she's stopped going to the swimming pool.

3
Jude   I tried to clean the inside of my laptop and I've put all the bits back but it isn't working.
Matthew   Well, I'm not surprised! I warned you not to .... in the first place.

4
Paul   I get so bored since I retired from my job.
Julia   Well, why don't you .... golf?

5
Ali   What's this figure here, £30?
Ryan   It's what you get when you .... £15 .... from £45.

6
Freya   You look exhausted these days.
Daniel   Yes, teaching 28 hours a week really .... me.

7
Imogen   Ollie left very suddenly, didn't he?
Layla   Yes, he just .... without even saying goodbye.

To the surprise of everyone at the party, Ollie suddenly took off without saying goodbye.

13 Up

A Read this text about someone complaining about having to do housework. Notice how the particle *up* sometimes expresses the idea of completing or totally finishing something.

> I spent all morning yesterday **clearing up**[1] my study. There were books and papers everywhere. Then I had to **sweep up**[2] the rubbish and dead leaves on the terrace. After that I tried to **tidy up**[3] my bedroom. There were dirty clothes all **jumbled up**[4] in a pile on the floor. I had to **hang up**[5] four jackets and several pairs of trousers I'd left lying on chairs, and then I **loaded up**[6] the washing machine. That took me an hour. Then I discovered the washbasin was **clogged up**[7] in the bathroom, so I had to clear that. By that time I'd **used up**[8] all my energy and I was too tired to do anything, so I just fell asleep on the sofa.

[1] making a place tidy and clean, especially by putting things where they usually belong
[2] remove rubbish or dirt, usually from the floor, using a brush
[3] make a room or a group of things tidy by putting things in the correct place
[4] (adjective) mixed together in an untidy way (from the verb **jumble up**)
[5] hang something, especially clothes, on a hook
[6] to put a lot of things into a machine or vehicle
[7] blocked
[8] finished a supply of something

Note how the particle *up* can be used for emphasis:

Eat up your vegetables!   **Drink up** your juice!   Seth's **used up** all the milk.

These three sentences could be written without *up*, but using *up* emphasises the meaning of 'finish it all or completely'.

B Read this social media chat between Robert and Georgia.

> **Robert** 17:02
> Hi Georgia, what's new?
>
> **Georgia** 17:03
> My sister Eliza **showed up**[1] at last. She's been promising to come for weeks.
>
> **Robert** 17:03
> Great. ☺
>
> **Georgia** 17:04
> Yeah, she **turned up**[2] yesterday evening.
>
> **Robert** 17:04
> What's she doing these days?
>
> **Georgia** 17:05
> She's just **opened up**[3] a restaurant serving exotic food from different countries. It's in that shopping mall in Dunston, you know.
>
> **Robert** 17:06
> Wow! That's original. It'll certainly **liven** Dunston **up**[4] a bit – it's such a boring place. So, what's the **set-up**[5]? Is she the only person involved?
>
> **Georgia** 17:07
> No, she has a business partner and they **divide up**[6] the work – and the profits!
>
> **Robert** 17:08
> Sounds like fun. ☺
>
> **Georgia** 17:08
> Yeah, but she says it's hard work. She spends half the day **chopping up**[7] food and cleaning the kitchen.
>
> **Robert** 17:09
> Mm. Maybe we're better off working in office jobs …

[1] arrived, especially at a place where people were expecting her
[2] arrived
[3] started a new shop or business
[4] make something more interesting and exciting
[5] (noun) the way that something is arranged (from the verb **set up**)
[6] separate something into smaller parts or groups
[7] cutting something, especially food, into small pieces

Exercises

13.1 **Look at the picture and answer the questions.**

1 What does the woman need to tidy up?
2 What does she need to sweep up?
3 What must she hang up?
4 What are jumbled up on the floor?
5 How might she feel when she has cleared everything up?

13.2 **Choose the best verb from B to fill the gaps in this email. Use a different verb in each gap and write it in the correct form.**

●●●   ✉   Reply   Forward

Hi, Gina!

How are things with you? Hope all's well. Has your cousin .... (1) up yet? We certainly need him around to .... (2) this place up a bit! Besides which, I need his help in the garden. An old tree blew down last week and I need to .... (3) up the branches. When he eventually .... (4) up, let's try out that new club that's .... (5) up in Market Street.

Love, Esme

13.3 **Choose the correct word to complete these sentences. Sometimes there is more than one possible answer.**

1 Sam .... up too much time on the first exam question and didn't finish the paper.
   a) clogged   b) used   c) divided   d) showed
2 Guess who .... up at midnight last night!
   a) showed   b) livened   c) hung   d) turned
3 Please could you .... up these onions for me?
   a) divide   b) turn   c) chop   d) clog
4 Sofia spent ages .... up the lounge.
   a) clearing   b) tidying   c) hanging   d) turning
5 A new supermarket is .... up near us next month.
   a) turning   b) showing   c) opening   d) hanging
6 The bath is .... up with hair. It's disgusting!
   a) jumbled   b) swept   c) chopped   d) clogged
7 Could you .... up the leaves on the front steps, please?
   a) hang   b) clear   c) use   d) sweep
8 When the old man died, his things were .... up among his children.
   a) chopped   b) divided   c) cleared   d) used

13.4 **In some of the phrasal verbs in A and B opposite, the verb can be used on its own without the particle *up* to make a grammatical sentence with more or less the same meaning.**

1 In which cases could the *up* be left out?
2 In the sentences where the particle is not essential, what extra meanings, if any, do you think the *up* adds?

14 Out

A

Out meaning not in

Many phrasal verbs with *out* have an association with the basic meaning of *out*, i.e. not in.

phrasal verb	meaning	example
leave out sth/sb or **leave** sth/sb **out**	not include something or someone	For homework do exercise 8 but **leave out** number 10.
cut out sth or **cut** sth **out**	remove by cutting, usually from paper or cloth	She **cut** the pieces **out** from the dress material.
show out sb or **show** sb **out**	lead a visitor who is leaving to the door of a room or building	Let me **show** you **out** – it's quite hard to find the exit from here.
see out sb or **see** sb **out**	go with someone to the door of a room or building when they are leaving	Don't worry, I can **see** myself **out**.
let out sb/sth or **let** sb/sth **out**	allow a person or animal to leave, usually by opening a locked or closed door	The door will be locked but the receptionist will **let** you **out**.
lock out sb or **lock** sb **out**	prevent someone from entering a building by locking the door	I forgot my keys and was **locked out** of my own house!
lock yourself **out**	accidentally prevent yourself from getting into a building by leaving the keys inside when you shut the door	I've **locked** myself **out** so often that I've hidden a spare key in the garden now.

B

Out meaning to the end or completely

Sometimes *out* in phrasal verbs gives an idea of completing or doing something to the end.

I **sorted out** my room on Sunday. [arranged things that were untidy]

I **cleared out** [made tidy by removing unwanted things] all my wardrobes and threw away all my **worn-out** shoes. [adjective: used so much that they had become damaged, from the verb **wear out**]

Unfortunately, I'd **run out** of furniture polish, so I couldn't do any polishing, but I'll do that next weekend. [there was none left because it had all been used]

C

Other uses of *out*

Here are some other phrasal verbs and expressions which use *out*.

He **spread out** the photos on the table so everyone could see them. [arranged on a flat surface]

The band has a new album **coming out** next month. [available for people to buy]

Would you like to **try out** the bike before deciding whether to buy it? [test to find out if it works or decide whether you like it]

My husband's business is so busy at the moment that I'm **helping out** in the office. [helping, especially by doing work or giving money]

I always feel I **lost out** because I never learnt a musical instrument as a child. [did not have an advantage that others had]

I feel totally **stressed-out** at work at the moment. [adjective: very worried and anxious]

I've been working so hard for so long, I feel like screaming. I think I'm suffering from **burnout**. [noun: the condition of being ill or tired because you have been working too hard]

Exercises

14.1 **Rewrite these sentences using phrasal verbs from A.**

1 I'll take you down to the exit, if you like.
2 For some reason my name was omitted from the guest list.
3 My keys are inside the car and I can't get into it.
4 He can find his own way to the exit – there's no need to take him there.
5 She collected advertisements from the magazines that would give her money off her shopping.
6 The security guard opened the gate so we could leave the building site.

14.2 **Complete these sentences using phrasal verbs. Write the verbs in the correct form.**

1 I .... out by not learning a foreign language at school. I meet so many people I just can't communicate with.
2 Would you like to .... out my tennis racket? It's a new model.
3 My business is growing so fast I need someone to .... out at weekends. I don't want to suffer from burnout.
4 I got .... out yesterday. I left home without my keys and my flatmate had gone away for the day.
5 I .... out a job advertisement from the paper last night and now I don't know where I put it.

6

Chloe	Right, Archie, I'm leaving now.
Archie	I'll come with you and .... you out. Our new office building is a bit complicated.
Chloe	Oh, it's OK, I can .... myself out.
Archie	Well, actually you can't. They lock the street door at 6 p.m., so I'll have to come and .... you out.

14.3 **Write a sentence about each picture using phrasal verbs from this unit.**

1   2

14.4 **Choose which sentence from a–e below best fits the gaps 1–5 in the text.**

I wanted to find out more about the history of my town for a college project. (1) So I decided to go to the local records office. I got out some books, newspapers and some old maps which they had. (2) I decided to make a pile of things to scan. (3) There was a huge amount of material, too much in fact. (4) So I hurried and just chose the most important things to scan in the time I had left. (5) I will go back and do them some other time.

a) So I sorted out the most important items.
b) Unfortunately, I had to leave out the very big maps.
c) I'd cut out some articles from the local paper, but I needed more information.
d) Time was running out; the office closed at 5.30 p.m. – I felt very stressed-out.
e) I spread them all out on a big table.

15 Off

A Leaving places

Off sometimes combines with verbs to express the idea of something or someone leaving a place.

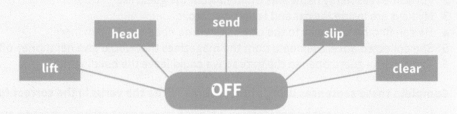

example	meaning
The space shuttle will **lift off** at 09.00 hours.	leave the ground (of a spacecraft)
We should **head off** at about six tomorrow.	start a journey or leave a place
I've **sent off** the documents to the lawyer.	send a letter, document or parcel by post
Let's try and **slip off** before the meeting finishes and go for a drink.	leave a place quietly so that other people do not notice you going
Why did he just **clear off** without saying goodbye? **Clear off**! This is private property.	leave a place quickly (informal)

B Ending or changing state

Off sometimes expresses the idea of moving towards an ending or a change of state.

I'll come and **see** you **off** at the airport tomorrow. [go to the airport in order to say goodbye]

My cousin has **sold off** his share of the company he started with a friend. [sold all or part of a business]

After lunch Grandpa **dozed off** on the sofa. [gradually started to sleep, especially during the day]

Mr Prosser suddenly looked very pale and **broke off** in the middle of his lecture. [suddenly stopped speaking]

Please could you **run off** 20 copies of the agenda for the meeting this afternoon? [if you run off copies of something, you print them]

She's so clever. She can **run off** a statement for the press in half an hour. It would take me all day! [quickly and easily write something that is usually difficult to write]

Note that **run off** with the meaning of leave somewhere quickly could also have been included in A above.

C Other expressions with *off*

What he said has **put** me **off** the idea of going to Blandville for a holiday altogether! [made me not like something]

His description of the hotel was very **off-putting**. [adjective: made something sound unattractive or unpleasant, from the verb **put off**]

Maybe we should **hold off** and go to Paris or somewhere in the spring? [delay doing something]

I think I've managed to **turn** him **off** the idea of building a model railway track in the back garden. [make someone decide that they are not interested in something]

She didn't get offended by the comment; she just **laughed** it **off**. [laughed about something unpleasant in order to make it seem less important or serious]

English Phrasal Verbs in Use Intermediate

Exercises

15.1 Complete these sentences, using verbs from A or B. Write the verbs in the correct form.

1 The company is not doing very well – isn't it time you .... off your shares in it?
2 We were talking to Matilda when she suddenly .... off in the middle of a sentence and ran out of the room.
3 I thought it was very rude of him just to .... off like that without saying goodbye.
4 Would you like me to come and .... you off at the station?
5 I thought I'd .... off fairly soon – I've got to get up early tomorrow, but thank you for a lovely party.
6 I was so tired that I just .... off in front of the television.
7 You mustn't forget to .... off that birthday card this afternoon.
8 A large crowd gathered to watch the rocket .... off.

15.2 Replace the underlined words in these sentences with phrasal verbs from the opposite page.

1 It won't take him long to <u>do</u> the letters you asked him to do.
2 I often <u>fall asleep</u> in boring lectures.
3 Let's try and <u>leave quietly</u> before the others wake up.
4 In the middle of a long speech, the actor suddenly <u>stopped</u> and ran off the stage.
5 I've <u>put</u> all the Christmas presents for abroad <u>in the post</u>.
6 The school disco <u>has given</u> her <u>quite negative feelings about</u> discos in general.
7 Tell that boy in our front garden to <u>leave at once</u> – he's annoying the dog.
8 Fortunately, he <u>didn't take</u> the criticism of his acting <u>seriously</u>.
9 I'll <u>print</u> a copy of the report for you.

15.3 Answer these questions using full sentences.

1 If someone criticised your hairstyle would you laugh it off or get very upset?
2 What kind of programmes are most likely to make you doze off in front of the television?
3 If you go on a journey on your own, who usually sees you off?
4 Can you run off an English essay quickly, or does it take you a long time?
5 Why might a lecturer break off in the middle of a talk?
6 If you plan to slip off during a party, how are you intending to go?
7 If someone tells some young people to 'clear off', how do you think that person probably feels about them?
8 Name something that might put you off eating your dinner.

15.4 Rewrite these sentences using a phrasal verb from the opposite page that means the opposite of the underlined verb. Make any other necessary changes so that the sentences make sense.

1 I'm going to <u>meet</u> Artem at the airport tomorrow.
2 I've just <u>received</u> a letter from Elizabeth.
3 The rocket is due to <u>land</u> tomorrow at noon.
4 I hope I've managed to <u>interest</u> him in the idea of redecorating the house.
5 I <u>woke up</u> when all the others went off to play tennis.
6 We're planning to <u>arrive</u> in the early evening.

16 On and in

A On

On in phrasal verbs sometimes has a clear link with the basic physical meaning of *on*.

Never buy shoes without **trying** them **on**! [putting on a piece of clothing to see whether it fits and whether you like it]

| Leo | Do you think Dan's really feeling better or is he just **putting on** a brave face? [pretending to have a particular feeling or behave in a way that is not real or natural for someone] |

| Ben | No, I think he's fine now. I don't think his cheerfulness is **put-on**. [adjective: pretend or not genuine, from the verb **put on**] |

| Sam | I've got something **weighing on*** my mind at the moment. Could you give me some advice? [worrying, upsetting] |

| Mia | No problem. Tell me all about it and I'll do what I can. |

On is also used with verbs where there is an idea of dependence.

You can always **rely/depend/count on*** Max! [be confident that someone will help you]

*In these four verbs *upon* may be used instead of *on*. *Upon* sounds slightly more formal.

On in phrasal verbs also often contains an idea of *further*.

Just because you've failed one driving test, you mustn't stop having lessons. You must **keep on** trying. [continue to do something]

When you've finished with the magazine, just **pass** it **on** to someone else. [give]

B In

Here are some of the many phrasal verbs that use *in*. In each case there is a link with the basic physical meaning of *in*.

phrasal verb	meaning	example
call in	visit a place or person for a short time, usually when going somewhere else	Please **call in** and see us when you are next in town.
take sth **in** or **take in** sth	make a piece of clothing narrower	This skirt is too big for me now – I'll have to **take** it **in**.
rub sth **in** or **rub in** sth	put a substance on the surface of something and rub it so that it goes into the surface	**Rub** the cream **in** gently with the tips of your fingers.
lock sb **in** or **lock in** sb	prevent someone from leaving a room or building by locking the doors	Make sure you leave the office by 6.30 p.m. or you'll be **locked in**.
push in (informal)	rudely join a line of people who are waiting by going in front of some of the people who are already there	It's so annoying when people **push in** at the bus stop.
sink in	start to be believed (used about something unpleasant or surprising, which usually has implications)	Be patient with Evie – it'll take a long time for the terrible news to **sink in**.

Exercises

16.1 **Rewrite the underlined parts of these sentences using phrasal verbs from A.**

1 I read the gardening article you gave me and then <u>gave</u> it to a friend who's also interested in plants.
2 Do you think she's really angry, or do you think she's just <u>pretending</u>?
3 He looks very pale and tired. Something is clearly <u>worrying</u> him.
4 It's a lovely jacket. <u>See if it fits you and how it looks on you</u>.
5 I'm <u>not going to stop</u> working until I've finished this report.
6 You can <u>be sure that William will be there when you need him</u>.

16.2 **Look at these remarks by different people and then read the statements 1–5 below. If the statement is true, tick (✓) the box. If the statement is false, put a cross (✗) in the box and explain why it is false.**

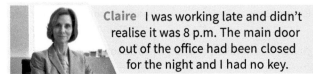
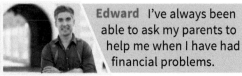

Claire I was working late and didn't realise it was 8 p.m. The main door out of the office had been closed for the night and I had no key.

Edward I've always been able to ask my parents to help me when I have had financial problems.

Richard I've got some mosquito bites. Have you got any cream that'll stop them itching?

Anwar Oscar doesn't seem to be answering his phone. I'll tell him the news when I see him tomorrow.

Alice My new skirt was far too loose, so I reduced the waistband by three centimetres.

Charlotte I've got a lot of problems which are worrying me at the moment.

1 Anwar has decided to keep on phoning Oscar. ☐
2 Alice decided not to take her skirt in. ☐
3 Charlotte has a number of things weighing on her mind. ☐
4 Richard wants to rub in some cream. ☐
5 Edward can't really count on his parents' support. ☐
6 Claire got locked in. ☐

16.3 **Correct the mistakes in these sentences. There is one mistake in each sentence.**

1 Hey, that man just pushed on – that taxi should have been ours!
2 Heidi's bad news has been weighing my mind on all day.
3 I need time for to sink in the news.
4 I couldn't leave the room because someone had locked me out.
5 Phrasal verbs may seem hard but you must keep in trying.
6 You'll never guess who called at the office in today!

Over to you

Go to the Cambridge University Press dictionary website at www.dictionary.cambridge.org. Find one more meaning for each of these verbs and write an example sentence: *pass on, take in* and *rub in*.
If you do not have Internet access, try looking in a good monolingual or bilingual dictionary.

17 Down and over

A Different meanings of *down*

general meaning of down	example	meaning of phrasal verb in example
move in the direction of the ground	We'll have to **chop/cut down** that old tree. It's dead.	cut through it so that it falls to the ground
heaviness which causes difficulty	We were **weighed down** with luggage, so we couldn't run to catch the train.	carrying too much
	I was **loaded down** with books, so I took the bus home.	carrying too many things
put on paper	Just **note down** the main points, not everything the lecturer says.	put something on paper or on an electronic device, especially something that someone says
	I'll **note down** your phone number, or else I'll forget it.	write something on a piece of paper or type it on an electronic device so that you do not forget it
reduce a number or amount, or not let it rise	I'm taking these tablets to **keep** my blood pressure **down**.	stop the number, level or size of something from increasing
	I'm trying to **cut down** on burgers and chips as I've started to put on weight.	eat or drink less of a particular thing, usually in order to improve your health
stop an activity	The car factory has **shut down**, and 2,000 people have lost their jobs.	closed and stopped working
	That nice Italian restaurant in town has **closed down**. What a pity!	stopped doing business

B *Over*

Read Hamad's email to Jessica about a report at work.

> Jessica,
>
> Could you please **read over**[1] Bethany's latest report and just **look over**[2] the figures in the appendix? We can **go over**[3] it together when we meet tomorrow. Then I'll add our comments and **hand** the whole thing **over**[4] to the sales team.
>
> Thank you,
>
> Hamad

[1] read something from the beginning to the end in order to find any mistakes or to understand it better

[2] quickly examine something

[3] talk or think about something in order to explain it or make sure that it is correct

[4] give something to someone else

Listen to this voicemail.

Hi, Mum. I'm **staying over**[1] at Aisha's tonight – she's a bit miserable because she didn't win the tennis championship. I'm sure she'll **get over**[2] it soon, though. She also **fell over**[3] and hurt her knee quite badly. Anyway, I'll see you tomorrow. Bye.

[1] spending the night somewhere else rather than going home (*staying* on its own would also be possible here)

[2] recover from an illness or disappointment

[3] fell to the ground (*fell* on its own would also be possible here)

Exercises

17.1 **Read the sentences using phrasal verbs from A and then answer the questions.**

1 Jamie is weighed down with luggage.
   What do we know about Jamie's luggage?
2 She's trying to cut down on chocolate.
   Does she still eat chocolate?
3 Alexander took down everything we said.
   Did Alexander remember or write what was said?
4 The garage has shut down.
   Has the garage shut for the evening?
5 They chopped down the bushes in front of their house.
   Why might they have decided to do this?

17.2 **Complete these newspaper headlines with the correct verbs from the box. Write the verbs in the correct form.**

chop	cut	go	hand	keep	shut

1 **LOCAL CAFÉ** .... **DOWN BY HEALTH INSPECTORS**

2 **DOCTORS WARN TEENAGERS TO** .... **DOWN ON FAST FOOD**

3 **REBEL TROOPS** .... **OVER WEAPONS**

4 **TWENTY OAKS** .... **DOWN TO MAKE WAY FOR BYPASS**

5 **GOVERNMENT PROMISES TO** .... **DOWN INFLATION**

6 **MINISTERS TO** .... **OVER REPORT IN DETAIL TOMORROW**

17.3 **Answer these questions about phrasal verbs with *down* and *over*. Use a dictionary if necessary.**

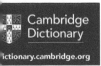
Cambridge
Dictionary
ictionary.cambridge.org

1 Which three phrasal verbs in the email on the opposite page are often used with *through* instead of *over*? Does using *through* instead of *over* change the meaning at all?
2 Can you see any meaning for *over* that connects the three verbs in the voicemail?
3 Match each of the phrasal verbs below with the correct general meaning of *down* from the table in A.
   a) I need a holiday. Stress and overwork are **wearing** me **down**.
   b) Let me **take down** your details.
   c) A lot of fences **blew down** in the hurricane last night.
   d) The police are trying to **crack down** on street crime.
   e) The government is doing all it can to **hold** prices **down**.
4 Explain what these phrasal verbs with *over* mean in the sentences below.
   a) Amy is very good at **putting over** her point of view in meetings.
   b) I haven't got enough room. Can you **move over**, please?
   c) Can you **check over** these figures for me, please? It's important that there are no mistakes.
   d) Don't put your glass of wine on the floor. Someone is sure to **knock** it **over**.
   e) Make sure the milk does not **boil over**.

18 Around and about

Around and *about* are often interchangeable in phrasal verbs: both particles are equally possible with all the verbs in A below and with some of the verbs in B. Note also that *round* can sometimes replace *around*.

Phrasal verbs with *around* and *about* often express the idea of acting in a relaxed way, or without a particular purpose or without concentrating.

Most of the verbs in this unit are informal.

A Spending time

phrasal verb	meaning	example
wait about/around	stay in one place without doing anything as you wait for something to happen	If you can **wait around** for about an hour, we should be able to tell you your results.
laze about/around	relax and enjoy yourself by doing very little	For the first week of our holiday we usually just **laze about** on the beach.
sit about/around (somewhere)	spend time sitting down and doing very little	Please let me help you. I don't like just **sitting about** all day.
hang about/around/ round (somewhere) (informal)	spend time somewhere without doing very much	There are always a lot of rather suspicious-looking people **hanging round** outside that bar.
mess about/around	spend time playing or doing things with no particular purpose	Tim spends his weekends **messing around** in the garage repairing things.
	behave stupidly, waste time doing unimportant things	The pupils were given extra homework for **messing around** in class.
mess sb about/ around (informal)	treat someone badly or waste their time, e.g. by changing your mind or not doing what you promised	He's been **messing** her **around** for ages and just won't commit to the relationship.
lie about/around	spend time lying down doing very little	I hate the way she just **lies around** all day watching TV while I'm working.

B Being in a place

Fans were **milling about/around/round** the hotel lobby hoping to see the film star and get her autograph. [walking around a particular place or area, usually while waiting for something]

Meanwhile photographers and journalists were **standing about/around/round** chatting to each other. [spending time standing in a place waiting for someone or doing very little]

Tyler   Can you **stick around** this afternoon? [informal: stay somewhere for a period of time] If so, I'll **take** you **around/round** the office and introduce you to the other account managers if you like. [visit a place with someone showing them the most interesting or important parts]

Anna   No, it's all right, thanks. The boss has already **shown** me **around/round**. [gone with someone to a place that they have not visited before and shown them the interesting parts]

Exercises

18.1 **Draw lines to match the verbs in the left-hand column with the best definitions in the right-hand column.**

1 mess
2 hang
3 lie
4 sit
5 laze

about/(a)round

lie down doing very little
spend time sitting down and doing very little
relax, enjoy yourself and do very little
behave stupidly or waste time
spend time somewhere not doing very much

18.2 **Now use the verbs from exercise 18.1 to fill the gaps in these sentences. Write the verbs in the correct form and use each verb once only.**

1 She just .... around on the sofa all day chatting to friends online.
   I wish she'd get a job.
2 We could be .... round here for hours waiting for a taxi. Let's walk.
3 After the meeting we were just .... around chatting for a while.
4 My idea of a perfect weekend is just .... around at home with a good book.
5 I wish the kids would stop .... about.

18.3 **Rewrite the underlined words in these sentences using phrasal verbs from the opposite page.**

1 Do you want to <u>stay here</u> after the meeting? I finish work at 5 p.m. and I could <u>go with you and show you the most interesting places in</u> the old town.
2 Nothing much happened at the demonstration. We just <u>stood in one place not doing much</u> and held our banners up.
3 They spend most weekends just <u>doing things without much purpose</u> in their boat; they don't really sail it seriously.
4 On my first day, the boss <u>went with me through</u> the workshop and introduced me to various people I'd be working with.
5 At the drinks party people were just <u>wandering here and there</u> hoping to find someone they knew.
6 Look, I'm sorry, I don't want to <u>cause you problems and waste your time</u>, but I wonder if we could postpone our meeting till next week?

18.4 **Here are some other phrasal verbs with *about/around*. Read the sentences and try to explain in your own words what they mean. Use a dictionary if necessary.**

1 I've got to go now but I'll **see** you **around**.
2 Don't **order** me **about**! I'm not your servant, you know.
3 My suitcase got a bit **bashed about** on the plane.
4 He told the kids to stop **fooling around**.
5 Assistant: Can I help you?
   Customer: No thanks. I'm just **looking around** the gallery.

Cambridge Dictionary
ictionary.cambridge.org

19 For and with

Note that with all the verbs in this unit the particles *for* and *with* must go before the object of the verb.

A   *For*

Each response in the dialogues below contains two phrasal verbs with *for*. Learning verbs in pairs associated with the same context can help you remember them.

Hannah	I've been given the chance to apply for that new post in head office. What do you think?
Dylan	I think you should **go for** it [try to get or achieve it]. We'll all be **rooting for** you [informal: showing support for you in a competition, or hoping that you will succeed].

Eleanor	How's your new babysitter?
Julian	We **couldn't ask for** a better babysitter [the new babysitter is the best of her kind]. She just **lives for** our kids and they just adore her [believes that the kids are the most important people in her life].

Zoë	I saw you going into Victoria's flat with her this morning. Is anything wrong?
Leah	Her washing machine had flooded the kitchen. She **sent for** a plumber and got it fixed but it left a terrible mess [send someone a message asking them to come to see you]. We had planned to go into town and I was **calling for** her on the way there, but in the end we stayed at home and tidied the mess in the kitchen [visiting her place in order to collect her].

Joey	What does 'R' mean on that sign?
Finlay	I think it **stands for** 'restaurant' [is the first letter of a word or name and is used to represent it]. Let's stop. You must **be dying for** something to eat [informal: be wanting something very much, especially food or drink].

B   *With*

phrasal verb	meaning	example
could do with sth/sb	need or want something or someone (informal)	I **could do with** a cup of coffee.
deal with sth	if something [e.g. a book, film, article] deals with a particular subject or idea, it is about that subject or idea	His latest book **deals with** the civil war of 1984–1989.
stick with it	continue doing something even though it is difficult (informal)	I know studying for a PhD is hard, but I think you should **stick with it**.
go with sth	if one thing goes with another, they suit each other or they look or taste good together	That shirt **goes** really well **with** your blue jacket.
put up with sb/sth	accept unpleasant behaviour or an unpleasant situation, even though you do not like it	I don't know how she **puts up with** her sister's bad temper.
catch up with sb	meet someone you know, after not seeing them for a period of time	I hope to **catch up with** Ava when I'm in Berlin. I haven't seen her for years.

Exercises

19.1 Look at the phrasal verbs in A. Then match the questions 1–6 with the appropriate answers a–f below.

1 These shoes are a bit expensive – do you think I should buy them?
2 Oh dear, look at that accident.
3 What did you think of the restaurant?
4 Do you know what CV means?
5 Would you like to go to a café?
6 Who are you supporting in the league?

a) Couldn't have asked for anything better!
b) Yes, go for it!
c) Quick! Send for an ambulance!
d) Yes, I'm dying for an ice cream.
e) We're rooting for the Reds, as usual.
f) Sure! It stands for curriculum vitae.

19.2 Complete these sentences with an appropriate verb. Write the verb in the correct form.

1 He .... for a doctor as soon as he felt the pains in his chest.
2 Martha .... for her work, so she's going to find it very hard when she has to retire.
3 These boots don't really .... with this skirt, but they're comfortable.
4 You .... for a nicer teacher. She's so patient and kind.
5 I'll have to have a word with Gina. I can't .... up with her rudeness any longer!
6 Your hair is too long – you .... with a haircut.
7 You should .... with the course. It would be a shame to give up now.
8 I love going back to my home town and .... up with all my old friends.

19.3 Use a phrasal verb from the opposite page to complete these dialogues.

1 **Anna**   This fish tastes delicious with your tomato sauce.

  Isabelle Yes, they do .... well .... each other, don't they!

2 **Charles** Shall we go to the concert together?

  Sarah   Good idea. I'll .... you on the way there.

3 **Felix**   I've bought two bottles of water.

  Elliot   Great, I'm .... something to drink.

4 **Fran**   I thought the film was great.

  Millie   Yes, I thought it .... the theme of love really sensitively.

5 **Michael** Let's meet for a coffee and a chat next week.

  Darcy   Yes, I can't wait to .... you.

19.4 Rewrite these sentences using phrasal verbs from the opposite page.

1 I couldn't tolerate such noisy neighbours as yours.
2 It's been such a busy week. I can't wait for the weekend.
3 Evelyn's shoes match her handbag perfectly.
4 All the students at his university were hoping Austin would win the golf championship.
5 I have the best job you could imagine.
6 Her grandson is the most important person in Stella's life.

A Through

Through in phrasal verbs gives an idea of going from one side of something to the other, or from the beginning to the end of something. Note that with most of these phrasal verbs *through* must go before the object of the verb.

If you **sleep through** a loud noise or activity, it does not wake you.

> I'm sorry I'm late. I'm afraid I **slept through** my alarm.

If you **live through** something, you experience a difficult situation or event.

> People who have **lived through** a war often have rather a different outlook on life.

If you **flick through** a magazine or book, you look briefly at its pages.

> I usually **flick through** a magazine before buying it.

If you **look through** something, you read it quickly and not very carefully.

If you **go through** something, you carefully read or discuss it to make sure that it is correct.

> I'll **look through** the report tonight and then we can **go through** it properly tomorrow.

If you **take** someone **through** something, you explain it or show them how to do it.

> Don't worry – Jack will **take** you **through** the job before we leave you on your own.

If you **see through** a person who is trying to trick you, you realise what they are really like or what they are trying to do.

> He is so charming that few people **see through** him and realise that he is just a conman.

B Back

Back in phrasal verbs or expressions usually conveys the idea of returning.

If you want to return something that has been delivered to you, e.g. by post, perhaps because it is the wrong size or is damaged, you **send** it **back**. If you go to the shop to exchange it in person, you **take** it **back**. Shops **take back** things they have sold you if you find they are not in good condition when you get home. If you buy goods in a shop with a debit card and ask for **cashback** (noun), the shop will give you cash from your bank account. If you **call/phone/ring** someone **back**, **text** someone **back** or **email** someone **back**, you are replying to a phone message, text message or e-mail from them. If emails **bounce back**, they didn't get to their destination and have been sent back. If you **bounce back** from something, you start to be successful again after a difficult period.

Note that with the verbs above, *back* can go before or after the object of the verb.

If someone, especially a child, **answers** (someone) **back**, they reply rudely to someone they should be polite to.

> **Mother** Say thank you to Mrs Brown.
>
> **Child** Say thank you yourself.
>
> **Mother** Don't **answer** me **back** like that.

An interesting use of *back* is in the expression: We **go back** ten years. This is an informal way of saying: We have known each other for ten years.

If you **bite back**, you do something bad to someone because they did something bad to you. However, if you **bite** something **back** or **bite back** something, you stop yourself from saying something that shows your true feelings or thoughts.

> When Emma is criticised, she doesn't hesitate to **bite back**.

> When Callum asked me what I thought of his lime-green suit, I had to **bite back** my initial response.

Exercises

20.1 **Write what you could say in these situations using phrasal verbs with *through*.**

1 Your boss asks you to explain to a new member of staff how things are done in the office, step by step. What could you say to the new person?
2 A friend warns you that another person, Leo, is trying to trick you. Reassure the friend that you realised what Leo was really like the first moment you met him.
3 You arrive late for an important meeting. You set your alarm clock but didn't wake up when it rang. Apologise and explain what happened.
4 You have done some calculations at work, and there seems to be a mistake. Ask a colleague to read the figures carefully to see if they can see any mistakes.
5 A colleague offers to read in detail a 12-page report you have written. Tell them that that will not be necessary and that you'd be grateful if they just looked at it very briefly. (Give two possible answers.)
6 A friend asks you why a person you know always seems so sad. Explain that that person has experienced some terrible things over the last few years.

20.2 **Complete these sentences using verbs or expressions from B.**

1 This new jacket just doesn't look right on me; the colour is all wrong. If I .... it back to the shop, do you think they'd .... it back? I bought it over 30 days ago.
2 I had to .... back some angry words when they told me I had lost my job.
3 I bought this clock online, but it's not as nice as it looked on the computer screen. I think I'll .... it back.
4 I don't think he'll just accept his brother's insults. He's the sort of person who will .... back if he's attacked.
5 We're old friends. We .... back to the 1980s when we were at college together.
6 Kids nowadays seem to lack respect for their parents and won't hesitate to .... back.
7 I haven't got any cash. I'll get .... when we go to the supermarket.
8 I got the email address wrong, so my message .... back.

20.3 **Complete the sentences using an appropriate phrasal verb from the opposite page.**

1 James rang while you were out. Please could you ....
2 I don't like these trousers I bought today. I think I ....
3 Harry missed his train this morning because he ....
4 Ella isn't really reading the magazine; she's just ....
5 I wanted to tell her how upset I was, but I managed to ....

Mr Taylor was one of those people everyone could see through immediately.

21 Into and away

A Into

Read the entries in Amelia's personal diary. Each entry has a phrasal verb with *into*.

APRIL	
7 Mon **Ran into** Maria in town today. Nice to see her again.	met someone I know when I did not expect to meet them
8 Tue Car problems again today! Must **look into** getting a new one.	investigate and examine the facts about a problem or situation
9 Wed Poor old Julia! The boss told her he didn't like some work she'd done and she **burst into** tears.	suddenly started to make a noise, especially to start crying, laughing or singing
10 Thu The boss wants to have lunch with me. Anna says I shouldn't **read** anything **into** it, but I'm suspicious of his motives.	believe that an action, remark, or situation has a particular importance or meaning, often when this is not true
11 Fri Met Liam today. He **went into** his marriage problems in great detail. Felt sorry for him.	described and discussed something in a detailed way
12 Sat Decided to **throw** myself **into** doing some gardening now that spring is here!	start doing something with a lot of enthusiasm and energy
13 Sun Saw Liam again. Told him I was busy as I didn't want to **enter into** another discussion about his private life.	start to become involved in something, especially a discussion. (Note that you enter a room, not enter into a room.)
14 Mon The boss wants us all to **buy into** his ambitious new plan for the company, but I'm not convinced.	completely believe in a set of ideas

B Away

phrasal verb	meaning	example
tidy away sth or **tidy** sth **away**	put things in cupboards and drawers, etc. after you have been using them	Mum told me to **tidy away** all my things before my aunt came to visit.
pack away sth or **pack** sth **away**	put something into a bag or container, or in the place where it is usually kept	The Scouts **packed away** their tents and left the camping ground.
tear sb **away** (usually + **from**)	force someone to stop doing something they enjoy in order to do something else	I'm sorry to **tear** you **away** from your computer, but I need your help.
stay away from sth	avoid something that has a bad effect on you	I think I should **stay away from** desserts. I'm putting on weight.
turn away	move your face so you are not looking at something	When they show an operation on TV, I have to **turn away**.
lock yourself **away**	go to a room or building where you can be alone, usually so that you can work	I decided to **lock** myself **away** in my room till I'd finished my essay.
run away (often + **from**)	secretly leave a place because you are unhappy there	Did you ever **run away** from home as a child?

Exercises

21.1 **Match the beginning of each sentence with its ending.**

1 At the supermarket yesterday, Julia ran — into his words.
2 Harvey is getting over his broken heart by throwing himself — into all that alternative medicine stuff.
3 When she saw me dressed up as a pirate, she burst — into the causes of the war.
4 He doesn't think before he speaks, so don't read too much — into the argument.
5 In your essay you should have gone more fully — into what happened.
6 We were disagreeing about the film and then Robyn entered — into laughter.
7 The police are doing all they can to look — into his studies.
8 I don't really buy — into Jake.

21.2 **Complete these sentences using a phrasal verb with *away*. Write the verb in the correct form and add, if necessary, a reflexive pronoun (e.g. myself, yourself).**

1 I once terrified my parents by .... from home.
2 Please .... your games and books. It's time for dinner.
3 You really should .... Stanley. He's a bad influence on you.
4 She was so upset that she .... in her room until the next morning.
5 I always .... when there's a penalty. I can't bear to watch.
6 Please could you .... from the computer? I need some help in the garden.

21.3 **Complete these sentences in any way that makes sense using one of the phrasal verbs from the opposite page.**

1 I was very surprised when Claudia burst ....
2 It makes sense to stay ....
3 My best friend always throws ....
4 Sometimes I'd really like to run ....
5 I find this job so stressful. I really should look ....
6 When I went to the town centre last week, I ran ....
7 Before moving house I spent weeks packing ....
8 Whenever visitors are coming, I usually tidy ....

21.4 **Here are some more phrasal verbs with *into* and *away*. Read the sentences 1–5 and match the phrasal verbs with the definitions a–e below. Use a dictionary if necessary.**

Cambridge
Dictionary

tionary.cambridge.org

1 As soon as Nathan saw me he **launched into** a long account of his travels.
2 Because it is so expensive in this country at the moment, tourists are **keeping away**.
3 Trying to cross the room in the dark, he **banged into** a small table and knocked it over.
4 It isn't a person in that field, it's a scarecrow – the farmer wants to **scare** the birds **away**.
5 I **bumped into** your sister in town this morning.

a) knock against something, usually by accident
b) meet someone you know when you have not planned to meet them
c) start doing or saying something (e.g. a speech or a story) in a very enthusiastic way
d) make a person or animal so frightened that they go away
e) not go to a place

21.5 **Can you see any basic meanings for *into* and *away* in the phrasal verbs in this unit that might help you learn them?**

A | At work

Kate works as a nurse. When she starts work she has to **clock on**[1], and when she leaves she **clocks off**[2]. If records show that she has worked an extra-long shift, then she is able to **take** time **off**[3] at a later date. She was planning to take a holiday in July this year but has had to **bring** it **forward**[4] as July is going to be a particularly busy time for her hospital this year. Kate loves her work, but her hospital is understaffed and she hates to always **be pushed for**[5] time. She finds it almost impossible to **fit in**[6] time to talk to the patients although she feels that is an important part of her job. She can chat for a few minutes but then she has to **press on**[7] with her other duties. The hospital employs many nurses from overseas. When their work permits **run out**[8] after three years, they have to reapply for a further work permit.

[1] record the time she arrives at work (also **clock in**)
[2] record the time she leaves work (also **clock out**)
[3] spend time away from work
[4] change the date or time of something so that it happens earlier than expected
[5] not have enough of something, usually time or money
[6] find time to do something or see someone
[7] continue doing something in a determined way
[8] come to an end (of the period of time of a document or agreement); more formal equivalent is *expire*

B | At leisure

When Kate does have spare time, she likes to relax. She usually **hangs out/around/round**[1] with friends she was at school with. They love **whiling away**[2] their days off together, going round the shops or just chatting at one of their homes. Sometimes they go away for a weekend and **muck about**[3] at Kate's aunt's cottage in the countryside. Last time they did that, a colleague of Kate's **latched on to**[4] them and went too. The others didn't really like her at first, especially as she always kept them **hanging on**[5] while she got ready, but now they all like her very much.

[1] spends a lot of time (informal)
[2] spending time in a relaxed way, either because they are waiting for something or have nothing special to do
[3] waste time doing silly things (informal)
[4] spent time with them, especially when they did not want her with them
[5] waiting, usually for a short time (informal)

Exercises

22.1 **Complete these sentences with a verb from A.**

1 I'm afraid I'm a bit .... for time today. Could you give me a lift?
2 Oh dear! My passport has .... out. I must renew it before our trip.
3 I usually .... on at 9 a.m. every day, but if my train is late it might be 9.15.
   I .... off at 5 p.m., but sometimes I can finish a bit earlier on Fridays.
4 Mr Chan wants to .... the meeting forward to this week as he's busy
   all next week. I'm not sure if we can .... it in this week as we're very busy too.
5 If we .... on after lunch, we can probably finish the report by 5 p.m.
6 I'm going to .... some time off next month and go and stay with my parents.

22.2 **Write an appropriate question to fit each answer.**

1 .... ?
   Oh, I usually just hang out with friends, or sometimes I do some sport.
2 .... ?
   Well, he never studied; he just spent all his time mucking about, so it's no surprise.
3 .... ?
   No, she's not a friend. She just latched on to our group and followed us.
4 .... ?
   Oh, it's great for whiling away the time if you're waiting for a plane or a train.
5 .... ?
   Let's just hang on for five minutes. I want to speak to someone.

22.3 **Correct the mistakes with the phrasal verbs in these sentences.**

1 We had to wait an hour for the next train, so we went for a walk to while off the time.
2 A young French woman latched to me at the party last night. I think she wanted to
   practise her English.
3 I clock on work at 7.30 a.m. every morning.
4 We have to finish this job by six o'clock. We'd better press up with it.
5 I just don't know how we're going to fit three meetings on before the summer break.

Sometimes I get tired of just hanging out with other bats.

Over to you

Write a description of how you spend your work and leisure time using as many of the phrasal verbs in this unit as you can.

A The past

Charnbury Life HOME | EVENTS | *MUSEUMS & GALLERIES* | DINING

Journey into the past at the

Charnbury Folk Museum

If you're young, come on a journey into the past before you were born. If you're a senior citizen, let us **take you back**[1] to your childhood. **Think back**[2] to what everyday life was like 50, 60, 100, 200 years ago, before computers, before TVs, before fridges and washing machines. Many of our exhibits **date back**[3] to the early 19th century.

Is that old vacuum cleaner in your attic just a **leftover**[4] from a **bygone**[5] era, or is it a piece of industrial history? Come and find out.

Address: Palmer Square, Charnbury Tel: 0211 4684536

[1] make you remember a period or an event in the past
[2] think about things that happened in the past
[3] have existed since a particular time
[4] (noun) something which exists from an earlier time
[5] (adjective) from a time which does not exist any more

Leftover (noun) and **bygone** (adjective) are formed from the verbs **be left over** and **go by**.
We used some balloons that **were left over** from the Christmas party to decorate the house for her birthday. [still existed/were unused from an earlier time]
As time **goes by** you realise that your parents' advice was in your best interests. [passes]
Note that **bygone** also exists as a noun, but it is usually always in the plural **bygones**.

B Time moving

I'm sorry to **hold you up** but you must sign these forms before you go in. [delay you]

If there are no **hold-ups**, we should arrive by about seven o'clock. [noun: delays]

Leo, can you **hurry the kids up**. The coach is about to leave. [make them act more quickly]

Mum walks so fast. It's quite hard to **keep up with** her. [go at the same speed as someone]

The meeting **dragged on** and everyone got irritable. [continued for too long]

I'm sorry I'm late. My French lesson **ran on**, so I didn't leave school till 4.30 p.m. [continued for longer than expected]

Three weeks **passed by** before I got a reply to my letter of complaint. [went past]

It's difficult to plan for the future. Nobody knows what **lies ahead**. [will happen in the future]

> **Tip**
>
> If a phrasal verb has a noun or adjective form associated with it, learn them together and record them together in your vocabulary notebook, e.g. *leftover* and *be left over*.

Exercises

23.1 Write the best phrasal verb expression from the options below to complete this text.

The film is a time travel adventure and I found it very entertaining, though my friend felt that it .... (1) a bit. At the beginning it .... (2) to the Iron Age where the hero is living an ordinary Iron-Age life. He eats a mysterious plant, however, and the years suddenly start .... (3) like minutes. Suddenly he is in the future and, as he is now a .... (4) from a .... (5) era, he finds it very hard to understand what is going on. This results in a number of amusing incidents. Although the plot is occasionally a little difficult to follow, I would certainly recommend it.

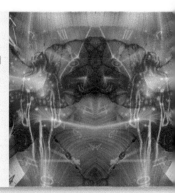

1	a) passed by	b) dragged on	c) held up	d) dated back
2	a) thinks back	b) hurries you up	c) takes you back	d) holds you up
3	a) going by	b) lying ahead	c) hurrying up	d) keeping up
4	a) bygone	b) hold-up	c) bygones	d) leftover
5	a) bygone	b) hold-up	c) bygones	d) leftover

23.2 Explain the difference in meaning between these pairs of sentences.

1 a) The lecture ran on.
  b) The lecture dragged on.
2 a) Ethan held us up.
  b) Ethan hurried us up.
3 a) This song takes me back to my childhood.
  b) This song dates back to my childhood.
4 a) It was not easy to keep up with the children as we went through town.
  b) It was not easy to hurry up the children as we went through town.

23.3 Here are some things people might say relating to time. What does the speaker mean in each sentence? Use a dictionary if necessary.

1 The older you get, the faster time goes by.
2 Music and smells have great powers to take you back.
3 Mr Jones is a leftover from a bygone age.
4 We should let bygones be bygones!
5 You never know what lies ahead.

23.4 Rewrite these sentences using the words in brackets. Write the words in the correct form.

1 The old oil lamps in my grandfather's house looked like things that had survived from a different era. (LEFTOVER, BYGONE)
2 The smell of marker pens always reminds me of my schooldays. (TAKE BACK)
3 The traffic was delayed on the motorway because of an accident. (HOLD-UP)
4 Sometimes, if the textbook is boring, the lesson seems to last longer than it should. (DRAG ON)
5 We can never know what the future will bring. (LIE AHEAD)
6 These pizzas were from the party. Nobody ate them. Would you like one? (LEFTOVER)

A | Describing where places are

example	meaning
We stayed in a lovely hotel which **was tucked away** in a little valley.	was in a quiet or hidden place that not many people see or go to (from **be tucked away**)
Our room **opened onto** a balcony with lovely views of the countryside.	opened in the direction of the countryside or had a view of it (from **open onto** sth)
Fields and woods **stretched away** to the horizon.	continued over a long distance (from **stretch away**)
We could see a few farmhouses which **were dotted around** the landscape.	were in different parts of an area and not close together (from **be dotted around**)
We felt we **were** completely **cut off** from the busy modern world!	very far away from other places and people (from **be cut off**)

B | People in locations

Read this conversation between two students.

Isla Come in, John.

John What a great room!

Isla Well, I like it. It was a bit dull when I moved in, but I bought these nice curtains which help to **brighten it up**[1]. In fact, I like it so much here that I'd rather **stay in**[2] than go out most evenings.

John You're lucky! The room I rent is so miserable that I **stay out**[3] as long as I can! I even **stayed on**[4] in the library tonight until it closed! Anyhow, I've come to bring you your file – you **left** it **behind**[5] at the seminar this morning.

Isla Oh, thanks. How silly of me. I'm glad you noticed it.

John Well, I **stayed behind**[6] to ask the professor some questions and then saw it lying there.

Isla Thank you very much. Would you like a coffee now you're here?

John Well, I can't stay now. But I'd love to **call back**[7] another time if that's OK?

Isla Sure, that'd be nice.

[1] make more attractive, often by adding colours
[2] remain at home, especially in the evenings
[3] come home late or not come home at night
[4] stayed in a place longer than planned
[5] left a place without taking something with you
[6] did not leave a place when others left it
[7] go back to a place to visit someone

> ### Tip
>
> Notice how three of the phrasal verbs in A are used in the passive: *be tucked away, be cut off* and *be dotted around*. Make a special note in your vocabulary notebook if any phrasal verb construction is used in a particular way, e.g. in the passive, as a noun or as an adjective, and write down a typical example sentence to help you remember it.

Exercises

24.1 Complete these sentences to describe these pictures using phrasal verbs based on the verbs in brackets.

The fields (stretch) …

There are small houses (dot) …

The room (open) …

The house (tuck) …

The house on the island (cut) …

24.2 Which phrasal verb from B opposite means …

1 the opposite of *go out*, as in meet friends or go to a restaurant?
2 not come home at night or come home late?
3 forget to take something with you when you go away from a place?
4 stay in a place when other people have left?
5 make something which is dull or boring more attractive or colourful?
6 stay somewhere longer than you planned?
7 go back to a place to see someone, often to visit someone briefly or to collect something?

24.3 Use the phrasal verbs from exercise 24.2 to complete these sentences. Write the verbs in the correct form.

1 I .... my memory stick .... at the computer class. I'll have to go back and see if it's still in the machine.
2 When you were a teenager, did your parents allow you to .... late?
3
    Assistant   I'm afraid the report isn't ready yet. It will be another couple of hours.

    Customer   OK. I'll .... tomorrow.

4 We've decided to paint the kitchen to .... it .... a bit. It's so gloomy and dull at the moment.
5 I'm really tired. I think I'll .... tonight and not go to the party after all, sorry.
6 The teacher asked the two badly behaved girls to .... after the lesson.
7 We loved the resort so much we decided to .... another week, even though our friends had gone home.

Over to you

Go to the Cambridge University Press dictionary website at http://dictionary.cambridge.org. In the search box, type *behind* and then search. From the list of phrasal verbs with *behind*, click on three that you are not familiar with and study the explanations.

25 Cause and effect

A Verbs with *off*

A number of phrasal verbs associated with cause and effect have the particle *off*.

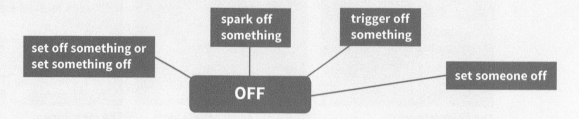

The terrorists **set** the bomb **off** in the middle of the rush hour. [caused an explosion]

We accidentally **set off** the burglar alarm when we came into the house. [made the alarm ring]

The scandal **set off** a series of events which caused the collapse of the government and a general election. [caused a series of events or a lot of activity, often without intending to do so]

You shouldn't have mentioned flying saucers. You've **set** him **off** now. He'll talk for hours. [made him start to talk about something he often talks about]

The ending of the play really **set** her **off**. I didn't know whether she was laughing or crying. [made her start to laugh or cry]

The crisis **sparked off** a bitter civil war. [caused something to suddenly happen or exist]

The Prime Minister's speech **triggered off** violent protests in cities up and down the country. [made something suddenly begin, often a difficult or violent situation]

B Other cause and effect verbs

Read these spoken extracts.

The new airport has **brought about**[1] a lot of changes on this island.

I don't know what **lies behind**[2] Mr Wild's attack on me. Maybe he's trying to **pay** me **back**[3] for something I said about him. Or maybe he's just **stirring** things **up**[4].

This photo **brings back**[5] memories of when we lived in Scotland, when I was a child.

The doctors still haven't **ruled out**[6] the possibility that he might have cancer.

I think most problems teenagers experience **spring from**[7] a feeling of insecurity.

[1] made something happen

[2] is the real reason for
[3] do something unpleasant to me because I have done something unpleasant to him
[4] causing arguments or bad feeling between people, usually on purpose

[5] makes me remember or think about something from the past

[6] decided that something is impossible

[7] are caused by

Exercises

25.1 Choose the best phrasal verb from the box to complete each sentence. Write the verb in the correct form.

bring back   lie behind   stir up   set off   spark off   spring from

1 That song always .... wonderful memories whenever I hear it.
2 I think my problems at work .... the fact that I never really wanted to go into accountancy as a career.
3 I wonder what really .... Maria's dislike of Zachary.
4 I don't like the way Naomi is always trying to .... trouble between us.
5 The film .... a lively discussion in the class.
6 The tragic pictures of the earthquake victims .... her .... and she just couldn't stop crying.

25.2 Fill the gaps in the paragraph below using the correct verb or particle.

> There has been a lot of discussion in the newspapers about what triggered
> .... (1) the recent explosion in the city centre. Some people believe that a
> bomb was .... (2) off by a terrorist group who hope to .... (3)
> about the downfall of the government. Others believe that the explosion was probably
> sparked .... (4) by an electrical fault and have .... (5) out
> any criminal activity. But the question still remains: was it a deliberate explosion set
> .... (6) by a group who wanted to .... (7) things up in order
> to .... (8) the government back for some injustice?

25.3 Which word from the box provides the best ending for these sentences?

suspects   fireworks   memories   feelings   reforms   violence

1 The police used DNA testing to rule out some
....

2 The political demonstration triggered off
....

3 That music brings back ....
4 The government plans to bring about
....

5 Violet's comments stirred up a lot of bad
....

6 At midnight on New Year's Eve we usually set
off some ....

25.4 Complete these sentences using a phrasal verb from the opposite page. Write the verb in the correct form.

1 Take no notice of what he says. He's always trying to .... trouble.
2 She vowed that one day she'd .... for all the heartbreak he had caused her.
3 I wonder what .... the protests last week.
4 The decision to increase taxes .... demonstrations all across the country.
5 Detectives still haven't .... the possibility of murder.
6 His therapist thought that his unhappiness .... a traumatic experience in his childhood.

26 Change

A ## Up meaning more or better

When *up* is used in a phrasal verb with an idea of change, it often adds an idea of becoming more or better.

The number of students getting good marks in their exams is **going up**. [increasing]

I was afraid no-one would come to my lecture, but the room is **filling up** nicely now. [becoming fuller]

Things were bad last week but the situation is **looking up** now. [improving]

Business was down at the beginning of the year but is **picking up** now. [improving after a bad period]

Would you like me to **heat up** the rice or will you have it cold? [make warmer]

Simon's been ignoring the situation for ages – it's time he **woke up to** what's happening. [became more aware of a situation or problem]

B ## Other phrasal verbs relating to change

When I look back over the last year, I see an awful lot of changes in my life. For instance, at work there has been an almost total **changeover**[1] of staff in the office. During the year we have also **phased out**[2] all the old computers and **phased in**[3] a completely new system of office administration. I wasn't sure how things would **pan out**[4] at first and there were a few problems to begin with. However, the arguments about the new system **blew over**[5] quite quickly.

[1] noun: a change from using or having one thing to using or having another (from **change over**)
[2] gradually stopped using
[3] gradually started using
[4] develop or happen
[5] became less important and were then forgotten

Dec 31

At the beginning of the year, my girlfriend left me and it took me a while to **get over**[1] that. But everything's fine with my personal life too now. One of the things I'm most proud of is the fact that I've managed to **give up**[2] caffeine so far this year. I didn't feel too good for the first few weeks, but that's all **worn off**[3] now. I **stuck with**[4] my new regime and now I feel fitter than I have for ages.

[1] begin to feel better after an experience that has made you unhappy
[2] stop a habit or stop doing or having something unhealthy
[3] gradually disappeared
[4] did as I had planned and did not change to something else (informal)

Tip

Sometimes it may help to learn phrasal verbs in pairs of opposites, e.g. *phase in* or *phase out* a new system; *heat up* or *cool down* food; *take up* or *give up* an activity; prices *go up* or *go down*.

Exercises

26.1 Look at these pictures and then complete the sentences about them below using phrasal verbs from A.

1 ![] Sales by month

2 ![]

3 ![] Sales by month

4 ![]

1 Sales have .... during the last few months.
2 I was in the kitchen .... some soup when I heard the phone.
3 Mobile phone use is .... all the time.
4 The bus isn't full yet, but it's ....

26.2 Complete these sentences using the two verbs from A opposite which you did not use in exercise 26.1.

1 It's time you .... to reality and went out and found a job!
2 The economic situation is definitely .... : exports have increased and unemployment is down.

26.3 Complete the word puzzle.

Across
1 change from one thing to another (noun)
2 We can't change it; we're .... with it.
3 I'm angry, but I'll .... over it.
4 The scandal will .... over after a few months.

Down
5 The firm will .... in a new pension scheme.
6 I'm not sure how the situation will .... out.
7 I think I'll .... up football and start playing golf instead.
8 I had an injection at the dentist's and it hasn't .... off yet, so I can't eat properly.

```
          6        7   8
      5
  1   H   N       O       R

  2

                  3

      4
```

26.4 Correct the mistakes with the phrasal verb expressions in these sentences.

1 The overchange to the new accounting system has caused endless problems.
2 There was a lot of trouble in the office last month, but it's all blown up now and things are back to normal.
3 Shall I hot up that pizza for you? I expect it's gone cold by now.
4 All these computers will be faced out over the next year and we'll get new laptops.

Success and failure

A

Read these extracts to understand the underlined phrasal verb expressions in the headlines.

Northcorp brings off $10m deal

Northcorp Telecommunications announced last night that the company had secured a $10m deal in the face of severe competition and despite many difficulties.

Umbrellas fail to catch on with teenagers

An attempt by a Japanese company to market a new range of jazzy umbrellas to teenagers has failed. Sales show that they have not become as popular as the company hoped.

Starfinder album takes off

The first album by the group which won the TV show *Starfinder* where bands competed for a record contract, has become instantly popular one day after it was released and is now number one.

Keira takes over as number one pop idol

18-year-old singer Keira Hoogan has been voted number one female performer in a national pop poll, replacing last year's winner, Francie Moon, as the country's most popular female artist.

Downfall of rebel group marks end of civil war

The failure of the rebel army to hold on to the western part of Kahuba and the rapid collapse of popular support for the rebels means the country's civil war is at an end.

Plan to build new stadium falls through

The President of the Football Association announced last night that the plan to build a new £950m national stadium has failed and the stadium will not be built.

Mini-balloon attempt comes off despite weather

An attempt to fly a mini hot-air balloon under Tower Bridge in London has succeeded, despite fog and rain which threatened to prevent the event.

Druma pulls off record attempt

ZAFI DRUMA yesterday succeeded in winning the 100m, 400m and 800m all on the same day at the International Athletics Championships in Mexico City, despite fierce international competition.

B

Read this speech by a headteacher to pupils who are leaving school.

When you leave this school, we hope you will **build on**[1] what you have learnt here. You must not expect to just **walk into**[2] a highly paid job, but most of you will, with hard work and self-discipline, succeed and achieve great things. Never be content to just **muddle through**[3], as so many people do, always trying to **catch up**[4] and failing to do so. Hard work, dedication and commitment will, in the end, **pay off**[5]. To **keep up**[6] with the competition, we all have to give 100% so that our country can **stay ahead**[7] in business and industry. It will be your job to make this happen. Good luck.

1. use a success or achievement as a base from which to achieve more success
2. get very easily
3. succeed in doing something even though you have difficulties because you do not really know how to do it
4. reach the same quality or standard as someone
5. be successful
6. make progress at the same speed as something or someone else in order to stay at the same level as them
7. continue to be more advanced and successful than other people

Tip

Where phrasal verbs fall naturally into two groups with opposite meanings, e.g. success versus failure, increase versus decrease, make two columns in your vocabulary notebook and fill them in as you meet new verbs that fit either column. Try doing this with the verbs on this page.

Exercises

27.1 **Find phrasal verb expressions from A on the opposite page that match these definitions.**

1 fail to happen
2 replace someone in a position of success
3 the sudden failure of a person or organisation
4 suddenly become successful or popular
5 succeed in achieving something difficult
6 happen successfully or as planned

27.2 **Decide whether these phrasal verbs are mainly associated with success or with failure by writing S or F in the box.**

1 bring off ☐
2 come off ☐
3 muddle through ☐
4 pay off ☐
5 catch up ☐
6 stay ahead ☐
7 take off ☐
8 fall through ☐
9 walk into ☐

27.3 **Fill the gaps in this school report with phrasal verbs from B opposite.**

SUBJECT	COMMENT
History	Ella's work in history is not very thorough but she does manage to .... somehow.
Maths	Ella has managed to successfully .... the work she did last year in order to make excellent progress this term.
English	Ella missed a lot of schoolwork through illness at the beginning of term, but she has managed to .... and is doing well now.
Geography	Ella has always been top of the class in geography and she has managed to .... this year too.
Physics	Ella has never found physics easy but her hard work is beginning to ....

27.4 **Rewrite these sentences using the words in brackets. Write the verb in the correct form.**

1 Beatrice immediately got a job in London. (WALK)

   ....

2 Aaron's hard work eventually brought him success. (PAY)

   ....

3 The company is hoping to make an important deal this week. (PULL)

   ....

4 Ruby never expected her singing career to meet with such instant success. (TAKE)

   ....

5 The project may well not happen because of a lack of funds. (FALL)

   ....

6 Harper finds it hard to make as much progress as the other kids in her class. (KEEP)

   ....

7 The new mobile phone design has become successful almost overnight. (CATCH)

   ....

8 Top software companies are finding it increasingly difficult to remain in front of their competitors. (STAY)

   ....

28 Starting and finishing

A Starting

If you …	then you …	example
set about sth/doing sth	start doing something that uses a lot of time or energy	The kitchen looked as if it hadn't been cleaned or tidied for months, but Jessica **set about** making it look as good as new.
set out	start a journey	We **set out** at 7 a.m. and didn't return until after dark.
start off or **start out**	begin life, existence or a profession in a particular way	Maisie **started out** as a model but soon realised that it was not the career for her.

Note that the noun the **outset**, from the verb **set out**, means the beginning, e.g. There were problems from the **outset** and things became progressively worse.

B Finishing

Joey **called off**[1] the building work his team was doing on the new company offices because he had heard that the company was going bankrupt. He knew the money was going to **dry up**[2], so he was not prepared to continue. Most of the team immediately **broke off**[3] what they were doing, but some of them first **finished off**[4] the task they were working on. Joey himself quickly **polished off**[5] the last of his paperwork and then **packed up**[6] too.

[1] decided to stop an activity that had already started
[2] end or stop coming
[3] stopped or interrupted
[4] completed the last part of what they were doing
[5] finished something quickly and easily
[6] collected his things together, usually after finishing doing something

Scarlett is trying to **give up**[1] caffeine. At first she **cut down**[2] to one strong cup of tea in the morning and another when she got home from work, and only five cups of coffee rather than fifteen every day, but she is finding it very hard to stop having any caffeine completely. She says that sitting down with a proper cup of tea helps her to **wind down**[3] after a hard day at work and that herbal tea doesn't have the same effect. She hopes her determination won't **fizzle out**[4] after a few weeks as she is very anxious not to **give up**[5] this new regime.

[1] stop doing or having something
[2] reduced the amount or number
[3] gradually relax after something that has made you feel tired or worried
[4] gradually end or disappear, usually in a disappointing way
[5] stop doing something before you have completed it, usually because it is too difficult

Exercises

28.1 Complete these comments by various people with words from the box below. Write the words in the correct form.

| set   fizzle   dry   start   give   polish   pack   cut   finish   call   break   outset |

1
I .... out as a chemist, but I knew from the .... that it wasn't what I wanted to do. So I .... it in and joined the navy instead.

2
I had 50 exam papers to correct that day, so I .... about marking them. I managed to .... off about 20 by 12.30, so I .... off for lunch and decided to .... the job off later.

3
I was putting on weight, so I decided to .... up fatty foods. I .... down on sweet drinks too, but I'm afraid my efforts .... out after a couple of weeks and now I'm back where I started.

4
Our research project was getting nowhere, and our funds were .... up. We didn't really want to .... the whole thing off, but we had no choice. We're very disappointed.

28.2 Answer these questions about yourself using full sentences with a phrasal verb.

1 What should you set about doing soon even though you don't really want to?
2 Can you think of something you were planning to do but then were forced to call off?
3 What helps you to wind down when you are tired or stressed?
4 What do you eat or drink too much of which you think you should cut down on?
5 What did you once start off doing but later gave up?

'You polished off all the cakes before I got here!'

Over to you

Go to the Cambridge University Press dictionary website at http://dictionary.cambridge.org and enter the word *start* in the search box. If you do not have Internet access, look up the word *start* in a good monolingual or bilingual dictionary. How many more phrasal verbs can you find based on *start*?

A

Actions and movement with *down* and *up*

Down in phrasal verbs about actions can mean towards the ground, towards a lower level or less intensely.

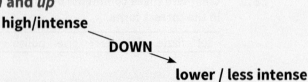

example	meaning
She **fell down** and broke her arm.	fell to the ground
Can you **get** that book **down** for me, please? You're taller than me.	get something that is above your head by reaching with your hand
Slow down! There's a police car behind us.	drive more slowly

Up in phrasal verbs about actions can mean towards a higher level, in a complete way or to a greater degree.

example	meaning
I must **wrap up** Stella's birthday present. Do you have any nice paper?	cover in paper, especially in order to give as a present
Can you help me to **tie up** this package? I don't want it to get damaged in the post.	put string or rope around something so that it is fastened together
Will you help me **blow up** these balloons for the party?	fill with air
Could you **pick up** that box and follow me, please? It has the exam papers in it.	lift using your hands
He felt very angry and **tore** her letter **up**.	tear into a lot of small pieces
Could you **move up** and let Isabella sit next to you?	move slightly so that there is enough space for someone else
I have a bad leg. I don't want to **slow** you **up**, so go ahead and don't wait for me.	make someone or something slower

B

Other action and movement verbs

Move over! I need to sit down. [change the place where you are sitting or standing so that there is space for someone else to sit or stand]

I'm just **popping out** for a newspaper. Do you want anything from the shop? [informal: leaving the place where I am to go somewhere for a short time]

I **reached out** for the light switch but couldn't find it in the dark. [stretched my arm in front of my body, usually in order to get or touch something]

Can you **help** me **on/off** with these boots, please? [help me put on / take off a piece of clothing]

Exercises

29.1 **Read these sentences and answer the questions.**

1 Could you get that saucepan down for me, please?
    Where do you think the saucepan is?
2 Emily has just popped out of the office.
    Is Emily going home for the day?
3 If Charlie moves up a bit, there'll be room for all of us.
    Where does Charlie have to move – a bit higher or closer to someone?
4 If Emily moves over, then Abigail can sit next to Matthew.
    Does Emily have to move more or less than Charlie in sentence 3?
5 Tear the cloth up into small pieces and soak them in the dye for a couple of hours.
    Is it necessary to use scissors to cut the cloth into small pieces?
6 Help your grandmother on with her coat, Julia.
    Is Julia's grandmother about to go outside or inside?

29.2 **Rewrite these sentences using phrasal verbs from the opposite page which have the *opposite* meaning to the underlined verbs.**

1 The children helped me to <u>unwrap</u> the parcel.
2 Can you <u>untie</u> Albert's shoe laces for him?
3 <u>Put down</u> the ball at once.
4 <u>Hurry up</u> – it's beginning to snow and there's ice on the road.
5 Annabelle loves <u>bursting</u> balloons!

29.3 **Look at these pictures and write answers to the questions about them using a phrasal verb from the opposite page.**

1

3

5

2

4

6

1 What has happened to the tree?
2 What's the woman doing?
3 What is the boy doing?
4 What's the boy doing?
5 What's the woman doing?
6 What's the woman doing?

29.4 **Choose the correct verbs to complete these sentences.**

1 Their heavy rucksacks .... the climbers up.
2 In the darkness of the cinema, he .... out and took her hand.
3 I'm just going to .... out to the post office. I won't be long.
4 Let me .... up your travel pillow for you now that we're on the plane.

A Destroying

Here are some phrasal verbs which relate to the concept of destruction.

phrasal verb	meaning	example
fall apart	break into pieces because of being too old or too weak	Take care with this priceless old book. It's beginning to **fall apart**.
pull down sth or **pull** sth **down**	destroy a building or other structure because it is not wanted any more	They are planning to **pull down** the old police station and build a new one.
screw up sth or **screw** sth **up**	twist or crush paper or material with your hands	You can tell she's nervous – look how she's **screwing up** those scraps of paper.
tear apart sth or **tear** sth **apart**	pull something violently so that it breaks into two or more pieces	The customs officers **tore** the bag **apart** and found the hidden drugs.
tear down sth or **tear** sth **down**	violently destroy a building or other structure because it is not wanted	I can't bear to watch them **tearing down** the school we used to go to.
knock over sth/sb or **knock** sth/sb **over**	hit or push someone or something, usually accidentally, so that they fall to the ground or onto their side	As he was dusting the room, he **knocked over** a vase and spilt water all over the table.
put out sth or **put** sth **out**	make something that is burning, e.g. a fire, stop burning	We managed to **put** the fire **out** before the fire brigade arrived.
root out sb/sth or **root** sb/sth **out**	find and get rid of the thing or person that is causing a problem	The government says it will **root out** crime and the causes of crime.
stamp out sth or **stamp** sth **out**	get rid of something that is considered wrong or harmful	The government says it is doing all it can to **stamp out** the problem of drugs.

B Reacting to destruction and negative situations

HOME | **LOCAL NEWS** | WORLD NEWS | SPORTS

FIGHT TO SAVE VILLAGE HOME

Meanborough local council has decided to destroy a lovely old cottage with a beautiful rose garden in the village of Wareholt in order to widen the main road. However, the villagers are equally determined to **fight back**[1]. The authorities want to evict an 82-year-old lady, Mary Jakes, who has lived all her life in the cottage. They are **bending over backwards**[2] to persuade her to go and live in a modern old people's home in the nearest town and have offered to move her at their cost.

Mary does not want to move and villagers are doing all they can to **see** her **through**[3] her difficult time. Mary may seem old and harmless, but she has **turned on**[4] several officers from the council who have tried to get her to change her mind. There was a recent **setback**[5] for Mary when she was told that she couldn't stay in the cottage because repairs needed to be done to the roof. However, her neighbour, a builder, quickly **saw to**[6] it and her roof is now in good repair, so she is still in the cottage and hopes to win her battle.

[1] defend themselves when something or someone attacks them
[2] trying extremely hard, often to help or please someone
[3] help or support someone during a difficult period in their life
[4] criticised them very strongly or attacked them
[5] noun: problem which caused time to be wasted
[6] did what needed to be done to solve the problem

Exercises

30.1 **Complete these sentences using verbs from the table in A opposite.**

1 The border police have tried unsuccessfully to .... out illegal immigration.
2 When the thefts at the school happened, the headteacher promised to .... out the person or persons responsible.
3 We got a lovely old chair from my grandmother's house when she died, but it was .... apart so we had it restored.
4 She read the letter then .... it up and threw it angrily into the wastepaper basket.
5 I got so excited I .... over my coffee cup and made a terrible stain on the tablecloth.

30.2 **Which phrasal verbs do these pictures illustrate? Write a sentence to describe what the animals or people in each picture are doing using the appropriate phrasal verb from the opposite page.**

30.3 **Rewrite the underlined parts of these conversations using phrasal verbs from B opposite.**

1
Pedro	I'm sorry you didn't get the funds you applied for to do your research.
Gisela	Yes, well, it was a bit of <u>a disappointment and I did waste a bit of time because of it</u>, but I've applied for a different grant and hope I'll get that.

2
James	Are you managing to survive without working?
Dan	Well, my parents have lent me some money to <u>enable me to survive</u> while I'm studying.

3
Lauren	Teachers suffered very badly under the last government – their salaries fell and their conditions got worse.
Eloise	Yes, but they <u>are not just reacting passively any more</u> now and their union is much stronger.

4
Nicole	Did you get much support from Mr Crombie?
Dominic	Oh yes, he <u>did absolutely everything possible</u> to help me.

5
Tom	I hear you experienced Faith's bad temper this morning!
Jayden	Yes, I made an innocent comment and she just <u>reacted really furiously</u>.

6
Alexa	The scanner's not working again.
Cameron	OK, don't worry, I'll <u>go and fix it</u>.

31 Communication

A Managing subjects and topics

Sophia Brown is speaking to her colleagues at a weekly business meeting. She gives an outline of what she's going to say.

Well, there are a couple of matters which I want to **bring up**[1] today for discussion. But before we **get on to**[2] those questions, I just want to **run through**[3] the schedule for next week's sales conference, which you all have copies of. Someone asked me if we could talk about the new computer system, but I'd prefer to **leave** that **aside**[4] for today and **come back to**[5] it another time. I'm sure I don't need to **spell out**[6] how important it is that we're all thoroughly prepared for next week's conference, so maybe we can **deal with**[7] that first. So, let's have a quick **run-through**[8] of the schedule and discuss each event in turn.

[1] start to talk about
[2] start talking about after discussing something else
[3] repeat something, usually quickly, to make sure it is correct
[4] not discuss it so that we can discuss something else
[5] return to discuss it at a future time
[6] explain in detail
[7] discuss or give our attention to
[8] noun: a practice or repetition to make sure something is correct (from the verb **run through**)

Note that some of the phrasal verbs above can have the object before or after the particle:

bring sth **up** or **bring up** sth   **leave** sth **aside** or **leave aside** sth   **spell** sth **out** or **spell out** sth

B Communicating and interacting with others

In these dialogues the second speaker uses a phrasal verb to repeat the first speaker's meaning.

Jensen	I wish they had done what they said they would do.
Nancy	Yes, they should have **kept to** what they promised and not changed their minds.
Freddie	I don't know who to ask for help or advice on this matter. It's very delicate.
Louis	Yes, it's difficult to know who to **turn to**, isn't it?
Anna	Lucy was extremely enthusiastic and excited about coming to work for us.
Flora	Yes, she was absolutely **bubbling over** with excitement when I spoke to her.
Ellis	She acts as if she was the boss, telling everyone what to do.
Mia	Yes, she's always **ordering** people **about/around**.
Sienna	I saw a sign saying that the car park will be closed tomorrow. Can you tell everybody else, please?
Ronnie	Yes, I'll **pass** the news **on***. I'll send an email to everyone in the office.
Harry	I see Grace said no to the job.
Zoë	Yes, she **turned** the offer **down***.

*The object can also appear after the particle in these two phrasal verbs.

Exercises

31.1 Look at the picture and answer the questions below.

Connor There's something else I'd like to bring up now.

Oscar I'd like you to spell things out a bit more for us.

Gabriel Let's run through the weekend programme once more.

Sara Could we perhaps come back to this next week?

Alice Let's leave that aside for now.

1 Which speaker wants to introduce a new topic now?
2 Which speaker would welcome a fuller explanation?
3 Which two speakers want to deal with a topic later on?
4 Which speaker would like to repeat something to make sure everyone understands it?

31.2 Choose the best phrasal verbs from the opposite page to complete these sentences.

1 I'm sorry, but I'm going to have to .... your invitation as I'll be away then.
2 Karl is such a bossy person, always .... people ....
3 Let's .... this question .... for now and return to it when we've all read the report.
4 How on earth did we .... such an extraordinary topic of conversation?
5 If she has a problem, she knows she can always .... her aunt for help.
6 Elizabeth is thrilled with her new flat – she is .... with enthusiasm.
7 In this essay I plan to .... the causes of the French Revolution from a new perspective.
8 Let's try to .... the agenda and not get distracted.
9 Could you .... a message to Leo when you see him later?

31.3 Here are some more phrasal verbs connected with communicating. Try to explain the meanings of the verbs in bold. Use a dictionary if necessary.

1 They won't be able to hear you at the back of the hall. You'll have to **speak up**.
2 Class 2B seem to spend most of their time in my lessons looking out of the window – I just don't know if I am **getting through to** them or not.
3 Although I think most of the staff agree with me, no-one else is prepared to **speak up**.
4 The arrangements for the conference are rather complicated and I hope I'll be able to **get** the details **across** to everyone.
5 I'm sorry to **butt in**, but I couldn't help hearing you mention that you come from Edinburgh.
6 Jack was halfway through his speech when he **dried up**.

32 Describing people and places

A Describing people

Francesca and I love going to smart restaurants where we have to **dress up**[1], though she always finds it hard to decide what to **put on**[2]. Her favourite evening dress is long, red and tight-fitting, and she has to get me to help her **do up**[3] the zip. As we live in Moscow, we have to **wrap up**[4] well before going out in winter and she **puts** a long fur coat **on**[5] over her dress. As soon as we arrive anywhere, she goes straight to the ladies' room to **freshen up**[6].

[1] put on formal or special clothes
[2] put a piece of clothing onto your body
[3] fasten
[4] dress in warm clothes

[5] see note 2
[6] brush your hair, refresh your make-up or have a quick wash

B Describing places

When we arrived in the town, we were surprised to see how **rundown**[1] it looked. The streets **were littered with**[2] rubbish. However, one building in the town centre **stuck out**[3]. Its tidy window boxes and fresh paint **set** it **apart**[4]. There was a beautiful old lamp **sticking out**[5] from one corner. When we went closer, we found it was the Town Museum.

[1] (adjective) shabby, in a poor condition
[2] (always passive) contained a lot of something, usually something negative
[3] was noticeable because it was different

[4] made it different, usually better, than others of the same type
[5] coming out beyond the edge or surface

C Comparing and contrasting people and things

Owen I can never **tell** one twin **from** the other, can you?

Eva No, I can never **tell** them **apart**.

Lewis Joey will always **stand out** in a crowd. [look different from others]

Evan Yes, I'm sure he'll never **blend in**! [look or seem the same as those around him so he is not noticed]

Her handbag and boots **go** very well **together**.

Exercises

32.1 **Complete these sentences using a phrasal verb from A.**

1 You've had such a long journey. Would you like some time to .... before we go out to dinner?
2 It's a very informal party. You don't have to ....
3 Will you help me .... my dress? I can't reach the buttons at the back.
4 It's freezing cold today, so if you're going out, do .... well and .... a scarf.

32.2 **Correct the mistakes in these sentences. Think about the meaning as well as the grammar of the sentences.**

1 I don't want to wear my new jacket tonight. You can put on it if you like.
2 Although the house looked rundown from the outside, it was very shabby inside.
3 If you're going out in the snow, make sure you wrap on well.
4 Do you think this scarf and coat get together OK?
5 He hates the way his ears stick off.
6 It takes me a long time to get the kids ready in the morning because Sam and Layla can't do on their own shoes yet.
7 Joseph and his brother are so alike – I can't see one from the other.
8 It's a very formal party, so you don't need to dress up.

32.3 **Complete this text using words from the opposite page.**

> The city council are trying to improve some of the older, ... (1) parts of the city. They're trying to construct new buildings which will blend .... (2) with the existing architecture. There's one new building that .... (3) out, which I like very much. It has a beautiful decorated façade and little statues which .... (4) out from the roof, which .... (5) it apart from all the other buildings.

32.4 **Some of the phrasal verbs from this unit can be used in a metaphorical way. Try to work out the metaphorical meaning of these phrasal verbs from their basic meaning by answering the questions below.**

1 Military history **is littered with** examples of armies being destroyed because of generals or politicians making silly mistakes.
  Are there many or few examples of silly mistakes in military history?
2 I thought Tom Hanks's performance in that film really **stood out**.
  Did the speaker think that Tom Hanks's performance was ordinary or special?
3 The quality of Daisy's descriptive writing really **sets** her work **apart** from that of the other students in the class.
  Is Daisy's writing better or worse than that of the other students?
4 I can't **tell** John's voice **from** his father's on the phone.
  Does John's voice sound like his father's on the phone?
5 Bringing a new actor into the series might **freshen** things **up**.
  Does the speaker think that the new actor will spoil or improve the series?

33 Describing public events

A review of an event

About Town

HOME | CINEMA | *THEATRE* | MUSIC | DINING

COMEDY AT THE LONDON ARTS CENTRE

The show **was** fully **booked up**[1] for weeks, and when it opened last night, the public **poured in**[2] and very soon the London Arts Centre was **packed out**[3]. But why? What had they come to see? Comedians who **take off**[4] politicians and who could easily **stand in**[5] for the real leaders who run our country. The show was **put on**[6] by its creators to protest against the recent election and to send a message to the government about the result. The show was timed to **tie in with**[7] National Democracy Week. It was a good idea, but the standard of the performances was third-rate and an embarrassing number of people simply **walked out**[8] before it ended. There were some amusing moments when the performers **sent up**[9] the Prime Minister, but overall it was a dismal show. Despite the large **turnout**[10] for the show's first night, I doubt it will attract many people during the rest of its seven-day run.

1 if an event, person or place is booked up, there is no space or time available for someone
2 arrived or entered somewhere in very large numbers
3 (adjective) very full
4 copy the way a person or animal behaves, often in order to make people laugh
5 play the role of someone for a short period of time
6 organised
7 if one event ties in with another, it is planned so that both events happen at the same time
8 left the performance before it had ended because it was viewed negatively
9 made someone or something seem stupid by copying them in a funny way
10 (noun) the number of people who came to watch or take part in an event or activity

B Other verbs connected with events

phrasal verb	meaning	example
call off sth or **call** sth **off**	cancel something, especially because it no longer seems possible or useful	We decided to **call off** the sports event as we'd only sold 20 tickets.
cram into/in somewhere	go into a place even though it is too small and becomes very full	The hall seated 200, but more than 300 **crammed into** it for the meeting.
pass off	happen, especially in a good way	The demonstration **passed off** peacefully despite fears that there would be violence.
put off sth or **put** sth **off**	postpone to a later date	We had to **put off** the match because the rain was so heavy.
put back sth or **put** sth **back**	arrange something for a later time	We've **put** the time of the staff meeting **back** so more people can come.

Tip

It is often a good idea to learn a group of phrasal verbs together by connecting them in a story, as in the review in A above. Make up your own stories for verbs you have written down in your vocabulary notebook.

Exercises

33.1 **Answer the following questions about the phrasal verbs from A using full sentences.**

1 If a performance is booked up, can you get tickets for it or not?
2 If people are said to pour into (a place), what do you know about the number of people?
3 If people cram into a room, what is the room then like?
4 What kinds of events might be put on to tie in with National Poetry Week?
5 Is a comedian more likely to send up celebrities or post office workers?
6 When would an actor need someone to stand in for them?

33.2 **Choose the correct word to complete these sentences.**

1 It was so cold in the hall that a few people .... out before the end of the concert.
   a) turned b) walked c) poured d) packed
2 The class went to see the performance of *Macbeth* because it .... in well with the project they were doing on Scottish history.
   a) crammed b) stood c) tied d) booked
3 We were delighted when we saw how many people had .... out for the meeting.
   a) turned b) taken c) stood d) walked
4 The teacher was worried about the play her young class was putting on for the parents, but fortunately, everything .... off without any problems.
   a) took b) passed c) walked d) called
5 Isla is very good at .... off the teachers in her school.
   a) sending b) calling c) taking d) putting

33.3 **Replace the underlined words with a phrasal verb from the opposite page.**

1 The concert has been <u>cancelled</u> because the main performer is ill.
2 My aunt has a job going round different schools <u>substituting</u> for teachers who are sick.
3 This year the Drama Club is going to <u>present</u> a performance of *Hamlet*.
4 That actor is very good at <u>imitating</u> the royal family.
5 The shops are usually <u>very crowded</u> during the sales.
6 My uncle has arranged his trip to this country to <u>coincide</u> with my parents' anniversary.

33.4 **Complete this email, using the correct phrasal verbs from the opposite page.**

● ● ●   ✉   Reply   Forward

Hi Dexter.

You must go and see the show that the Students' Arts Club is .... (1) this week. It's brilliant and it .... (2) very well with the study of satire that we're doing at the moment in our literature lectures. We were lucky to get tickets as we'd been told that it .... (3), but we managed get the last two and to .... (4) the hall along with at least 2,000 other people. The actors were so good at .... (5) the bureaucracy in this college and Ben Hurley was brilliant at .... (6) the Dean. No-one .... (7) early – not even the Dean, who seemed to be enjoying himself as much as everyone else! It's been so popular that the play planned for next week has been .... (8) till next month so the Club can hold some extra performances.

---

34 Describing situations

A   Dialogues commenting on situations

Maya   It's such a cold day. I wish I could **get out of** the bike ride Jack's planned. [avoid doing something that you should do, often by giving an excuse]

Alex   Why don't you suggest cancelling it? I'm sure the others would also prefer not to go in weather like this.

Oscar   I have identical twins, Flora and Florence, in my class – I always **mix** them **up**. [confuse two people or things by thinking that one person or thing is the other person or thing]

Stan   Yes, I **muddle** them **up** too. It doesn't help that their names are so similar. [confuse two people or things in your mind]

Megan   I really don't like sharing an office with Bethany – she thinks the whole world **revolves around** her and her insignificant problems. [thinks she's more important than anyone else]

Anna   Yes, I know. I think she is one of the most self-centred people I've ever met.

John   We've been **running up against**[1] quite a lot of problems here recently.

Leah   I know. As soon as we deal with one problem, another immediately **crops up**[2], and I now feel I can't **bank on**[3] things **turning out**[4] well in the end.

[1] beginning to experience
[2] suddenly appears, usually when you are not expecting it
[3] depend on something happening
[4] happening in a particular way or having a particular result

B   An island revolution

Milly   The situation at work is so annoying at the moment! There's been a small **mix-up**[1] of orders and everyone is making a great drama out of it.

Tom   Oh come on! You can **rise above**[2] that. Just **back off**[3] and let others handle things.

[1] (noun) mistake caused by confusion
[2] not allow something bad that is happening or is being done to you to upset you or affect your behaviour
[3] stop being involved in a situation, especially to let others deal with it themselves

Holidaymakers who were **caught up**[1] last week in a revolution on the Caribbean island of St Maria have now returned home. The situation first **hotted up**[2] when rebels seized the Presidential Palace. The returning tourists report that they were all **thrown together**[3] in one of the largest hotels and were not allowed to leave until the situation **calmed down**[4].

[1] (always in passive) involved in a situation, often when you don't want to be
[2] (informal) became more exciting, with a lot more activity (compare with **heat up** which is used about food, see Units 26 and 60)
[3] forced to be together and get to know each other
[4] became more peaceful

Exercises

34.1 **Match the statements on the left with a suitable response on the right.**

1 I'm so worried about what David is doing.	I've run up against that problem too.
2 All the pages are in the wrong order in this report.	I know, but I'm sure everything will turn out all right in the end.
3 Sometimes the printer will only print black and white.	I wouldn't bank on it.
4 I need you here next Monday.	I know, but try to rise above it.
5 I do hope the bus arrives on time.	I must have mixed/muddled them up. Sorry.
6 I feel so angry about what's happened.	OK. I'll see if I can get out of my trip to London.

34.2 **Complete these sentences with a suitable word.**

1 When you're a teenager it's easy to think the whole world .... around you and your personal problems.
2 There was a .... with the reservation – our room had been double-booked.
3 I think you should .... off a little and let her do what she wants.
4 Problems at work tend to .... up when you're least expecting them.
5 I hope everything .... out well for you in your new job.

34.3 **Replace the underlined words with phrasal verbs from the opposite page.**

1 I was in the capital city a month before the economic crisis exploded, but things were already beginning to become agitated and more intense, even then.
2 He went to the country as a news reporter but became unintentionally involved in the civil war which started shortly after his arrival.
3 I might never have met David, but we had no choice but to live and work together during our military service and we've been friends ever since.
4 The situation in Lostrania has become more peaceful now, but it's still too dangerous to go there for a holiday.
5 Try not to get so involved. Let them sort it out.
6 You can't trust him to help you.

I know!

Venus

Earth

Because she's such a big star she thinks the whole world revolves around her.

Over to you

Choose five of the phrasal verbs from this unit and use them in sentences about situations you have been in recently.

A Referring to information in academic writing

This table shows phrasal verbs which are useful in academic writing.

phrasal verb	example	meaning
come under sth	be included in or may be found in	Sanderson (2008) studied mistakes involving prepositions, tenses and other items which **come under** the heading of grammatical errors in second language learning.
draw on/upon sth	use information or your knowledge or experience of something to help you do something	In designing the experiment, Freya Farr **draws upon** earlier studies done in America and Asia.
point out sth (often + **that**)	present a new fact, especially one that is important in the present discussion or situation	Willis (2011) **points out** that economic statistics often show a sharp rise just before a serious recession.
turn to sth/sb	begin to think, speak or write about a subject	I should now like to **turn to** another issue which is often neglected: parental control.

B Noticing and understanding information

In these conversations, the second person repeats what the first person says using a phrasal verb.

Zara I didn't fully understand what he was saying for a few minutes.

Ed Yes, it took me a few minutes to **latch on** to what he was talking about.

Rory I found it difficult to understand the full importance of the decision.

Amber Yes, me too. I found it hard to **take in** its significance at first.

Julia We must be careful to notice any difficulties that occur once we start the project.

Mason Yes, we'll have to **watch out for** possible problems.

Liam Could you try and get some information about how to contact George Phelps?

Ellie Yes, I'll try and **find out** his contact details.

Olivia Sofia, will you make sure that Ava has scanned those documents for me?

Sofia Yes, I'll **check up on** her right away and see if she's done them.

Dan Frankie, I can't find that market report we wrote about three years ago.

Frankie OK, I'll try and **track** it **down**. It must be on the system somewhere.

C Other verbs connected with information

Eliza What's the capital of Ecuador?

Blake Oh, I know it isn't Bogotá – that's the capital of Colombia and it isn't Caracas – that's the capital of Venezuela. Oh, I don't know. I **give up**. [stop trying to think of the answer to a joke or question]

Eliza It's Quito.

I said something that upset Ivy. I didn't mean to, it just **slipped out**. [I didn't intend to say it]

The total on the bill and the total on the credit card statement should **match up**, but don't [be the same]. There must be a mistake.

Exercises

35.1 Look at A and B. Then complete this book review using the phrasal verbs from the box below. Put the verbs into the most appropriate form.

| check up on   come under   draw on/upon   point out   track down   turn to |

Book Review — *Land Tracks* by Michael C. Whitmore

Land Tracks is an unusual book about the history of our nation. The author has managed to .... (1) a number of previously unpublished sources. He has .... (2) these to argue that the current political situation in the land owes a great deal to the separate histories of the two main groups of people who make up our population. After analysing the historically suspicious relationship between these two groups, the author then .... (3) the relationship between our country and our neighbouring island. He .... (4) that traditionally the relationship between our two nations has always been based on trust and respect. The writer uses his imagination quite freely, and the book should really .... (5) the heading of fiction rather than non-fiction. It is a very interesting work, although anyone seriously wishing to investigate our history should .... (6) many of the facts presented by this author.

35.2 Correct the errors in this paragraph. There are seven in total. Each error is a matter of either an extra word or wrong word order.

Hannah and Ben were playing a game. Hannah had thought of a famous football player and Ben was trying to find who it was out. He turned his mother to but she pointed it out that she knew absolutely nothing about football. He would have to try to track the answer himself down and to watch out any clues for that Hannah might deliberately give. After ten minutes Ben still hadn't latched up on to who she was talking about, so he gave himself up and Hannah told him the answer.

35.3 Find three collocations for these verbs from the opposite page. Use a dictionary if necessary.

EXAMPLE Someone might watch out for ......*problems*......, ...*difficulties*...... or ......*danger*........ .

1 You might check up on .... , ... or ....
2 You might point out .... , ... or ....
3 Someone might find out .... , ... or ....
4 You might take in .... , ... or ....
5 .... , ... or .... might slip out.

35.4 Some of the phrasal verbs on the opposite page are used in a metaphorical rather than a literal way. In the sentences below these verbs are used in a literal way. What do they mean?

1 As they drove through the town, Martha's father **pointed out** anything he thought might interest the children.
2 In the scene at the end of the film, **watch out for** the man sitting in the café behind Leonardo DiCaprio – that's my brother!
3 The dog quickly **tracked** the rabbit **down** to where it was hiding under the garden shed.
4 Ethan managed to **slip out** of the house without anyone noticing.
5 Polly **turned to** the man on her left and started chatting to him about his work.

Cambridge Dictionary

dictionary.cambridge.org

36 Solving problems

A Talking about problems

Tom	What's the matter? Why are you looking so worried?
Emily	I've got a few problems at work and I don't know what to do about them.
Tom	Well, why don't we **talk** them **over**[1] together? That might help you to **sort yourself out**[2].

Emily	OK, thanks. Well, first of all, Julia was going to give a very important presentation tomorrow, but she says she's ill and isn't going to be able to do it. I think she's just **bottled out**[3] as it's for such an important client. Feeling a bit ill was just the perfect **let-out**[4] for her. I'd do it myself but I'm busy with meetings all day.
Tom	Well, that **calls for**[5] quick action if the presentation is tomorrow. You'd better do it yourself if it's so important. Just cancel your other meetings.
Emily	I guess I'll have to. The next problem is that personal belongings have been going missing from people's desks during the day.
Tom	Oh dear. You should **deal with**[6] that problem as quickly as possible. Let's make a list of action points …

[1] discuss something before making a decision
[2] spend time dealing with your personal problems
[3] (informal) decided not to do something because she was afraid
[4] (noun) excuse or way of avoiding doing something she said she'd do
[5] needs or deserves a particular action or quality
[6] take action to achieve something

B Finding a solution

Now read what Emily did about her problems at work.

She **faced up to**[1] the fact that she would have to do the important presentation herself, so she immediately contacted her personal assistant to ask him to **see about**[2] postponing her meetings for the next day. As for the thefts, she realised that the solution to finding the office thief **lay in**[3] working out exactly who could have been in the office when each of the thefts took place. So she **came up with**[4] a plan that enabled her to check who had been there at each of the times concerned. That **narrowed down**[5] the suspects to two people. She questioned them both and soon found out who had taken the belongings.

[1] accepted that a difficult situation existed
[2] deal with something or arrange for something to be done
[3] would be found in (from the verb **lie in** something)
[4] thought of or suggested something that might solve a problem
[5] made something, usually a list or choice, smaller and clearer by removing what is irrelevant or less important

Exercises

36.1 **Match the newspaper headlines 1–5 with the stories a–e below.**

1 NEW POLICE SQUAD TO DEAL WITH ILLEGAL IMMIGRANTS
2 Garcia bottles out of contest with Paterson
3 POLICE NARROW DOWN SUSPECTS IN MURDER CASE
4 Education Minister to talk over problem with teaching unions
5 GOVERNMENT SEEKS LET-OUT ON ELECTION PROMISE

a) Three men are to be interviewed in the Oxford area following new information. Up to now there
    has been no real …
b) If possible, ministers would like to be able to drop the pledge without angering the public …
c) The team will be stationed at ports of entry and will have the task of checking anyone suspected
    of having arrived …
d) The fight was arranged for September in Las Vegas, but now it will not take place.
    A spokesman for the 28-year-old …
e) The minister said she would go into the discussions with an open mind, and that all the issues …

36.2 **A father is talking to his son who he thinks is very lazy. The underlined expressions have got
mixed up. The particles are correct, but the verbs are incorrect. Put the correct verbs in.**

> It's time you <u>faced</u> yourself <u>out</u>. You're 27 now and you still haven't got a job! You've got to <u>come
> up to</u> reality. It's about time you realised that the secret of success <u>talks in</u> taking positive action.
> Over the next couple of days, I will expect you to <u>lie up with</u> a few ideas about how you're going
> to improve your situation. Why don't you go and <u>sort about</u> that job Uncle Robert offered you at
> his factory? I've offered to help <u>deal</u> things <u>over</u> with you, but you never seem to want my help.
> Yet you don't <u>see with</u> things yourself!

36.3 **This is how Tom and Emily's conversation in A continued. What do you think the five underlined
phrasal verbs mean?**

> **Emily** Well, it's just <u>dawned on</u> me that the thefts have always happened on the top floor. So it
> couldn't be anyone who never goes up there. That actually <u>rules out</u> quite a lot of people.

> **Tom** Think some more about exactly where and when things were stolen and you'll probably
> find that the answer <u>jumps out at</u> you.

> **Emily** Thanks, Tom. It's good to <u>work through</u> things with you! It really helps me to
> <u>sort</u> things <u>out</u>!

Over to you

> Choose five of the phrasal verbs from this unit that you would particularly like to learn. Look them up in a
> good dictionary, for example go to the Cambridge University Press dictionary website at
> http://dictionary.cambridge.org, and copy out any useful example sentences that you find there.

37

Decisions and plans

A Thinking about things and deciding

If ...	you could ...	meaning
someone offered you money for your bike, but you weren't sure if you wanted to sell it or not	**sleep on** it	wait until the next day before you decide what to do about it
	decide to take the money and **do without** the bike	manage without it
you were offered a good job in a town far away from where you live	**weigh up** the pros and cons	think carefully about the advantages and disadvantages involved before making a decision
	run it **by** your parents or a good friend (informal)	tell your parents or a good friend so that they can give their opinion
you were getting tired of paying rent to live in a flat	**plan ahead** and start saving money to buy a house	make decisions or plans about something you will do or might do in the future
	think ahead, and consider how you would like to live in 10 or 20 years from now	think carefully about what might happen in the future
someone offered you the chance to invest all the money you've saved in a company they were starting	**think** it **over** and tell them your decision at a later date	think carefully about the idea before making a decision
	think through the possible risks of giving all your savings away	think carefully about the risks and consider the possible consequences

B Other verbs connected with planning and deciding

We should **allow for** possible delays on the motorway and leave an hour earlier. [consider or include something when making plans or judging a situation]

Having to pay extra for all our meals at the hotel was something we didn't **bargain for**. [expect something to happen and be prepared for it]

I'm sure he'll **opt out** of doing the bungee jump at the last minute. [choose not to do something you have planned]

I'm sure he'll **chicken out** of doing the bungee jump at the last minute. [informal: decide not to do something you have planned because you are frightened]

I **have** so many things **on** in the evenings that it would be too much to be on the school committee too. [have arrangements to do things]

My husband seems to **be** completely **set against** moving to the country. [be opposed to]

I **could do without** having my family coming to stay this weekend. I just want a quiet weekend. [informal: said when something is annoying you or causing problems for you because your situation at that time makes it difficult for you to deal with it]

Exercises

37.1 Complete this dialogue using verbs or particles from A.

Sarah Do you think you're going to take that job in New York, Isaac?

Isaac Well, I've been thinking it .... (1) and trying to .... (2) up all the positives and negatives, but I'm finding it really hard to come to a decision. I've run it .... (3) the family, but they all have different views. My younger child is really keen on the idea but the older one isn't. My wife says we have to think .... (4) and imagine how things would be for the kids when they're a bit older.

Sarah So how long do they give you to .... (5) through all the implications and come to a decision?

Isaac Unfortunately, I have to make up my mind by next week.

Sarah Well, why don't you .... (6) on it. Things might seem clearer in the morning.

37.2 Answer these questions about yourself using full sentences.

1 When you have an important decision to make in your personal or your professional life, who would you usually run it by first?
2 If you are worried about a situation at work, do you usually think it over immediately or decide to sleep on it first?
3 You have enough money for only one of these – a special holiday or a car. Which would you prefer to do without?
4 In what ways do people plan ahead for their retirement?
5 What sorts of things might people chicken out of doing?

37.3 Rewrite these sentences using the word in brackets so that the sentences keep the same meaning.

1 We should take into consideration the fact that he is still only young. (ALLOW)
2 I really can't help you as I have a lot of things to do today. (ON)
3 He wants to stop having art classes at school next year so he can do extra music. (OPT)
4 We didn't expect Max to turn up at the party with a lot of his friends. (BARGAIN)
5 My son is determined not to go to university. (SET)
6 I would really prefer it if we didn't have people coming for dinner this evening. (WITHOUT)

37.4 Correct the mistakes with the phrasal verbs in these sentences.

1 I was going to do the parachute jump, but I chickened off in the end.
2 I have on a lot of things this weekend.
3 In judging her work, you should really allow her inexperience for.
4 If we buy the flat, we'll have to make without holidays for a few years.
5 Let's run our plan through Sarah before we make our final decision.
6 I could make without having to go to a conference this weekend.
7 In deciding how much holiday money we need, we should allow the fact for that food is very expensive there.

38 Disagreeing

A Disagreement at work

There was an **outcry**[1] at work today because the boss announced that he wanted us all to take a pay cut. We had a union meeting at lunchtime, and we all agreed to **stick together**[2] and refuse to agree to his requests. Our union leader **spoke out**[3] very clearly to our boss and to the local press this afternoon. We're sure that the boss will have to **give in**[4] in the end. Although in some ways I'd rather **stay out of**[5] it myself, I have no choice but to support my fellow union members.

[1] (noun) public expression of anger and disapproval
[2] support each other, especially in a difficult situation
[3] publicly expressed an opinion, usually to oppose or criticise something or someone
[4] finally agree to what someone wants after a period of refusing to agree
[5] not become involved in an argument or discussion

B Private disagreements

Read Grace's email to an advice column.

Dear Eva,

Please can you help me. My big sister and I always used to be good friends, but we **fell out**[1] when I started going out with a new boyfriend. Now she is always trying to **put me down**[2] and it is really beginning to **get to**[3] me. My boyfriend usually tries to **stick up for**[4] me, but then she just laughs at him too. Four years ago my boyfriend went out with my sister for a few months, but surely she doesn't **hold** this **against**[5] us? What can we do?

Grace

[1] argued with each other and stopped being friends
[2] make me feel stupid or unimportant by criticising me
[3] make me feel upset or angry
[4] defend me when I am being criticised
[5] like or respect them less because they have done something wrong or something that she does not like

C Back

The verb **back** is often used to refer to the position you take in an argument or decision.

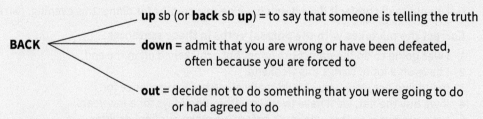

BACK

up sb (or **back** sb **up**) = to say that someone is telling the truth

down = admit that you are wrong or have been defeated, often because you are forced to

out = decide not to do something that you were going to do or had agreed to do

Examples:

When I make my point at the meeting, please **back** me **up**.

The government **backed down** on its controversial plans to increase income tax.

Lottie had agreed to come sailing with us tomorrow, but she's **backed out**.

Exercises

38.1 In this radio interview a protester is angry about a plan to build a new road through some beautiful woodland. Complete the interview using verbs from the opposite page.

Reporter	Now, Mr Humfry, you have .... (1) out recently against the new road plan. Do you think your protest campaign can change the decision?
Protester	Well, there are a number of different groups opposed to this plan, and if we .... (2) together we can force the authorities to rethink.
Reporter	But do you really think the authorities will be prepared to .... (3) down over this? The minister has said the road plan must go ahead.
Protester	This isn't a small protest. There's been a massive public .... (4). People are not willing to see their environment destroyed by road building. The Highways Department must listen to us or face the consequences.
Reporter	The consequences? Do you mean violent protest as with the Knox Bridge?
Protester	Not violent protest, no. We have always emphasised to our members that if violence erupts they should .... (5) out of it and keep our protest peaceful. We condemn violence. No, I'm talking about a huge, non-violent wave of protest.
Reporter	And you think that, in this way, the government will be forced to .... (6) in?
Protester	Yes, I believe they will simply have to listen.

38.2 Use a phrasal verb from the opposite page to complete these dialogues so that Speaker B agrees with Speaker A's statement.

1 A: Apparently, Toby agreed with Liam's version of the events.
   B: Yes, he ....
2 A: I hear Ryan and Oliver have had a serious argument.
   B: Yes, it seems they've ....
3 A: Georgia always defends Mia when people criticise her.
   B: Yes, she ....
4 A: I think we should withdraw from the project.
   B: Yes, I agree. I think we ....
5 A: Chloe is always criticising Adam and making him look small.
   B: Yes, she's always ....
6 A: We shouldn't feel negative towards Violet just because she acted stupidly.
   B: No, we shouldn't ....
7 A: I think not getting the job is really beginning to upset Rosie.
   B: Yes, I think it's really ....

38.3 Complete these sentences using a phrasal verb from the opposite page.

1 Harry says he won't come to the fancy dress party with me, but I'm sure he'll eventually ....
2 Why have Heidi and Sarah .... ? They used to get on so well together.
3 I just don't have enough money for the holiday we were planning in Canada. I'm going to have to ....
4 My best friend and I have always .... , through good times and bad times.
5 The boss's constant criticisms are really .... me and I'm going to start looking for another job.

39 Persuading

A   Verbs with *talk* and *put*

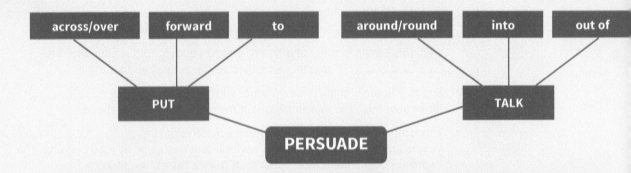

If you …	then you …	example
put across/over sth or **put** sth **across/over**	explain or express something clearly so that people understand it easily	He's an excellent teacher. He **puts** his subject **across/over** so well.
put forward sth or **put** sth **forward**	state an idea or opinion, or suggest a plan, so that it can be considered or discussed	The company has **put forward** a plan to build a new hotel in the city centre.
put sth **to** sb	suggest an idea or plan to someone so they can consider or discuss it	Your proposal is interesting. I'll **put** it **to** the committee tomorrow.
talk sb **around/round**	persuade someone to agree with you or to do what you want them to do	Mum won't let me go away with my friends, but Dad might be able to **talk** her **around/round**.
talk sb **into** sth/doing sth	persuade someone to do something which they may be unwilling to do at first	She **talked** me **into** going jogging every day before work.
talk sb **out** *of* sth/doing sth	persuade someone not to do something	My sister wants to leave college but my parents are trying to **talk** her **out of** it.

B   Other verbs connected with persuading people

PRIME MINISTER **CALLS FOR**[1] WAR ON DRUGS

Minister **brushes aside**[2] opposition to new tax plan

UNION BOSS **BRINGS** EMPLOYER **ROUND**[3] TO PAY DEAL

Doctors **press for**[4] shorter working hours

CITY **ROPES IN**[5] LOCAL INDUSTRY TO SUPPORT ENVIRONMENT PLAN

"I was just **having** the media **on**[6], and they **fell for**[7] it," says star who faked his own death

[1]   says a particular thing should be done, usually in order to change or improve a situation
[2]   refuses to listen to what someone says, or refuses to think about something seriously
[3]   persuades someone to agree with you or to do what you want them to do
[4]   try to persuade someone, usually someone in authority, to give you something or to allow something to happen
[5]   (informal) persuades someone to help you with something, especially when they do not want to
[6]   (informal) persuading someone that something is true when it is not, usually as a joke
[7]   were tricked into believing something that is not true

Exercises

39.1 **Choose the correct particle to complete each sentence.**

1 The minister put the new proposal .... the Prime Minister.
   a) forward   b) to   c) across/over
2 I was hoping to leave at 4 a.m., but my parents talked me .... it.
   a) into   b) round   c) out of
3 Have you managed to talk your dad .... lending you the money to buy a car yet?
   a) into   b) round   c) out of
4 The new manager has some interesting new proposals that he wants to put .... at the staff meeting tomorrow.
   a) forward   b) to   c) across/over
5 The lecturer was no good at putting his ideas .... and I found it impossible to follow his talk.
   a) forward   b) to   c) across/over
6 My brother doesn't want to go skiing, but I think I'll be able to talk him ....
   a) into   b) around/round   c) out of

39.2 **Write the phrasal verbs presented on the opposite page into one of these categories.**

presenting an opinion or trying to persuade	successfully persuading	people's reactions to persuasion

39.3 **Read the sentences below and answer the questions about them.**

1 The headteacher brushed aside the parents' criticism that the children were being given too much homework.
   How did she take the parents' criticism?
2 Jessica was just having Daniel on when she said she was going to work in the USA.
   Where is Jessica going to work?
3 The parents were roped in to help organise the school sports day.
   Did the parents decide that they wanted to help organise the sports day?
4 Harry fell for Sarah's story that all her money had been stolen.
   What do we learn about Sarah?
5 The Party is calling for constitutional reform.
   Does the Party want constitutional reform or not?

39.4 **Complete the text using phrasal verbs from the opposite page. Sometimes there is more than one possible answer.**

If you're a politician .... (1) change, you're trying to .... opponents
.... (2) to your way of thinking. You will probably try to do this by .... (3)
your plans as clearly as possible, and you'll doubtless also try to use the media to .... (4)
the changes that you want. Indeed, you will .... (5) all the supporters you can find to
help you .... others .... (6) voting for your proposals.

40 Praising and criticising

A Praising and criticising

Max	Now that you've been in our company fora month, what do you think of the other people in your department?
David	Well, there is one **outstanding**[1] person and that's Jessica. She's a first-class personal assistant. She **stands out**[2] from the others.
Max	That's good to hear. What about Lucas? What do you think of him?
David	He's very able, but I wish he wasn't such a **show-off**[3]! I don't know who he's trying to impress.
Max	It's just all the other staff, I think. He always **shows off**[4] more when lots of people are around.
David	Yes, but otherwise his performance is fine – his work certainly **measures up**[5].
Max	So there are no real problems then?
David	Well, I am very worried about Sophie. She seems to be **screwing** everything **up**[6] at the moment. I'd had such good reports of her that it really surprised me. I tried asking her what she was **playing at**[7], but she just refused to talk about it.
Max	Why don't you have a word with Jessica? Perhaps she can find out what's wrong.

[1] (adjective) extremely good, or of a very high standard
[2] is much better than other people or things
[3] (noun) person who tries to impress in an annoying way
[4] tries to make people admire his abilities or achievements in a way other people find annoying
[5] is good enough
[6] (informal) making a mistake with everything, or damaging or spoiling everything
[7] (always used in the continuous form; always used in questions) doing; when you ask what someone is playing at, you are surprised or angry about their behaviour

B Ways of criticising

If you **lay into** someone, you criticise or attack them in an angry way.

  The headteacher really **laid into** the new teacher for arriving in school so late.

If you **pick on** someone, you choose one person from a group of people to criticise or treat unfairly, especially when they are smaller or weaker than you.

  Arthur was a quiet, studious child and the big boys in the class used to **pick on** him.

If you **hit back**, you criticise or attack someone who has criticised or attacked you.

  Jack is constantly criticising his sons – I'm sure they'll **hit back** eventually.

If you **take out** something **on** someone or **take** something **out on** someone, you treat someone badly because you are upset or angry, even though they have done nothing wrong.

  Of course Maryam is upset at losing her job, but she shouldn't **take** it **out on** her family.

If you **rub** something **in** (informal), you talk to someone about something which they want to forget because they feel bad about it.

  I know it was all my fault. I just wish everyone would stop **rubbing** it **in**!

Exercises

40.1 In the dialogue in A opposite there are two phrasal verbs which have related noun or adjective forms. Write down the phrasal verbs and their related forms and explain the connection between them.

40.2 Read these remarks by different people and then answer the questions below by writing the correct name in the box.

I decided I had to defend myself against all the criticisms, so I did.

Paula

I couldn't believe how aggressively she attacked me and criticised me.

Imogen

Everyone was treating me badly because of what happened, but I had no part in it.

Laura

He chose to attack me because I'm junior to him and can't defend myself.

Logan

I wanted to forget the whole incident, but he insisted on reminding me of it.

Ahmed

1 Who felt that someone was rubbing it in?

2 Who felt that they had to hit back?

3 Who felt someone had picked on them?

4 Who felt that people were taking it out on them?

5 Who felt that someone laid into them?

40.3 Rewrite each sentence using the word in brackets.
1 Dan won the prize as his short story was clearly the best. (STOOD)
2 Molly got the sack because her work just wasn't good enough. (MEASURE)
3 What on earth does Phoebe think she's doing? She's behaving so oddly. (PLAYING)
4 I wish Ed wouldn't try to impress all the time! (SHOW)
5 If you make such a stupid mistake again, you'll lose your job. (SCREW)
6 I know I was stupid but please don't remind me. (RUB)
7 Seth's father spoke very angrily to him for scratching his new car. (LAID)
8 Why does everyone always blame me for everything? (PICK)

41 Exclamations and warnings

The exclamations and warnings on this page are all typical of informal, spoken English.

A

Reactions and responses

Ahmed	I just wanted to ask you a couple of questions.
Sara	Fine. No problem. **Fire away**! [something you say to tell someone you're ready for them to start asking you questions, or to start speaking]
Darcy	Oh, everything is so awful at the moment.
Leah	Oh, **lighten up**, will you! You'll make everyone as miserable as you! [something you say to tell someone to stop being so serious or annoyed]
Amy	Evelyn wants you to give a talk to her students next Monday.
Dan	Evelyn? Next week? **Hang on / hold on**! Who's Evelyn? Is she someone I know? [something you say when you are confused or surprised by something and you need time to think]
Clara	I feel like killing Tyler! I'm never, ever going to speak to him again!
Hannah	**Steady on**! I know he acted stupidly, but he's not a bad person really. [something you say to tell someone that you think what they are saying is too extreme]
Dylan	You see, what I want to say is, well, I mean, it's like, er, it's difficult to say it.
Felix	**Come on**! **Spit it out**! What is it? [**come on** something you say to encourage someone to do something you want them to do, especially to hurry up, to try harder, or to tell you something; **spit it out** something you say to encourage someone to tell you something which they do not want to tell you]
Louis	Some of the students are very poor and can't afford textbooks.
Katie	Poor? **Come off it**! They have enough money for mobile phones. [something you say to tell someone that you do not believe them or that you disagree with them]

B

Commands and warnings

example	comment
Watch out! / **Mind out!** / **Look out!** There's a car coming!	said to tell someone to be careful so that they can avoid danger or an accident
Go on! / **Hurry up**! We've not got all day!	said to encourage someone to do something or to tell someone to do something more quickly
You're doing very well! **Keep it up**!	said to encourage someone to continue to do something, especially to continue to work hard or well
Hold on. I'll get Mike for you. It's best if you speak to him.	said to ask someone to wait a moment

> ### Tip
>
> Many of the exclamations here are very direct and may be considered impolite if you say them to someone you don't know very well. Learn them so that you understand them when you hear or read them, but use them only with very great care.

Exercises

41.1 **Divide the exclamations and warnings on the opposite page into these groups:**

a) those that you could use to your boss or teacher
b) those that you could use only to close friends

41.2 **Choose the best response from those in the box to fit each of these dialogues.**

> Come off it!   Lighten up!   Steady on!   Mind out!
> Hold on!   Come on!   Spit it out!   Keep it up!

1
| Nicholas | I'm sorry, I just haven't had time to finish my essay. It's taken me ages to get hold of the books I needed for it. |
| Teacher | .... There are plenty of copies in the library. And you could have told me sooner if you had really been having problems. |

2
| Amelia | Can I speak to your sister, please? |
| Matt | .... I'll just go and see if she's home yet. |

3
Elliot	What's the matter with you?
Millie	There's something I've got to tell you but, well, I don't know where to begin.
Elliot	.... I haven't got all day.

4
| Bella | I'm never going to get all this work done. I hate my job. |
| Naomi | .... It won't take long if you hurry up a bit. |

5
| Anna | Look at the picture on the side of that lorry! |
| Tom | .... You're going to hit the car in front of you! |

6
| Aisha | That was a stupid thing to do. You're fired! |
| Harvey | .... You know I'm one of your best workers. |

7
| Archie | Now I've been in the office for a month, I'd like to know if you are pleased with my work. How am I doing? |
| Rob | Very well! .... You'll soon be getting a promotion. |

41.3 **Answer the following questions.**

1 Which exclamation on the opposite page is connected with the idea of shooting a gun?
2 Which exclamation is connected with the idea of forcing out the liquid in your mouth?

41.4 **Divide the exclamations from the box below into pairs that have approximately the same meaning. What is the basic meaning for each pair? Describe a situation when each pair of expressions might be used.**

> Watch out!   Hold on!   Mind out!   Hurry up!   Go on!   Hang on!

42 The classroom and learning

A Things the teacher says

With all the verbs in these examples, the particle can go either before or after the object, e.g. **give in** your homework or **give** your homework **in**.

Indices and logarithms

$$a^m \times a^n = a^{m+n}$$
$$(a^m)^n = a^{mn}$$
$$\log(AB) = \log A + \log B$$
$$\log(A/B) = \log A - \log B$$
$$\log(A^n) = n \log A$$
$$\log_b a = \frac{\log_c a}{\log_c b}$$

The teacher says ...	The teacher wants:
Hand/Turn in your worksheets at the end of the lesson, please.	... the students to give her their work at the end of the lesson.
Rose, **give/hand out** these worksheets, please.	... Rose to give each student a worksheet*.
Jon, **clean off / rub out / wipe off** what's written on the board, please.	... Jon to clean the board.
Work out the answers without using a calculator.	... the students to do some maths without using calculators.
Cross out any rough work when you have found the answer.	... the students to put a line through any rough work.
Take care not to **miss out** /omit any of the exam questions.	... the students not to forget to answer any of the exam questions.
Take turns to **act out** your dialogues in groups of four.	... the students to perform the actions and say the words of their dialogues.
Please **put** your books **away**.	... the students to store their books where they are usually stored.

*Sheets of paper that everyone in a class or lecture receives a copy of are called **handouts**. These might be worksheets (i.e. have exercises on them) or they might contain a text or some reference material.

B Other classroom phrasal verbs

Charlotte was ill for a month and so she **fell behind** with her schoolwork [failed to do her schoolwork by a particular time]. She is going to find it difficult to **catch up** [reach the same standard as the rest of the class].

Pupils often **play up** when a teacher is new or inexperienced. [behave badly]

Although Isabelle had done good work throughout the year she **messed up** her exam. [did her exam badly]

The teacher cleared the books from the table and **spread out** the map. [opened out something that was folded]

Tip

Listen carefully to instructions in English from your teacher and note down any phrasal verbs they use. If you are not sure what they mean, ask them for an explanation.

Exercises

42.1 Look at these pictures and write a sentence to describe what the student is doing in each case.

42.2 Would Tim's parents be pleased or not if their son's teacher told them the following?

1 Tim was playing up in class last week.
2 Tim messed up his homework.
3 Tim has been helping a classmate who has fallen behind.
4 Tim has caught up with the rest of the class.
5 Tim didn't hand in his homework.
6 Tim missed out some important stages in his work.

42.3 Complete this story using appropriate phrasal verbs from the opposite page. Write the verbs in the correct tense.

Last term Alexa missed three weeks of school and so she ....(1) with her studies. She did all she could to try to ....(2) with the other students, but she couldn't manage it. When it came to the maths test at the end of term, she just couldn't ....(3) the answers. She spent all her time on half of the question paper and ....(4) the other half, so inevitably she failed. Because she had ....(5) the test, her parents decided she'd better have a maths tutor over the holidays. In this week's test she came top of the class.

42.4 Rewrite these sentences using more informal phrasal verbs instead of the underlined verbs.

1 At the end of the lesson we have to <u>store</u> our books in our bags.
2 Students often <u>misbehave</u> when they are bored in class.
3 The teacher <u>erased</u> the new words from the board and then tested us.
4 We have to <u>submit</u> our registration forms for the exam on Friday.
5 I usually <u>omit</u> my middle name when I am filling in forms.
6 Some people were <u>distributing</u> leaflets about a demonstration in the town centre.
7 My partner and I had to <u>perform</u> our dialogue in front of the whole class.

42.5 Answer these questions using full sentences.

1 Why are you often asked to cross out rough work in an exam?
2 If a teacher gives out a sheet listing all the kings and queens of Britain, is that a worksheet or a handout or both?
3 Why do most students carry an eraser in their pencil cases?
4 How easy would it be for you to work out how many euros are equal to 250 US dollars?
5 What do you think is the reason for pupils playing up in class?

43 Student life: courses and exams

A Enrolling on courses

Look at this information leaflet for students at Welney College. Then look at how David explains the system informally to a friend using phrasal verbs. The numbers (¹, ², etc.) help you to match the phrasal verbs with their meanings.

Welney College
—— Promoting excellence ——

- Autumn term ends[1] on 18 December. Spring term begins[2] on 8 January.
- Students wishing to register for[3] spring term courses should do so before 12 December.
- Any student not completing a course[4] will not receive credits for that course.
- Course essays must be submitted in a final form[5] seven days before the end of a course.
- Students failing more than 30% of their total coursework will be expelled[6] from the college.

A. Ashworth, Academic Administrator

David:
– We **break up**[1] on 18 December and **go back**[2] on 8 January, so we've got about a three-week break.

– But we've got to **sign up**[3] for courses for next term before 12 December.

– You have to go to all the lectures; if you **drop out**[4] before the end, you don't get the credits.

– And you have to **write up**[5] your course essay and submit it a week before the course ends.

– If you fail 30% or more of your courses, they **throw** you **out**[6] of the college.

B Before an exam

How to... take tests

Six tips for exam success

- **Keep up**[1] all the skills you need for the exam so that you don't have to do a lot of work at the last minute.
- **Brush up on**[2] some of the things you learnt a long time ago; they may possibly **come up**[3] in the exam.
- Don't just **mug up**[4] on the key points you need for the exam and hope that you'll **scrape through**[5] with little effort.
- On the other hand, don't try to do everything. **Swotting up**[6] on everything you have done all term means you will have to revise a lot of useless things too.
- Concentrate on **polishing up**[7] the most important areas and your best skills.
- Don't fool yourself that you'll pass the exam on the basis of what you've **picked up**[8] during the lectures and classes. You will need to revise!

[1] continue to do something
[2] practise and improve your skills or your knowledge of something, usually something you learned in the past but have partly forgotten
[3] if a question or a subject comes up in an exam, that question is asked or questions about that subject are asked in the exam
[4] (informal) quickly try to learn the main facts about a subject, especially before an exam (often + *on*)

[5] manage, with a lot of difficulty, to succeed in something
[6] (informal) learning as much as you can about something, especially before an exam (often + *on*)
[7] practising and improving your skills or your knowledge of something
[8] learnt by absorbing it rather than studying it

Exercises

43.1 **Rewrite these sentences using the words in brackets so that they keep the same meaning.**

1 I'm going to register for a course in statistics next year. (SIGN)
2 Several students did not complete the Moral Philosophy course. (DROP)
3 Our course finishes on 20 June. (BREAK)
4 He was forced to leave university after one term. He'd done no work at all. (THROW)
5 I can't come out tonight. I have to have my essay finished for tomorrow. (WRITE)
6 My next term at college starts on 12 September. (GO)

43.2 **Which of these would make most students happy and why?**

breaking up	dropping out	being thrown out
scraping through	mugging up	swotting up

43.3 **Choose the best phrasal verb from the opposite page to complete this email.**

> ● ● ● ✉ Reply   Forward
>
> Dear Auntie Megan,
>
> At last my first year exams are over. It's such a relief. I feel as if I've done nothing but
> .... (1) for them for ages. Although I'd .... (2) with work quite well
> during the year, I still needed to .... (3) everything that we had covered, of course.
> Fortunately, everything that I hoped would .... (4) in the exam paper did. So I hope
> I've done OK and haven't just .... (5). Now all I have to do is .... (6)
> one course assignment, which I need to hand in by the end of term.
>
> We don't .... (7) till the end of the month and so I won't be home till then. We
> don't .... (8) until the end of September, so it'll be a lovely long break. I look forward
> to seeing you soon.
>
> Love,
>
> Kelly

43.4 **Correct the ten phrasal verb mistakes in this paragraph. Either the wrong particles or the wrong verbs have been used.**

Alfie hardly worked up at all for his exams. He brushed over on the history of the French Revolution, but no questions on the French Revolution got up in the exam. He was afraid that he would be thrown off university for failing his exams. However, he did just manage to scratch through them and so he will be in college when we return back next term. He has promised to try to keep through with work next year as he is planning to sign in for a couple of quite difficult courses, including business studies. He'll have to polish over his French because the business studies course involves spending a term in France working in a business. He thinks he can just lift up the language when he gets there, but I think he should study it before he goes because he only has school French.

> ### Over to you
>
> Go to the Mini dictionary at the end of this book and find more phrasal verbs with *break*. Is there a common theme in their meaning? If so, what is it?

44 Student life: reading and writing

A Reading

Now, your homework for the weekend. Can you all please **read up on**[1] air pollution for next week. You'll find a good chapter in your textbook on page 40, but you don't need to read it all – just **dip into**[2] it. Now please **turn over**[3] the worksheet on your desk. Nancy, will you please **read out**[4] the paragraph at the top of the sheet?

[1] read a lot about a particular subject in order to learn about it
[2] read small parts of a book or magazine

[3] turn a page so that you can see the other side
[4] read aloud

B Writing

phrasal verb	meaning	example
write out sth or **write** sth **out**	write something again in a better or more complete way	In the exam, make notes in rough first and then **write** your essay **out**.
note down sth or **note** sth **down**	write or record words or numbers, often so that you do not forget them	**Note down** your password somewhere safe.
jot down sth or **jot** sth **down**	write or record something quickly on a piece of paper or an electronic device so that you remember it	Jack **jotted down** Lucy's address in his phone.
scribble down sth or **scribble** sth **down**	write something very quickly on a piece of paper	I only had time to **scribble down** a few notes before I made my speech.
fill in sth or **fill** sth **in**	write or record all the necessary information on an official document, e.g. a form	Please **fill in** this registration form and return it by 18 September.
fill out sth or **fill** sth **out**	write or record all the necessary information on an official document, e.g. a form	Let's **fill out** this questionnaire together.

C Improving a piece of writing

Dad   Your essay's good, but I think it would be better if you **cut out**[1] this paragraph here. Also it'd be a good idea to add a paragraph **summing up**[2] your main points at the end. This paragraph here is a bit strong – why not **tone** it **down**[3] a bit? And your point about crime **crops up**[4] in several places – why not deal with it in just one paragraph? And you only **touch on**[5] the issue of government control. Surely that deserves a bit more space? In fact I really think you should try to **set** your whole argument **out**[6] better!

Daughter   Why don't you just write it then, Dad!

[1] removed
[2] describing briefly the most important points
[3] make it less critical or offensive
[4] appears

[5] mention briefly (also **touch upon**)
[6] give all the details or explain clearly, especially in writing

Exercises

44.1 **Match the verbs on the left with an object from the right. There may be more than one answer.**

1	scribble down	a)	a subject
2	fill in/out	b)	a book or an article
3	jot down	c)	the page
4	note down	d)	a rough draft of an essay
5	write out	e)	the times of the trains to London
6	read up on	f)	the answer you have written
7	dip into	g)	a form or a questionnaire
8	read out	h)	a few very quick notes
9	turn over	i)	someone's phone number on a piece of paper

44.2 **Use the phrasal verbs from exercise 44.1 to complete these sentences. Write the verbs in the correct form. There may be more than one possible answer.**

1 I get nervous when I have to .... what I've written in class.
2 I haven't read the book in detail. I just .... it.
3 The witness managed to quickly .... the registration number of the car before it drove away at high speed.
4 I've made some notes for my speech; now I'm going to .... in full.
5 There are three forms to .... for this visa application.
6 We should .... the departure times for flights to Rio de Janeiro.
7 I'll have to .... international law for the exam.
8 Now .... and let's see what's on the next page.
9 Hang on, I'll just .... your address in case I forget it.

44.3 **Look at this student essay and the teacher's comments in the margin. Then complete what the teacher might say to the student using phrasal verbs from the opposite page.**

1 Delete this sentence.	The problems of pollution in the world cannot be solved overnight, since smoke from factories is a necessary evil, and cars and planes will always be noisy. Cleaning the environment is expensive. ~~Large passenger aircraft make more pollution and noise than other planes.~~① People's health is affected.② Governments are completely stupid on questions of the environment.③ It is very expensive to improve the environment.④
2 You only mention this very briefly, but it's an important issue.	
3 This is too strong!	
4 This point has already appeared once in your essay.	
5 Summary needed!	⑤ ....

Teacher I've put a line through this sentence; you should .... (1). And you only .... (2) the question of health; you should have written more. Also you should .... (3) what you say about governments; it's too strong. Then this last point has already .... (4) once; you don't need to repeat it. And finally, the essay ends too suddenly. You should .... (5) your arguments.

A Talking informally about your work or career

Well, to **get ahead**[1] in a job like mine you have to be prepared to **take on**[2] a lot of responsibility and work long hours.

[1] be successful in a job
[2] accept a particular job or responsibility

When the boss first **took me on**[3], he **filled** me **in**[4] on what the job involved, but he didn't tell me I would have to do so much travelling!

[3] began to employ me
[4] gave me the information I needed in order to do something

Well, I **stood down**[5] as chairman in 2015, and Martha Wilmott **took over**[6]. As you all know, she has **carried out**[7] some important reforms in the company and has been very successful.

[5] left an important job or official position so that someone else can do it instead
[6] started doing a job or being responsible for something that someone else was doing or was responsible for before you
[7] done or completed something, especially something important

I'm 60 now, so I think it's time for me to **step down**[8] and **hand over**[9] to a younger person.

[8] leave your job, especially so that someone else can do it
[9] give someone else responsibility or control

B More work-related phrasal verbs

Ellen	Nicole, do you think you could **fix up** a staff meeting for me? [provide or arrange something for someone]
Nicole	Yes, I'll do that. When were you thinking of?
Ellen	Well, let's **pencil** it **in** for Friday morning and see whether everyone else is free then. [arrange for something to happen on a particular date, knowing the arrangement might be changed later]

William	Why are you back home already? Did you **knock off** early today? [informal: stop working, usually at the end of a day]
Callum	I wish I could say that. The truth is I've just been **laid off**. [lost your job because there is no work for you to do; from the verb **lay off** someone or **lay** someone **off**]
William	Oh, I'm sorry to hear that.

Abigail	Did you ever **follow up** that phone call you had with the oil company? [do something in order to make the effect of an earlier action or thing stronger or more certain]
Michael	No, I really should do something about it.

Maisie	It's amazing how much we can get done when we all **pull together**, isn't it? [work as a group in order to achieve something]
Nathan	Yes, although sometimes it's also good if people just **leave** you **to** it. [informal: go away from someone so that they do something by themselves or so they can continue what they are doing]

Exercises

45.1 **Write down phrasal verbs from the opposite page which are:**

a) connected with finishing work (four answers)
b) connected with making arrangements (two answers)

45.2 **Complete this text using verbs or particles from the opposite page.**

Eloise has been .... (1) on more and more responsibility at work. She was only taken .... (2) two years ago, but she has already managed to .... (3) out a very successful reorganisation of office procedures. Her boss just .... (4) her to it, and Eloise then filled him .... (5) when she had arranged everything. She has always been very good at getting people to .... (6) together and at motivating them. She's someone who will really get .... (7) and make a successful career. In fact I'm sure that when the boss eventually .... (8) down, he'll .... (9) over the running of the company to her. He can be sure it will be in safe hands!

45.3 **Write suitable answers to the questions below using phrasal verbs from the opposite page.**

1 Shall I tell you what's been going on while you were on holiday?
  Yes, please ....
2 Could you deal with the enquiries we've had in response to our advert?
  Certainly, I'll ....
3 Could you arrange an appointment for me with the bank manager?
  Yes, I'll ....
4 Why did you stand down as Director?
  Well, I've been doing it for years and I thought it was time to ....
5 Can we arrange a meeting for some time next week?
  Sure, why don't we .... ?

45.4 **Answer these questions about your own working life using full sentences.**

1 What kind of tasks do you have to carry out each day?
2 At what time do you knock off each day?
3 Do you know anyone who has ever been laid off?
4 What qualities do you think you need to get ahead in the job that you do?
5 What did you do to get taken on for the job that you now have?

A Being busy

Nikki	I haven't seen you for ages. Have you **been** a bit **tied up**[1] at work?
Tim	Yes, I've been incredibly busy. I was away for a conference and the work just **piled up**[2] while I was away. I've **been snowed under**[3] ever since. Although I **slave away**[4] till seven at night and even work at weekends, I still can't seem to **catch up with**[5] everything!
Nikki	Sorry I asked!

[1] been so busy that you are unable to see or speak to anyone else or go anywhere (informal)
[2] became more and more (used of something unpleasant, e.g. work, bills or debts)
[3] had so much work to do that I have problems dealing with it
[4] work very hard with little or no rest
[5] do something you did not have time to do earlier

B Working hard

Ellis	How are things going for you at work at the moment, Stella?
Stella	Well, we're **branching out**[1] into a new product line – children's clothes – so I'm pretty busy. At the moment I'm **working on**[2] some new designs for leisurewear. We're **working towards**[3] having a complete range for children of all ages. It's quite difficult but I'm sure I'll develop some good designs if I **keep at**[4] it.
Ellis	Well, you always were good at **sticking at**[5] things.
Stella	Well, I'd certainly rather do a project myself than have to **chase up**[6] other people to make sure they're doing what they promised to do. But sometimes you have to do that just to keep things **moving along**[7].
Ellis	Do you think you could **squeeze in**[8] lunch with me sometime?
Stella	Mm, possibly, but not till next week.
Ellis	That's fine. But don't try to **wriggle out of**[9] it at the last minute!

[1] starting to do something different from what you usually do
[2] spending time working in order to produce something
[3] trying hard to achieve
[4] continue working hard at something difficult or something which takes a long time
[5] continuing to work hard at something even though it is hard or takes a long time
[6] ask people to do something that they said they would do but have not done yet
[7] developing in a satisfactory way
[8] manage to see someone or do something when you are very busy and do not have much time available
[9] avoid doing something that other people think you should do, often in a dishonest way (informal)

Mr Benbow stuck at his job in the glue factory for 25 years before retiring.

Tip

When phrasal verbs have very strong visual images associated with the verbs they are made from, for example, *squeeze in*, *stick at* and *wriggle out*, try to picture the meaning of the verb alone to help you remember the meaning of the verb and particle together.

Exercises

46.1 Which phrasal verbs in A opposite do these pictures make you think of? Write the correct phrasal verb under each one.

1

....

3

2

....

4

....

....

46.2 Use the phrasal verbs from exercise 46.1 to rewrite these sentences. Use each phrasal verb once only.

1 I've been trying to get up to date with all the work I couldn't do when I was ill.
2 Sorry, I was incredibly busy all last week, so I couldn't go to any of the meetings.
3 Paperwork has just increased and increased recently. I don't know where to start.
4 I'm sorry I can't do the report this week. I'm just so incredibly busy.

46.3 Complete these sentences using the correct particles.

1 I've been working all day .... this essay and I still haven't finished it.
2 Whenever there's a difficult task to do she always tries to wriggle .... it.
3 Why should we slave .... till we're 65 and get nothing but a small pension?
4 Could we squeeze .... a quick meeting before lunch?
5 I must catch .... the housework before my visitors arrive this weekend.

46.4 Each line of the text below contains one mistake with a phrasal verb. Cross out the incorrect word and write the correct word in the box next to that line.

up

I need to chase ~~out~~ Austin's report so that we can

keep things moving away with the European sales

campaign. I know he's been working in it and I

know he's been working upwards the same goals

as all of us to branch up into new markets in Europe,

but he's not good at sticking for things and you

need to keep in it with campaigns like this one.

A   Formal and informal

Many phrasal verbs have more formal, non-phrasal equivalents.

phrasal verb	more formal equivalent	meaning	example
take out sth or **take** sth **out**	**withdraw**	get money from a bank	I **took** €100 **out** at the ATM yesterday. You may not **withdraw** more than €500 in 24 hours.
cut back sth or **cut** sth **back**	**reduce**	decrease the amount of money that is being spent on something	The government is **cutting back** on the education budget. The education budget is to be **reduced** next year.
pay back sb/sth or **pay** sb/sth **back**	**repay**	pay someone the money that you owe them	Lend me 50 pounds and I'll **pay** you **back** tomorrow. Poor countries find it very difficult to **repay** their debts.
come to sth	**total**	be a particular total when amounts or numbers are added together	The bill for the meal **came to** $86 altogether. Healthcare expenditure **totalled** $190 billion last year.

B   Paying bills and debts

I won't **pay off** the mortgage on my house until 2044. [pay back all the money owed]

My tax bill has arrived. I have to **pay up** by 30 December. [pay money owed, especially when you do not want to]

My kids **ran up** a phone bill of £600! [caused you to owe a large amount of money]

I know I already owe you £100. Can you lend me another £100 and I'll **settle up** with you when I get paid next week? [pay someone the money owed to them]

Other verbs connected with money

I've been offered a chance to go to New Zealand next year. So I've started **saving up**[1] already. I'm trying to **set aside**[2] a fixed amount each month so that I'll have enough.

It was a terrible holiday. Everything went wrong. And it cost us $3000, but I guess we'll have to just **write** that **off**[3]. We won't **get** it **back**[4].

They were **giving away**[5] free tickets at the Concert Hall today and I got one. Then I was in a bookshop buying a magazine and I **picked up**[6] a book on Italian cookery at a **knockdown**[7] price. It had been reduced from $40 to $20.

1. keeping money in order to buy something with it in the future
2. use money for one purpose and no other purpose
3. accept that an amount of money has been lost
4. it will not be returned
5. giving something to somebody without asking for payment
6. bought something when you have gone to a place to do something else
7. (adjective) very cheap

Exercises

47.1 **Rewrite these sentences using the word in brackets so that they keep the same meaning.**

1 The suspected criminal withdrew all the money from his bank account and has not been seen since. (TAKE)
2 As Sebastian's girlfriend has been working in Australia for the past two years, they have huge debts because of travel costs. (RUN)
3 The bill for the books we ordered totalled $70.85. (COME)
4 I lent him €500 a year ago and he still hasn't repaid me. (PAY)
5 Now that I've lost my job, we're going to have to reduce what we spend on our weekly trip to the supermarket. (CUT)
6 If you pay the restaurant bill with your credit card, I'll give you my share later. (SETTLE)

47.2 **Complete this email using words from the box.**

aside	back	down	off	up

Hi Alfie,

I've got some exciting news. At last I've saved .... (1) enough money to come and visit you in Canada. What's more, my parents have agreed to write .... (2) the money I borrowed from them when I was at university. They don't expect to get it .... (3) unless I'm rich and famous one day! Anyway, I've been setting .... (4) money for the trip all year and at last I can afford it. I've heard you can get tickets at knock.. (5) prices on the Internet, so I'll try and do that.

Looking forward so much to seeing you soon,

Lydia

47.3 **Choose the correct word from a–d to complete the text below.**

My financial situation is in a bit of a bad way at the moment. First of all I owe my brother some money and he says I have to pay .... (1) before the end of the month. I've .... (2) up so many other bills that I don't know how I'm going to pay them .... (3). I wanted to sell my car, but it's so old and rusty that I can't even .... (4) it away. At work they're threatening to .... (5) back our opportunities for overtime. I don't know what I'll do then.

1 a) back   b) up   c) off   d) out
2 a) cut   b) saved   c) run   d) picked
3 a) back   b) up   c) off   d) out
4 a) give   b) settle   c) take   d) write
5 a) pay   b) knock   c) set   d) cut

47.4 **Answer these questions using full sentences.**

1 What, if anything, are you saving up for?
2 How much money do you usually take out at a cash machine?
3 What would you expect the bill for a night in a hotel in your country to come to?
4 Do you have any big debts, and if so, when do you hope to pay them off?
5 What sorts of things might you pick up at a flea market?

48 Money: buying and selling

A Shopping and buying goods

Tom	That leather bag's £220. Shall I see if he'll sell it cheaper?
Lily	Yes, why don't you try and **beat** him **down** to £200. [make someone reduce the price of something]
Keira	Did you manage to get that car you wanted for a lower price?
Zac	Yes, the dealer **knocked** 10% **off** the price because I offered to pay cash. [reduced the price by a certain sum]
Harper	This is a nice old vase. Is it an antique?
Beatrice	Yes it is, but I **picked** it **up** for €50. It was a real bargain. [bought it at a cheap price]
Fran	It would be nice to buy something for our teacher now that the course is ending.
Paco	Yes, we should **club together** and get her some flowers or a nice gift. [put our money together as a group]
David	I'm not going to buy stuff at those gift shops again. They really **ripped** me **off** last time. [informal: cheated me by making me pay too much]
Robyn	Yes, a lot of those tourist shops are a real **rip-off**. You can get the same things in ordinary shops for half the price. [noun: from the verb **rip off**]
Albert	Shall we buy the computer here? It comes with a two-year guarantee.
Pilar	No, let's **shop around** a bit. It may be cheaper in another computer store or online. [look at different shops and compare prices]
Aaron	Jensen is selling Adele's autograph for $200. Should I buy it?
Matthew	If I were you I'd **snap** it **up**. It will probably become very valuable in the future. [slightly informal: buy it quickly because the price is good]
Megan	The car failed its annual test yesterday. Two of the tyres are badly worn.
Simon	Oh no! Now we have to **fork out for** two new ones! [informal: pay for something, especially when you do not want to]

B Other buying verbs

Learn these verbs in pairs to help you remember them.

We should **stock up** on fruit and vegetables and not buy so much junk food. [buy large quantities of]

We should never **skimp on** healthy foods. [spend too little money on or use too little of]

We **splashed out** [spent a lot of money on something we didn't really need] on lots of new furniture last month and **ran up** [caused ourselves to have to pay] a huge bill.

I've had this email about an online offer. They're **selling off** printers. [selling to get rid of them]

Should I buy one right away in case they **sell out**? [have none left]

> ### Tip
>
> Sometimes you meet pairs of phrasal verbs which you can link together into one sentence or a pair of connected sentences, as in section B on this page. Try to learn as many pairs of phrasal verbs in this way because it will help you to remember them more easily.

Exercises

48.1 Fill the gaps with appropriate verbs from the opposite page.

1 He wanted $4000 for his old car, but I managed to .... him down to $3750.
2 We're going to have to .... out a lot of money this year; the kitchen needs a new floor and the roof needs to be repaired.
3 We mustn't .... on the food and drink for the party. We don't want our friends to think we're mean!
4 I .... up an interesting old book about my village in a second-hand bookshop. It was only five pounds.
5 The tickets for the rock concert are bound to .... out really quickly. I think we should get online as soon as bookings open.

48.2 Answer the questions below using phrasal verbs from the box.

| splash out (on sth) | club together | stock up (on sth) | knock off | shop around |

1 You're going to stay on a small island for three days where there aren't any shops. What can you do to make sure you have enough food for your stay?
2 Your sofa and armchairs are beginning to look very old. You have some money you'd like to spend. What could you do?
3 You want to buy your friend's bicycle but you think the price is too high. What could you ask your friend to do?
4 You want to buy a laptop, but the prices seem to be very different for the same model in different shops and online. What should you do?
5 Your classmate Sara is ill in hospital and you think it would be nice to send her a bunch of flowers from the whole class. What could you suggest?

48.3 Correct the mistakes with the phrasal verbs in these sentences. There is one mistake in each sentence.

1 She became addicted to online shopping and ran into huge credit card bills.
2 We were ripped out in that restaurant. They charged us for four desserts when we only had two.
3 He sold over his share in the business and went travelling round the world.
4 When he offered me his tennis racket for only $100, I snapped it off because it was still in excellent condition.
5 We had to fork for a new washing machine because our old one broke down.

48.4 Answer these questions about nouns formed from phrasal verbs. Use a dictionary if necessary.

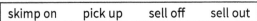

1 On the opposite page, you are shown the noun form of one of the phrasal verbs. Which one is it?
2 Look at the box below. Which of these phrasal verbs from the opposite page also have noun forms, and if so, what do the noun forms mean? Use a dictionary if necessary.

| skimp on | pick up | sell off | sell out |

A   Starting and doing business

Local Entrepreneurs

Tim Benson **started up**[1] his own business in his first year at university. He **set up**[2] a small company **hiring out**[3] bicycles to other students. He was very successful and claims that his profits **ran into**[4] thousands of euros a month, a lot of money for a student. As a **spin-off**[5] he used to sell cycling clothes and equipment to the students, and that also was a good earner for him. 'I was really happy with that **set-up**[6],' says Tim, 'as I loved cycling myself.'

1   created (a business or other organisation)
2   started (a company or organisation)
3   allowing people to use for a short time in exchange for money
4   reached a particular level
5   (noun) extra business in some way related to an earlier successful business
6   (noun) business arrangement

B   Ups and downs in business

Read this conversation about Mason's business activities.

Bobby   Doesn't Mason own his computer business any more?

Lauren   No, he **sold up**[1] and used the money to buy a small chain of clothing **outlets**[2].

Bobby   Really? Has he done well?

Lauren   Yes. His **turnover**[3] was so big he managed to **take over**[4] a jewellery company that had been a success but was **winding down**[5] because of bad management. They were no longer able to pay for the **upkeep**[6] of the stores.

Bobby   Wow! How much did he have to pay of his own money?

Lauren   Well, he **poured** a lot of money **into**[7] it – he **puts** it **at**[8] around a billion – but he saved it from **going under**[9] and it's making a profit now. In fact he says the profit on wedding rings alone **runs to**[10] several hundred million. He says he's glad he decided to risk the **takeover**[11].

Bobby   So he's a rich man now then?

Lauren   He's very rich, but you know something? He still drives around town in that old car of his!

1   sold a business (or house) in order to go and do something else (or live somewhere else)
2   (noun) shops
3   (noun) amount of money or business made by a company in a period of time
4   get control of a company by buying most of its shares
5   gradually reducing the amount of work being done until it closes completely
6   (noun) cost or process of keeping a building or something in good condition
7   provided a lot of money for something over a long period
8   roughly calculates at a particular amount
9   failing financially
10   reaches a particular amount, usually a large amount
11   (noun) act of gaining control of a company

Tip

Business English uses a number of specific phrasal verbs that are either rarely used in other contexts, e.g. *to start up, to sell up*, or are used in other contexts with different meanings, e.g. *to turn over*. If you have a particular interest in Business English, make a special collection of these as you come across them.

Exercises

49.1 **Match the stories 1–6 with the headlines a–f below.**

1 The company has decided to wind down its operations in South America and to concentrate on its ...
2 The company was concealing massive debts but reached a point where it was bound to go under.
3 The takeover of Westin Engineering by Civic Technologies is to take place after all, it was announced today.
4 A company spokeswoman said profits were now running into nine figures. She confirmed that ...
5 Mr Donaldson has decided to sell up and retire to the south of France after 45 years in the business.
6 The lightweight clothes are a spin-off of space technology that sent men to the moon in the 1960s and 1970s.

a) COMPANY FOUNDER TO REALISE BIG PROFIT AFTER LONG CAREER
b) Company announces 800 million euro profit
c) Company benefits from decades-old science
d) Company to close overseas factories
e) COMPANIES WILL JOIN TO MAKE HUGE CORPORATION
f) Company financial crash was inevitable

49.2 **Complete these dialogues using phrasal verbs from the opposite page so that the second speaker agrees with and repeats more or less what the first speaker says.**

1   Jayden The government has put huge sums of money into agriculture.

    Henry   Yes, they've been ....

2   Lottie I seem to remember Hugh Morris began his business about ten years ago.

    Elise   Yes, you're right. He ....

3   Rosie   I would estimate that they've lost several million euros this year.

    Jamie   Yes, I'd ....

4   Isabella I hear Macron are establishing a branch in Oslo.

    Alicia   Yes, they're ....

5   Helena All the repairs on the old building are incredibly expensive.

    Connor Yes, the ....

49.3 **Complete these sentences using words from the box.**

hire out	turnover	take over	outlet	run to	set-up

1 Big companies often .... small ones.
2 These shops .... power tools by the hour.
3 Last year their .... was $100 million.
4 A new sportswear .... has opened on the edge of town.
5 I couldn't work there; the .... didn't appeal to me at all.
6 The cost of rebuilding could .... 10 million pounds.

50 Calling people

A Conversations on the phone or the Internet

Client	Can I speak to Mr Jones, please?
Assistant	I'm afraid Mr Jones is in a meeting.
Client	OK, I'll **call back**[1] later.

Client	Could you **put** me **through**[2] to Anabelle Parker, please?
Assistant	May I ask who's calling?
Client	It's David Brown. We were talking a few minutes ago but got **cut off**[3].

Sarah	It's a very bad line, isn't it?
Paul	Yes, it is. Why don't we end the call and I'll try calling you again?
Sarah	Do you think people could be **listening in**[4] on our conversation?
Paul	I don't think we can assume that any phone or Internet call is completely private.

[1] call someone for the second time, or call someone who rang you earlier
[2] connect a phone or Internet caller to the person they want to speak to
[3] were stopped from continuing the phone or Internet conversation because the connection broke
[4] secretly listening to a conversation

B Conversations about calling

Alex	Have you found out about costs for repairing the central heating yet?
Megan	No, I **called around** a couple of companies. [called several people, often in order to find out information]. None of them have **got back to** me yet with a definite figure. [talked to someone, usually to give them information that you were not able to give them before]
Alex	Well, if they don't **call back** [call someone who rang you earlier] soon, you'd better try **calling up** [calling] a few more places.

Luigi	Do you find it hard to **get through** to your parents in Tonga? [manage to talk to someone on the phone or on the Internet]
Marie	Not usually. If I call on the phone, my mum talks to me and then **puts** my dad **on** [give someone the telephone so that they can speak to the person who is on it], and he then **puts** me **on** speakerphone [turn on a loudspeaker on the phone so that everyone can hear the caller] so that I can talk to all my brothers and sisters. I can never get them to **hang up** [end a phone call, suddenly] and I don't want to **ring off** [end a phone call] either. If I call them on the Internet, it's great to be able to see all the family and talk to them at the same time, but the connection often isn't very good.

Frank	I don't feel very well today. I've got a terrible headache.
Scarlett	Oh dear. You'd better **call in** sick then. [call someone at your place of work to explain why you are not there]

> **Tip**
>
> You can use *phone* or *ring* instead of *call* if you are using the phone rather than the Internet, e.g. *ring back*, *phone around*, *ring up*, *phone in*.

Exercises

50.1 Rewrite the underlined words using a phrasal verb from the opposite page.

1 Why don't you <u>make phone calls to</u> several different companies to get the information you need?
2 It's difficult to <u>get a connection</u> to the customer helpline in the mornings.
3 I'm sorry, he's out right now. Can you <u>phone again</u> at about five o'clock?
4 Maryam <u>phoned the office</u> to say she's not feeling well.
5

> Kelly   Hi Uncle Jack, it's Kelly. How's everything?
>
> Jack   Hi! Fine thanks. Just a minute, I'll <u>give the phone to your aunt</u> so you can tell her all the news.

6 I'll <u>call you with my response</u> in a few days.
7 Is it OK if I <u>turn on the loudspeaker on the phone</u> so that everyone can hear your news?

50.2 Complete the word puzzle.

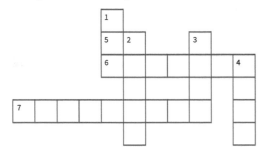

Down
1 Can I speak to Mr Walsh again please? I was speaking to him and we were .... off.
2 Hi, I've been meaning to .... you up for ages, but I didn't have your new number.
3 Hello, are you still there? Hello? I think she's just .... off.
4 Whoever it was, they just .... up; it must have been a wrong number.

Across
5 Why don't you call Sophia .... and invite her to the party?
6 Could you put me .... to the sales department please?
7 I can hear funny noises. Do you think someone's .... in on our call?

50.3 Here are some more phrasal verbs which you may need to use in connection with calling people. What do you think they mean? Use a dictionary if necessary.

Cambridge Dictionary
ctionary.cambridge.org

speak up   hold on   break up   switch on   switch off

50.4 Use the phrasal verbs from exercise 50.3 to answer these questions. Use each verb once.

1 How could you explain to a friend why they couldn't reach you on your phone when they tried to?
2 How could you tell someone you're speaking to on a phone that the signal is very bad and you have difficulty understanding what they're saying?
3 How could you ask someone to speak louder because there's a lot of background noise?
4 How could you explain to someone that you only got their message when you turned your phone on after the concert?
5 How could you ask someone to wait and not put the phone down while you have to interrupt the call for some reason?

A Feelings go up and down

Up and *down* phrasal verbs connected with feelings often refer to positive (up ↑) and negative (down ↓) emotions and emotional events, or a more emotional intensity (up ↑) or less emotional intensity (down ↓).

UP		DOWN	
example	meaning	example	meaning
Brighten up, will you! You're depressing everyone!	suddenly look or feel happier	She **broke down** when she was told the bad news.	was unable to control her feelings and started to cry
The film **cheered** us **up** considerably.	made us start to feel happier	**Calm down**! Losing your temper won't solve the problem.	stop feeling angry, upset, or excited
There's no point in **being hung up** about it; there's nothing we can do.	becoming very worried about something and spend a lot of time thinking about it (informal)	I need some time to **cool down** before I can see him again.	become calmer

B More verbs connected with feelings

● ● ●   ✉ Reply   Forward

There's obviously something you need to tell me that is making you very angry, so don't **bottle up**[1] your emotions. If you do, there is a danger that you will **tear yourself apart**[2].

[1] not allow yourself to show or talk about your feelings, especially feelings of anger and sadness (informal)
[2] make yourself feel very unhappy

● ● ●   ✉ Reply   Forward

I understand that the email has made you extremely angry, but don't get **carried away**[3]; proceed carefully. At work things are going to get better, and you should **jump at**[4] the chance of the new challenge which I know you will soon be offered.

[3] become so excited about something that you do not control what you say or do and you forget about everything else
[4] eagerly accept a chance to do or have something

● ● ●   ✉ Reply   Forward

You may be unwilling at first to take part in the activity holiday Kian has suggested, but talk about it with him and the other friends he's invited, and you may **warm to**[5] it a bit more. In fact, the idea could soon **grow on**[6] you and you'll find yourself doing something you never expected to do and **taking to**[7] it enthusiastically.

[5] become more enthusiastic about an idea
[6] you like something more and more, although you did not like it at first (informal)
[7] starting to like it

● ● ●   Reply   Forward

I can see that you **feel for**[8] Poppy, but be careful. She seems to have lots of problems and **hang-ups**[9], and you could soon become more involved than you want to. She will have to **pull** herself **together**[10] sooner or later; it's her life, not yours.

[8] feel sorry for someone who is unhappy or in a difficult situation
[9] feelings of embarrassment or fear about something, often when it is not necessary to feel that way (informal)
[10] become calm after being very upset or angry

Exercises

51.1 Read the sentences below. Decide which people are experiencing positive feelings and which are experiencing negative feelings.

1 Jude broke down when the doctor told her the results.
2 George is beginning to take to the idea of moving to Boston.
3 Faith has more hang-ups than anyone else I know.
4 Henry should calm down or he'll make himself ill.
5 Theo has cheered up a lot since I last saw him.
6 Mary doesn't seem to be able to pull herself together.
7 Thomas is very inclined to bottle up his emotions.
8 Anna has brightened up considerably since this morning.

51.2 Rewrite the underlined parts of these sentences using phrasal verbs from the opposite page.

1 The news that I didn't have to do the exam after all made me feel happier.
2 Look, Dominic. Try to be less angry! Getting angry won't solve the problem.
3 When she heard of her friend's death, she lost control of her feelings and wept.
4 She worries so much about silly little problems at work.
5 I wish you'd be a bit more cheerful! You're making me feel depressed!

51.3 Match the statements on the left with the most appropriate response on the right.

1 That new quiz show is growing on me now.
2 Would you like to try snowboarding?
3 Tom's marriage problems are tearing him apart.
4 Sam is so hung up about failing his exam.
5 If I win the lottery, I'll buy a flat in New York and one in Rio and …
6 I wish Nadia would brighten up a bit.

What more can we do to cheer her up?
I know – I do feel for them both.
Yes, I'm beginning to warm to it too.
Don't get carried away!
Yes, I hope he pulls himself together before his next attempt.
Sure, I'd jump at the chance.

51.4 Complete this email using verbs or particles from the opposite page.

Dear Esther,

I hope things are OK with you.

We've been having quite a difficult time here. Blake lost his job. After 20 years there, he .... (1) down when he was told. It seemed to .... (2) him apart and he has found it very hard to .... (3) himself together. However, thank goodness, he does seem to be brightening .... (4) a bit now. He's even beginning to take .... (5) the idea of doing a retraining course. Melissa was very angry at the way her father had been treated – she .... (6) for him so much. She's cooled .... (7) a bit now as she realises there is no point in getting too .... (8) up about it. Frankie has been great at trying to .... (9) us all up through all this.

Hope to hear from you soon.

Harriet

A   Talking about relationships

ask Eva

I've been **going out with**[1] my boyfriend for ten months now and we're planning to get married next year. But last week we **fell out**[2] over something really stupid. He heard a male friend of mine tell me my hair looked nice and he thought it was a **chat-up**[3] line. He got so jealous and wouldn't speak to me. Do you think a minor **falling-out**[4] like this is a bad sign for our future marriage, or am I worrying too much?

Faye

I think I've **fallen for**[1] the new guy who's just started work in our office. He **fitted in**[2] at once. He and I **get along**[3] really well, but he hasn't **asked** me **out**[4] yet. What should I do?

Florence

with Dr. Eva Fernandez

[1] having a romantic relationship with
[2] had an argument that damaged our relationship
[3] (noun, informal) a way of talking which suggests you are attracted to someone and want them to be attracted to you (from the verb **chat up**)
[4] (noun) argument (from the verb **fall out**)

[1] (informal) become very attracted to
[2] felt happy in a group of people because he was similar to them
[3] like each other and are friendly
[4] invited someone to go to a place like a cinema or a restaurant, usually to start a romantic relationship

B   Being attracted to someone

If you ...	then you ...
hit it off with someone	immediately like and become friendly with them (informal)
pair off with someone	start a romantic relationship with them
chat someone **up**	talk in a way that shows them that you are attracted to them and you try to make them attracted to you
go for a particular type of person or thing	like that type of person or thing

> **Tip**
>
> There are a lot of phrasal verbs which deal with relationships and how people get on with each other. Look occasionally at advice columns in a newspaper or magazine or online and note down any new ones that you find.

Exercises

52.1 Read the reply to Faye's letter and two other replies from the advice column. Fill the gaps.

Faye,

You say you're worried because you and your fiancé have (1) .... out. Well, take my advice, a temporary (2) .... with someone you love is not the end of the world. And your boyfriend shouldn't worry even if another man does try a (3) .... up line with you; if you love each other, such silly things will never threaten your marriage.

Pippa,

I get many letters from people in your situation. It can be hard when it feels like all your friends have (4) .... with boyfriends or girlfriends, and you're the only one who's still single. My advice to you is to stop worrying about the best way to (5) .... people .... at parties, and try to relax! Why not start a new class or join a club for a hobby you enjoy? That way you are more likely to meet the kind of guys you really (6) .... , and you never know what will happen next!

Connor,

You say you think you've (7) .... for the new student on your course, but that you're afraid she won't (8) .... in with your gang of friends. I suggest you (9) .... her out and then meet up with your friends later in the evening. If they don't (10) .... , then the choice is simple: either you lose her and keep your friends, or you keep her and perhaps lose 'friends' who aren't really true friends.

52.2 Correct the mistakes with the phrasal verbs in these sentences.

1 My friend and I fell away last week because she thinks I'm in love with her boyfriend.
2 The new student was finding it difficult to fit on, as he was older than the other students.
3 When George met his new colleague, he really fell to her and now he talks about her all the time.
4 Ethan and David hit it of immediately when they were introduced.
5 That girl over there was trying to talk me up.

52.3 Rewrite the underlined parts of this dialogue using phrasal verbs from the opposite page.

Annie	So what did you think of the film?
Jade	It was so romantic! I loved it, especially at the end where Chris finally <u>invited Lara to go out</u>.
Annie	That was sweet. But I didn't like it when Julie and Raul <u>started a romantic relationship</u>. She said at the beginning that she didn't normally <u>like</u> men who spend a lot of time at the gym. So it wasn't very realistic when she immediately <u>became very attracted to him</u>.
Jade	But it was because they <u>enjoyed a very friendly relationship</u> online first. She didn't know what he looked like! And then he <u>adapted well</u> to her group of friends, which always helps.
Annie	Yes, I suppose so. But my favourite storyline was Lena and Seth. The ones who were <u>having a romantic relationship</u> at the start but then had a big argument. It was so funny when he started <u>talking to her to try to attract her</u> at the carnival and she didn't know it was him – until he took off the lion costume!
Jade	Ha ha! Yes, that was definitely the funniest bit.

Read these letters from the advice column and the replies on the right.

I'm 19 and my boyfriend and I have just **split up**[1] after a year together. For the first six months everything was great, but then we just seemed to **drift apart**[2]. I didn't really want to **finish with**[3] him, but he decided to **break off**[4] our relationship. Should I ask him if we can start again and try to rediscover the magic of those first six months?

Nina

When two people **grow apart**[5], it's usually because they are basically different. The fact that he **broke off with**[6] you means he recognises that you don't really have a lot in common. You're young. Let him go!

[1] ended a relationship or marriage
[2] gradually become less friendly and the relationship ends
[3] end a romantic relationship (informal)
[4] end a relationship
[5] gradually become less friendly, often because you do not have the same interests and opinions any more
[6] ended a romantic relationship with someone

My parents **broke up**[1] last year and I've been depressed ever since. I see each of them regularly, and I love them, but I feel they have **let** me **down**[2]. Is there anything I can do to persuade them to **make up**[3] and live together again so that my sister and I can have a normal life like other kids?

Aidan

Aidan, a marriage **break-up**[4] is always very sad, but there's not much you can do. They are adults and they have made their own choices. You feel you're **missing out**[5] on a normal young person's life, but you're not alone. A third of all marriages in Britain end in divorce. Be brave and talk to your friends about it.

[1] their marriage or relationship ended
[2] disappointed me by failing to do what they agreed or what I expected them to do
[3] forgive each other and become friendly again
[4] (noun) the act or event of breaking up
[5] not doing or getting something you would enjoy or that would be good for you, or not having something other people have

A couple of years ago my uncle **ran off with**[1] another woman. She was much younger than him, in fact she was only 20 and he was 52. It ended in disaster. He left her last year and returned to his wife. But the neighbours all stare at him and laugh at him; it seems he'll never **live** it **down**[2]. He's doing his best to **settle down**[3] and be a good husband and uncle again, but I feel so unhappy for him. What can I do?

Elena

People can be very cruel, Elena, and your uncle may have to **settle for**[4] a lot more embarrassment before the neighbours forget what happened. The best thing you can do is to show your uncle that you love him and support him and show him that you accept him, and all his faults.

[1] secretly left a place with someone in order to live with them or marry them, especially when other people think this is wrong
[2] stop feeling embarrassed about something you did by waiting until people forget about it
[3] start living in a place where you intend to stay for a long time
[4] accept something, often something that is not exactly what you want or is not the best

Exercises

53.1 **Match the problems 1–6 with the responses a–f.**

1 My partner and I are so busy at work that we seem to be drifting apart. What should I do?

4 I always seem to pick girlfriends who let me down. What can I do?

2 How can I finish with my boyfriend without hurting his feelings too much?

5 I'm 35. Isn't it time I was thinking of settling down?

3 What can I do to get over the break-up of my marriage? I still love my wife.

6 I've decided never to get married. Do you agree with my friends that I will be missing out on a lot?

a) Become friends first – then you should know what she is really like before you take things any further.
b) The right time can arrive at any age – when you meet the right person.
c) Why not take up some new hobby together?
d) Why make such a major decision about your future now? You may feel very differently in a few years' time.
e) Time should slowly make things better for you.
f) Could you try to make him want to split up with you first?

53.2 **Rewrite these sentences replacing the phrasal verbs with another phrasal verb from the opposite page so that the sentences keep the same meanings.**

1 My sister and her husband broke up last year.
2 Millie was very upset when her boyfriend broke up with her.
3 We had been drifting apart for a long time, so it was better to separate properly.

53.3 **Complete these sentences using appropriate phrasal verbs from the opposite page.**

1 Whenever I quarrel with my girlfriend I can't wait to .... again.
2 We were all very shocked when Emily left her husband and .... her boss.
3 After leaving school my best friend got a glamorous job travelling all over the world, but now all he wants to do is get married and .... somewhere.
4 I am absolutely sure that I can trust her and that she will never .... me ....
5 It was so embarrassing when I spilt tomato soup all over my boss – I'm sure I'll never .... it ....
6 I think that children who are educated at home .... on the opportunity to make friends of their own age.
7 Elsa is determined to marry someone who is both handsome and rich, and she'll never .... less.
8 I can't understand why my girlfriend decided to .... our relationship.

> ### Over to you
>
> Look at the advice in an English language magazine online. Copy down any sentences that you find containing phrasal verbs.

54 Secrets and conversations

A Secrets

Josie You're **keeping** something **from**[1] me, aren't you?

Zachary Well, sort of. Lara really **opened up**[2] to me last night. She **poured out**[3] a lot of things but made me promise not to tell anyone and I can't **go back on**[4] my word.

Josie Go on. You can tell me, I won't **let on**[5] to Lara or anyone else.

Zachary No, I can't. In the course of her **outpouring**[6] she **owned up**[7] to something quite serious and I really can't tell you about it. You'd be far too shocked!

[1] not telling me about something
[2] started to talk more about herself and her feelings
[3] talked very honestly about what was making her unhappy
[4] not do something that you promised you would do
[5] tell someone about something that was supposed to be a secret
[6] (noun) long and emotional expression of what she was feeling
[7] admitted she had done something wrong

B Conversations

phrasal verb	meaning	example
keep on at sb	talk to someone about something many times, usually to complain about something they have done or not done	I wish you wouldn't **keep on at** me about my handwriting! No-one else has problems reading it.
talk down to sb	talk to someone as if they were less clever than you	The best teachers don't **talk down to** students but speak to them as equals.
play down sth or **play** sth **down**	try to make people believe that something is not very important or is unlikely to happen	There is no point in trying to **play down** the incident – too many people saw exactly what happened.
pin down sb or **pin** sb **down**	make someone give you exact details or a decision about something	She's the most infuriating woman – you can never **pin** her **down** to a date on anything.
have it out with sb (informal)	talk to someone about something they have said or done that has made you angry in order to improve the situation	Once Joel had **had it out with** Finn about his untidiness, things got much better.
wind up sb or **wind** sb **up** (informal)	tell someone something that is not true in order to make a joke or to annoy them	Stop pretending that you've lost your sister's new jacket. It's not fair to **wind** her **up** like that.
mouth off (informal)	talk about a subject as if you know more than everyone else or to complain a lot about something	Robert is always **mouthing off** about his boss behind his back, but he'd never say anything to his face.
shut (sb) **up** (informal)	stop talking or making a noise, or make someone else do this	Would you please **shut up** while I'm trying to concentrate on these papers.

> **Tip**
>
> You can sometimes fix phrasal verbs in your mind by writing them in true sentences about a person you know or an experience you've had.

Exercises

54.1 **Read these remarks by different people and then answer the questions below by writing the correct name in the box.**

> George   I'm determined to have it out with my parents. We can't go on in this way.

> Jason   My sister is always mouthing off about something. I wish she'd shut up.

> Michael   I think they were trying to play down the whole affair.

> Rebecca   The boss seems to have gone back on her word.

> Eleanor   Huh! My brother has owned up at last! It's about time!

> Gina   I felt my roommate was trying to wind me up.

1 Who is annoyed because someone talks about subjects as if they know more than everyone else or someone complains a lot about something?

2 Who thought someone told them something that wasn't true in order to make a joke or to annoy them?

3 Who is going to talk to someone about something they have said or done that has made them angry in order to solve the problem?

4 Who thinks someone is trying to make people believe that something is not very important or is not likely to happen?

5 Who is satisfied that someone has admitted they have done something wrong?

6 Who thinks someone has broken a promise to do something?

54.2 **Complete these sentences using words from the opposite page.**

1 I felt she was .... something from me. I asked her what it was, but she wouldn't .... on.
2 Oh, ... up, will you! Don't .... on at me all the time!
3 It's very difficult to .... him down. He never likes to make firm plans.
4 She's an excellent employer. She never .... down to her staff however inadequate they seem.
5 Georgina .... out her life story to me late last night. She's never .... up to me in that way before, and in her .... of emotion she revealed to me that she'd been in prison years ago.

54.3 **Read these sentences containing rather formal verbs and then write their more informal phrasal verb equivalents in the brackets. Use a dictionary if necessary.**

1 I promise I won't reveal (...) to Simon that you're moving out of the flat.
2 The government has reneged (...) on its promise to increase student grants.
3 I had a feeling he was concealing (...) something from me, something unpleasant.
4 She confessed (...) to having lied about the missing money.
5 I have finally decided to confront (...) Jamie. We simply can't continue with so much tension in the air.

Mr Harrison had a habit of talking down to people.

English Phrasal Verbs in Use Intermediate   **113**

Lucy has just had a new baby and is emailing her friend, Caitlin. Follow the correspondence between the two friends.

● ● ●   Reply   Forward

Hi Caitlin,

You'll be pleased to hear the new baby's doing fine. We've decided to **name** him **after**[1] his grandfather, Patrick. He has blue eyes and quite fair hair, so he **takes after**[2] his father. I find it hard to imagine myself **bringing up**[3] a child. Wish me luck for the next 18 years!

Love, Lucy

[1] give him the same name as someone else
[2] has a similar appearance or character as an older member of his family
[3] looking after a child and educating them until they are an adult

---

● ● ●   Reply   Forward

Hi Lucy,

Glad to hear everything's OK with the new baby. Babies **grow up**[4] so quickly and 18 years will seem like 18 weeks, I'm sure! Are you and Tom going to **carry on**[5] living in London, or are you thinking of moving closer to your parents? I know lots of people **end up**[6] moving out of the city when they have a family.

Take care,
Caitlin

[4] change from being a child to being an adult
[5] continue

[6] finally did something, especially without having planned to

---

● ● ●   Reply   Forward

Hi again,

We are thinking about moving house, but it's difficult because I don't know what would **become of**[7] our careers if we weren't living in London. But at the moment all I care about is that little Patrick will be a nice kid, that he won't **drop out**[8] of school or college, that he won't **wind up**[9] in a dead end job, and that he'll be healthy and happy, just like your kids.

Talk to you soon,
Lucy

[7] happen to
[8] stop going to classes before completing a course
[9] start to do or take something bad, usually because you are unhappy
[10] finally do something, especially without having planned to (like the verb **end up**)

● ● ●   Reply   Forward

Hi there,

I'm sure the little lad will **live up to**[11] all your hopes and expectations! A lot of 13-year-olds could **pass for**[12] 17 or 18 these days, and some of the values that were **handed down**[13] to us by our parents and grandparents are considered old-fashioned now. But I'm still optimistic. Do let me know how things go. Regards to Peter.

Love, Caitlin

[11] be as good as he is expected to be
[12] appear to be

[13] given or taught, by an older person to a younger person

Exercises

55.1 Which phrasal verbs in the emails on the opposite page could be replaced by the following synonyms? Write the phrasal verbs next to their synonym.

1 continue ....
2 looks like ....
3 not complete ....
4 transmitted ....
5 be as good as ....
6 happen to ....
7 raising ....
8 look as if they are ....

55.2 Answer these questions in full sentences using phrasal verbs.

1 Were you named after anyone? If so, who were you named after?
2 Who, if anyone, do you take after in appearance?
3 Who, if anyone, do you take after in character?
4 Do you think that children should be treated as adults while they are growing up?
5 What reason might someone have for dropping out of university?
6 Describe someone you know who could pass for someone older than they really are.
7 Do you possess anything that has been handed down from your great-grandparents?
8 Do you think that both parents have an equally important role to play in bringing up their children?
9 Until what age would you like to carry on working?

55.3 Complete this short biography using verbs from the opposite page.

Richard Potts was born 100 years ago today in the same small town in Wales that he lives in now. He was (1) .... after his maternal grandfather, Richard Jones, the distinguished sculptor, whom he was later said to (2) .... after in both character and appearance. The young Richard was orphaned at an early age and was (3) .... up by an aunt. He failed to (4) .... up to his relatives' hopes for him by (5) .... out of school at the age of 15. They were very concerned about what would (6) .... of him and, although there must have been plenty of temptations encouraging the young boy to (7) .... to gambling and drink, he resisted them all and (8) .... up taking a job in a coal mine. He impressed the managers so much that he eventually (9) .... up as a member of the board. He (10) .... on working until five years ago, when ill health forced him to retire, but he is still a familiar figure around the streets of his home town.

```
Over to you
```

Read an obituary or article about the death of someone famous from any English language newspaper and note down any phrasal verbs that you find in it.

A Symptoms

These speakers all describe health problems using phrasal verbs or in the case of *blocked-up*, an adjective based on a phrasal verb.

> I keep **throwing up**[1].

> I'm **fighting off**[4] a sore throat.

> My ankle has **swollen up**[7].

> I think I'm **coming down with**[2] flu.

> I've **put** my shoulder **out**[5].

> My nose is **blocked-up**[8].

> Sam's **going down with**[3] flu too.

> I can't **shake off**[6] this cold.

> I've **passed out**[9] a couple of times recently.

[1] (informal) vomiting
[2] becoming ill, usually with a disease that is not very serious, e.g. flu, a cold
[3] (informal) see note 2
[4] trying hard to get rid of
[5] dislocated or injured by making a bone move from its usual place
[6] get rid of
[7] become larger or rounder than usual
[8] (adjective) filled so that you are unable to breathe normally
[9] become unconscious; fainted

B One medical story

Maggie has had a hard time recently. Firstly, her sister **broke down**[1] after her divorce and was sick for several months. Maggie was still **caring for**[2] her when her brother was hit on the head by a tile that fell from a roof. He was unconscious for a couple of days. Fortunately, he **pulled through**[3] and has now more or less fully recovered although he does seem to have **slowed down**[4] a lot. No sooner were they both better than their grandfather **passed away**[5] and then just a few weeks later their grandmother **passed on**[6] too.

[1] became mentally or physically ill because of an unpleasant experience
[2] looking after someone who is too ill, too young, or too old to look after themselves
[3] recovered from a serious illness
[4] become less physically active than before
[5] died
[6] died

> **Tip**
>
> Try to learn phrasal verbs in chunks or longer phrases, e.g. *I'm coming down with flu; She's fighting off a cold; My nose is blocked-up*.

Exercises

56.1 Complete this text using particles from A.

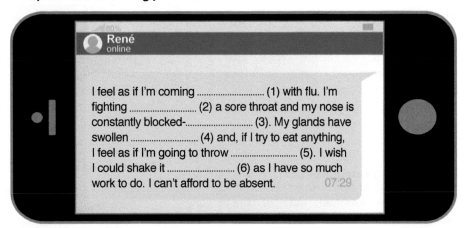

René online

I feel as if I'm coming .... (1) with flu. I'm fighting .... (2) a sore throat and my nose is constantly blocked-.......................... (3). My glands have swollen .... (4) and, if I try to eat anything, I feel as if I'm going to throw .... (5). I wish I could shake it .... (6) as I have so much work to do. I can't afford to be absent.   07:29

56.2 Rewrite the underlined parts of these sentences using a phrasal verb from the opposite page.

1 I've had a sore throat for a week now – I just can't <u>get rid of it</u>.
2 Megan hadn't eaten anything for 48 hours, and so it wasn't surprising that she <u>fainted</u> in the middle of her gym lesson.
3 The doctors were afraid that the 102-year-old man wouldn't survive the attack of pneumonia, but amazingly he <u>recovered</u> and was soon on his feet again.
4 I think <u>I'm just about to get</u> a cold – I feel a bit shivery.
5 My thumb <u>became bigger</u> after I accidentally hit it with a hammer.
6 The sea was so rough that many people <u>were vomiting</u> over the side of the ship.
7 People usually write letters of condolence to the relatives of someone who has <u>died</u>.
8 My grandmother is in great pain because she <u>has dislocated her hip</u>.
9 After the operation, her sister <u>nursed</u> her until she was completely recovered.
10 How do you think you <u>contracted</u> chickenpox?

56.3 Match the beginning of each sentence with its ending.

1 Andrew's uncle passed	for her elderly mother.
2 Beth is fighting	down a bit as they get older.
3 Erica is kept very busy caring	down with flu.
4 Flora's ankles swelled	off a bout of flu.
5 Most people usually slow	up during the long flight.
6 I think Gabriel is going	away last year.

56.4 Complete these sentences in any way that makes sense.

1 When her great-aunt passed away, Carla felt very ....
2 Jack broke down when ....
3 The last time I threw up was ....
4 You can get a blocked-up nose if ....
5 Kate's finger swelled up after ....
6 The best way to fight off a cold is to ....

> ## Over to you
>
> Look at a health advice page of an English language newspaper or magazine. Write down any phrasal verbs that you find there. Write them down in sentences to help you remember them.

57 Sport

A Sports items from newspapers

Weather delays Cup Final
The **kick-off**[1] of the Cup Final between Arsenal and Liverpool was delayed yesterday due to bad weather.

[1] (noun) start of a game of football

Driscoll to attempt record
Welsh swimmer Geraint Driscoll says he is **going for**[3] the world record in tomorrow's 100 metres freestyle event.

[3] will try to achieve something difficult [e.g. break a record, win a medal]

Archery: *England defeated*
ENGLAND were **knocked out**[2] of the European Archery Championship this afternoon in a surprise win by Sweden.

[2] forced to leave the competition because they were defeated

Dornton to play Harsfield
With both teams on 28 points, Dornton will meet Harsfield in a **play-off**[4] this Saturday at Dornton's home ground to decide who goes up to the first division.

[4] (noun) game to decide the winner, especially when the teams or competitors have the same number of points

B People talking about their sporting activities

I **work out**[1] at the gym three times a week to try to **burn off**[2] the calories and stay slim. I find it also helps me to **work off**[3] the stress of work.

[1] exercise in order to improve the strength or appearance of your body
[2] use or get rid of energy, calories or fat by doing a lot of physical exercise
[3] get rid of an unpleasant feeling, e.g. aggression or anger, by doing something energetic

Before I start a match I always do a **warm-up**[4]. Then after the match I make sure I **cool down**[5] and stretch properly.

[4] (noun) gentle exercises which prepare you for more serious exercise (from the verb **warm up**)
[5] become cooler

World-class marathon running can be very hard. You need great mental stamina, and you must never **give in**[6]. It's a great feeling when you **pull ahead**[7] of the rest of the field and know you're winning.

[6] accept that you have been defeated and agree to stop competing or fighting
[7] suddenly get in front of another person who was previously running at the same speed as you

Table tennis is a great sport. Anyone can **join in**[8]. We have a **knockout**[9] competition at work every month, just for fun.

[8] become involved in an activity with other people
[9] (noun) a competition in which only the winners of each stage play in the next stage, until one person or team is the final winner

Exercises

57.1 **Match the phrasal verb on the left with its more formal equivalent on the right.**

1 join in   attempt to achieve
2 give in   defeat
3 go for   surrender
4 pull ahead   participate
5 knock out   overtake

57.2 **Choose phrasal verb expressions from the opposite page to complete each of these notices from a sports club noticeboard.**

1 Always do a .... before doing any strenuous exercise.
2 Sign below if you would like to take part in next month's .... squash tournament.
3 Eat healthily. Remember you have to exercise for one hour to .... the calories from one slice of pizza!
4 Regular exercise helps to .... stress.
5 Don't forget to .... before running round the track.
6 Remember it's just as important to .... properly as it is to warm up.

57.3 **Answer these questions using full sentences.**

1 How often do you work out each month and what do you do when you work out?
2 How might you warm up before running a marathon?
3 Why would you be pleased if you pulled ahead of the other runners in a race?
4 Which sport is better for burning off calories and why – tennis or table tennis?
5 Would you prefer to join in a snooker game or a football game after work?
6 What kind of medal would a top athlete go for?

57.4 **Describe what is happening in these pictures using one of the nouns or verbs from the opposite page.**

1  2  3

57.5 **Here are three more phrasal verbs with sporting connections that were not on the opposite page. Can you choose the correct definition from the box for each of them?**

| was defeated by | progressed | told to leave |

1 If a footballer gets a red card, he is **sent off** the pitch.
2 England **went out** to Germany in the semi-finals.
3 Our team won the game and so they **went forward** to the next round.

A   Homes

phrasal verb	meaning	example
move out	stop living in a particular house or flat	Jack moved out of his college room last Monday.
move in	begin living in a new house or flat	A new family has moved in to the flat next door.
move in together	start living in the same house as someone	Sam and I have always been good friends, so when we both got jobs in Rio, we decided to **move in together**.
live on sth	have an amount of money in order to buy the things you need	I earn just enough to **live on**.
live off sth	have enough money for the things you need by taking it from a supply of money or another person	While Mia was unemployed she had to **live off** her savings.
put up sb or **put** sb **up**	let someone stay in your home for a short time	Would you be able to **put** me **up** when I'm in London next week?
sleep over	sleep in someone else's home for a night (noun) a sleepover	My daughter loves it when a school friend **sleeps over**. The kids **had a sleepover**.

Note: Do not confuse to **sleep over** with to **oversleep**. The verb to **oversleep** means to sleep longer than you should have done, e.g.

If I **oversleep** and am late for work again, I'll lose my job.

B   Daily routines

I've got a new job at the airport and have moved into a flat with a couple of friends. During the week I have to **get up**[1] early as I have to be at the airport by 6.30 a.m. I try to be very quiet in the mornings so I don't **wake up**[2] my flatmates. At the weekends I love **sleeping in**[3]. On Saturdays I sometimes **lie in**[4] till 11. I can't have a **lie-in**[5] if I'm playing football though, which I sometimes do on Saturday mornings. On weekday evenings I go to bed quite early, about 10.30 p.m. usually, but I **stay up**[6] at weekends. If I get home on Saturday night before my flatmates, I **wait up**[7] until they arrive home and we have a drink and a chat before going to bed.

I love sleeping in at weekends.

[1] get out of bed
[2] make them become conscious
[3] sleeping later in the morning than usual
[4] stay in bed later in the morning than usual
[5] (noun) longer time in bed in the morning than usual
[6] go to bed later than usual
[7] stay awake because you are waiting for someone to arrive

Exercises

58.1 **Look at these notices a–f on a college noticeboard and answer the questions below.**

a) Final-year students moving out after graduation have furniture to sell. Tel. 276544.

b) Living off your parents or off your savings? Earn extra cash by working at weekends. Call 896774.

c) Room available in student house. Five minutes from campus. Must be able to move in immediately. Ring 655491.

d) **Student grants are not enough to live on! Join our protest outside the Senate Building, Friday 2 p.m. Bring your friends!**

e) Time to move on? If you've just graduated and want careers advice, come to the careers workshop at 3 p.m., Thursday 25 May, room 12A, Hughes Building.

f) Engineering postgrad looking for like-minded, non-smoking student to move in to two-bedroom flat next month. Call 733208.

Which notice would you respond to if ...

1 ... your income was not sufficient to meet your needs and you were angry about it?
2 ... you felt you needed to take on a new challenge or start a new phase in your life?
3 ... you were looking for bargain items because you're going into an unfurnished flat?
4 ... you were about to leave your accommodation and had nowhere to live?
5 ... you were dependent on others for your income and wanted to earn some money of your own?
6 ... you wanted to share accommodation with someone who might become a friend?

58.2 **Are you a sleep lover? Fill the gaps in the online questionnaire and then answer the questions by ticking the boxes.**

Sleep Lover Survey

1 What time do you normally wake ....? ☐ 6–7 a.m. ☐ 7–8 a.m. ☐ 8–9 a.m. ☐ later

2 Do you feel sleepy if you .... up after midnight? ☐ yes ☐ no

3 Do you have a .... in at weekends? ☐ always ☐ sometimes ☐ never

4 Would you wait .... if a friend or relative you were putting .... was arriving very late? ☐ yes ☐ no

5 Do you enjoy .... in if you don't have to get up? ☐ yes ☐ no

6 How often do you sleep .... at a friend's house? ☐ often ☐ occasionally ☐ never

7 How often do you not hear your alarm and ....? ☐ every day ☐ sometimes ☐ never

58.3 **Complete these sentences using phrasal verbs from the opposite page.**

1 I'll be late back tonight, so please don't bother ....
2 Kate can't afford a hotel, so she's asked a friend to ....
3 I need an alarm clock to stop me from ....
4 We borrowed my uncle's van, so we didn't need to use a removal firm when we .... of our old house.
5 Gordon and Martin already knew each other well before they ....

59 Socialising

A Arranging social gatherings

Read the picture story below and note the phrasal verbs.

phrasal verb	meaning	alternative phrasal verb
ask sb **over/round**	invite someone to come to your house	**invite** sb **around/round/over**
come over	visit someone at their house	**come around/round**
bring along sb/sth or **bring** sb/sth **along**	bring someone or something somewhere	
pop in/into	go into a place just for a short time (informal)	
have sb **around/round**	if you have someone around, they come to your house for a social visit	**have** sb **over**

B Other socialising verbs

I met Peter the other day. He was **asking after** you. [ask for information about someone, especially about their health]

I'll **call round** and see Uncle Luke after work today. [visit someone who lives near to you for a short time]

Please **drop in/round** any time – I'm usually at home. [informal: make a short visit to someone in their home, usually without arranging it before]

The boss has **invited** me **out**. I wonder what she wants? [ask someone to go with you to a place, e.g. a restaurant or the cinema]

A: I'll **bring** that DVD **round** tomorrow that you wanted to watch.

B: Great! Could you also **bring round** that book I lent you?
[bring someone or something somewhere, especially to someone's house]

Exercises

59.1 Choose one of the phrasal verbs from A to report what Tim says in the sentences below.

EXAMPLE   Tim: Would you like to come to the cinema?
          He ...*invited me out*... .

1 Tim: Alice can come with you if you like.
   He said I could .... Alice .... if I liked.
2 Tim: You can both come to my place after the film.
   He .... us .... after the film.
3 Tim: I'll quickly go to the shop and get some biscuits on the way home.
   He said he would .... the shop for some biscuits on the way home.
4 Tim: I love it when people come to visit me.
   He said he loved .... people ....
5 Tim: You can borrow that DVD I was telling you about if my friend returns it before your party.
   He said I could borrow the DVD if his friend .... it .... before my party.

59.2 Correct the errors with the particles in these sentences.

1 My parents are always asking over you, so I'll tell them your news next time I see them.
2 Do drop out some time when you're passing our house and have a cup of coffee.
3 My uncle has invited me and a friend in to a smart restaurant to celebrate my birthday.
4 Of course you can bring your brother with when you come to our place tomorrow.
5 I often call about and see my grandmother on my way home from work.
6 I hope I'm not in trouble. The boss has just asked me to pop about to her office.

59.3 Explain the difference in meaning between these pairs of sentences.

1 a) I've got to pop up and see Owen in his office.
   b) I've got to pop down and see Owen in his office.
2 a) It's time I invited Alex and Ella over for a meal.
   b) It's time I invited Alex and Ella out for a meal.
3 a) Shall we call round and see Daisy this afternoon?
   b) Shall we drop round and see Daisy this afternoon?
4 a) I'll bring my niece round at the weekend.
   b) I'll bring my niece along at the weekend.

59.4 Write down four different ways in which you could invite someone to visit you at your place. Use a different phrasal verb each time.

59.5 Here are some more phrasal verbs connected with the theme of socialising. What do you think the phrasal verbs in bold mean? Use a dictionary if necessary.

Ivan   Did you enjoy your date with Paul?

Anna   Don't talk to me about Paul! He **stood** me **up**! I waited there for at least half an hour and then I decided to go to the cinema on my own. It was really annoying because my flatmate had wanted to **tag along** because she really wanted to see the film, but I wouldn't let her and then in the end I went all by myself. I thought I was going to have this lovely romantic evening! Paul has apologised and explained what happened, but I don't want to **run across** him for a while!

A Preparing food and drink

Martha was having a dinner party for some friends. A week earlier she had bought all the ingredients she needed, **measured** them **out**[1], prepared a chicken casserole and put it in the freezer to make sure it did not **go off**[2]. On the morning of the dinner party, she removed it from the freezer and **thawed** it **out**[3]. Then before her friends arrived she made sure that she **put** the chicken **on**[4] and she made a salad. She **heated up**[5] the casserole thoroughly, taking care that it did not **boil over**[6].

[1] weigh or measure a small amount of something from a larger amount of something
[2] become not good to eat because it is too old
[3] let it gradually become warmer so that it was not frozen any more
[4] began to cook food
[5] made it hot
[6] flow over the side of the pan

B Serving food and drink

When her friends arrived, Martha **poured out**[1] drinks and **handed round**[2] olives and other snacks. She went round the room **topping up**[3] glasses whenever she noticed that anyone needed a **top-up**[4]. Then they sat at the table and had the chicken casserole. Everyone said how well it **went with**[5] the salad and nothing **was left over**[6] at the end of the meal.

[1] filled glasses or cups with a drink
[2] offered something, especially food and drink, to each person in a group
[3] putting more drink into someone's glass or cup
[4] (noun) more drink poured into a glass or cup (from the verb **top up**)
[5] combined or tasted good with
[6] remained or was not eaten

C Styles of eating and drinking

As there were no **leftovers**[1] the next day, Martha decided to get a **takeaway**[2]. She ordered a curry to **take away**[3]. Martha's brother says that she **lives on/off**[4] curry because she eats it so often. Martha denies that, of course, but she admits that if ever she **eats out**[5] she always goes to a curry restaurant.

[1] (noun) food prepared for a previous meal but not eaten
[2] (noun) a meal that you buy and take somewhere else to eat. **Takeaway** is also the place where you buy a meal like this, e.g. a Chinese takeaway.
[3] buy prepared food in a shop or restaurant and take it somewhere else to eat
[4] only eats a particular type of food
[5] eats a meal in a restaurant, not at home

> **Tip**
>
> You will find quite a few more phrasal verbs on the food theme if you look at the instructions in a recipe book, e.g. *cut up* an onion, *take off* the skins of the tomatoes, etc. If possible look in an English language recipe book or search for some recipes on the Internet and make a note of any phrasal verbs that you find there.

Exercises

60.1 **Look at A and B opposite. Then complete these sentences with an appropriate phrasal verb.**

1 Your glass is half empty. Let me .... it up for you.
2 The pizza's cold. I'll .... it up for you.
3 The chicken's frozen. I'll put it in the microwave to .... it out.
4 When all the guests are here, I'll .... out the champagne.
5 No-one's eating the nuts and crisps. Shall I .... them round?
6 All you do is .... all the ingredients, put them in the breadmaking machine and switch it on.

60.2 **Use phrasal verbs from the opposite page to complete the second person's responses.**

1 Annie   This milk smells bad.

  Jake   Yes, I think ....

2 Erica   We need something to accompany the fish.

  Harry   Yes, we need something that will ....

3 Paul   It's time to start cooking the potatoes.

  Lily   OK, I'll ....

4 Maya   We'll have to keep the sauce on a very low heat.

  Oliver   Yes, we'll have to make sure it ....

5 Ellie   Let's go to a restaurant this evening.

  David   Good idea. It's ages since we last ....

60.3 **Answer the following questions.**

1 Three phrasal verbs on the opposite page also have noun forms. What are the verbs and what are their noun forms?
2 In the question 'Jessica, would you pass the biscuits round for me, please?', which phrasal verb on the opposite page means the same as *pass round*?
3 Which two phrasal verbs mean that you regularly eat one type of food to the exclusion of others?

60.4 **Complete these sentences with words from exercise 60.3.**

1 We've got some nice .... from the party last night. Shall I heat them up?
2 Some people seem to .... junk food. It can't be good for them.
3 Could you .... these snacks to the guests? Thanks. [two answers]
4 Amber, would you like a .... ? There's plenty more coffee in the pot.
5 Do you want to eat your food in the restaurant or .... ?
6 The food from the .... was as good as anything we could have cooked at home.
7 Nothing .... at the end of the meal.

60.5 **In some of these sentences it is possible to separate the verb and the particle. Where possible, write the alternative sentence.**

1 Would you hand round the peanuts, please?
2 I think my sister lives on fish and chips.
3 Don't forget to thaw out the gateau.
4 I don't think that chips go with caviar.

A The weather forecast

It will **brighten up**[1] in the north of England tomorrow morning, but the sun won't last long and the region will soon **cloud over**[2] again. Rain in the east will **clear up**[3] later. An area of high pressure means it should **warm up**[4] over the next few days in most regions, except in the far north, where it will actually **cool down**[5] a little because of strong north-easterly winds. On the south coast winds will **pick up**[6] during the afternoon, becoming strong by the evening.

[1] the sky will become lighter and the sun will start to shine
[2] the sky will become covered with clouds
[3] it will stop being rainy or cloudy

[4] become warmer
[5] become cooler
[6] become stronger

B Talking about the weather and its effects

Leo is talking about his camping trip to the Scottish mountains.

The weather was dreadful; we were there for a week and the storms just never **let up**[1]. We were **flooded out**[2] twice in our tent and ended up staying in a hostel. It just **poured down**[3] every day – one heavy **downpour**[4] after another. We **were rained off**[5] most days and couldn't do any serious walking. Then one day we thought the storms had **blown over**[6], so we climbed one of the highest peaks in the area. It started to snow. Luckily there was a cabin at the summit, so we took shelter there. We **were snowed in**[7] for two days before we could get out and go back down again. I shall never forget it as long as I live!

[1] stopped or improved
[2] had to leave a home or place because of a flood
[3] rained heavily
[4] (noun) a very heavy period of rain (from the verb **pour down**)
[5] if an outside activity is rained off, it cannot start or continue because it is raining
[6] become less strong and then ended
[7] were unable to leave that place because there was so much snow

Tip

Help yourself to learn phrasal verbs by drawing word diagrams based on one verb, e.g. *pick*, *blow*, or on one topic, e.g. *weather*.

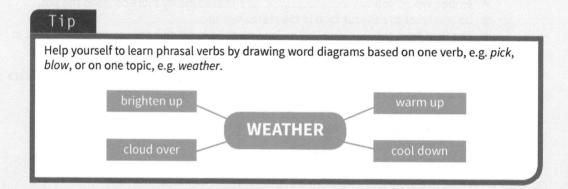

Exercises

61.1 **Complete these sentences using one of the phrasal verbs from A. Write the verbs in an appropriate form.**

1 There's a lovely blue sky now, but unfortunately the forecast says that it's going .... later in the day.
2 I hate it when it's so hot – I wish it would ....
3 Let's go and fly the kite – it'll be fun now the wind ....
4 The sea is quite cool in the mornings, but by midday it has usually ....
5 Let's go for a walk this afternoon if the rain ....
6 We could have a picnic lunch if the weather ....

61.2 **Match the weather situation on the left with the most logical consequence on the right.**

1 We were snowed in.   Some trees got blown down.
2 We were flooded out.   The teams were very disappointed.
3 The rain didn't let up.   All our carpets were ruined.
4 It cleared up later on.   We couldn't even open the front door.
5 A strong wind picked up.   We ate our picnic in the car.
6 The match was rained off.   We went for a walk in the evening.

61.3 **Complete these sentences with a noun or phrasal verb from the opposite page.**

1 It rained heavily all day. I've never seen such a ....
2 It's been pouring down all day. I wish it would ....
3 If the river breaks its banks, the villagers will be ....
4 No-one left their homes until the hurricane ....
5 Because of the storms, a number of football matches ....
6 It's too gloomy to take good photos now. Why don't you wait until it .... ?
7 It's very hot there in summer – even at night it doesn't ....
8 It's been terribly cold, but they have promised that it will .... next week.

61.4 **Some of the phrasal verbs on the opposite page can be used in a metaphorical way. Try to work out the metaphorical meanings and answer these questions.**

1 If Martina is brightening up a bit, is her mood getting more or less cheerful?
2 Would you suggest that someone should cool down if they are angry or if they are sad?
3 If an argument or scandal blows over, does it start or finish?
4 If an illness clears up, does it get better or worse?
5 If a party warms up, does it get more or less enjoyable?
6 If someone's face clouds over, do they start to look worried or happy?

> Over to you
>
> Write a paragraph about the weather you have experienced recently. Use as many as possible of the words presented on the opposite page.

A Going on a journey

Matthew had had a busy time at work, so he was glad to **get away**[1] from London for a month's holiday. He **set off/out**[2] last Saturday. His journey really **started off**[3] at St Pancras station when he **got on**[4] the Eurostar train to Paris. He was heading for a villa in the south of France but was planning to **stop off**[5] in Paris for a couple of days before continuing south.

[1] go somewhere for a holiday, especially when you need a rest
[2] started his journey
[3] began
[4] boarded
[5] visit for a short time when on the way somewhere else

B Travel in general

phrasal verb	meaning	example
check in	arrive at a hotel, say who you are and be given a key for your room	You go to reception and **check in** while I park the car.
check out	leave a hotel after paying and giving back the key of your room	I went to the hotel hoping to meet Sam, but he had already **checked out**.
get in	(of a train, bus, plane, etc.) arrive at a particular time	My train **got in** at 6.30 p.m.
pull in	(of a train) arrive in a station	The train **pulled in** exactly on time.
pull out	(of a train) leave a station	Unfortunately, the train I'd hoped to catch was **pulling out** just as I arrived on the platform.

C Air travel

Louise was lucky enough to get a cheap last-minute flight to New Zealand. She quickly packed her large suitcase and **carry-on**[1], and went to the airport. There weren't many people on the flight, so she **checked in**[2] immediately. The flight **took off**[3] on time and **touched down**[4] half an hour early. On her way home she is hoping to be able to **stop over**[5] in Hong Kong for a day or two.

[1] (noun) a small case or bag that you take on a plane with you
[2] showed her ticket at the official desk (the **check-in**) so she could be given a boarding card
[3] began to fly
[4] landed on the ground
[5] stop somewhere for a period of time when you are on a long journey

Exercises

62.1 Write sentences that mean the opposite of the sentences below using verbs from A.

1 Khalfan arrived home last Sunday.
2 Harriet got off the plane in Dubai.
3 My journey ended in a very exciting way.

62.2 Fill the gaps in this social media chat between Charlotte and her friend Lin.

Charlotte 12:03
Hi Lin, I've been finalising the plans for my trip. Want to hear?

Lin 12:03
Hi Charliotte – how's it going? Yeah. Tell me!

Charlotte 12:04
Well, I (1) .... off at Gatwick Airport. The travel agent has got me on a flight to Taipei on Tuesday afternoon. There's one that (2) .... off at 3.30 p.m., going via Amsterdam. If it's on time, we'll (3) .... down in Taipei at 3.55 p.m. the next day.

Lin 12:05
😊 I have to work afternoons and evenings that week. Can't you get a flight that (4) .... in earlier?

Charlotte 12:06
No, but don't worry about coming to meet me. I can (5) .... in at my hotel, and I'll (6) .... out early the next day and see you on Thursday morning. I'm going to (7) .... over for two days in Taipei and then go to Tokyo to see Noriko. I'll just (8) .... off there for one night and then it's on to Sydney to see Annabelle. I've bought a new (9) .... so I won't have to unpack my big suitcase until I get to Australia!

Lin 12:06
Wow! You'll be exhausted!!!!!!!!!!

Charlotte 12:07
Yes, but it'll be worth it! I really do need to (10) .... away; I've been studying so hard! Hey, must go. Talk to you after my lecture.

Lin 12:07
OK. Bye.

62.3 The phrasal verbs below have noun or adjective forms. Complete the table and write an example sentence for each noun or adjective form. Use a dictionary if necessary.

phrasal verb	noun/adjective form	example
touch down		
check in		
get away		
take off		
stop over		

62.4 Correct the mistakes with the phrasal verbs in this text. There are six mistakes in total.

> I went off for St Pancras station at 11 a.m. and there I got up the midday Eurostar train to Paris. It pulled off exactly on time and soon we were in the Channel Tunnel. After a couple of hours, we pulled over at Paris Gare du Nord station. Next day I checked off from my hotel and flew back. We touched in at Heathrow Airport at 11 a.m.

A Stopping to do things

Could you just **draw up** in front of the garage, and I'll put the boxes in the boot?

Could you **drop** me **off** here please? That's the restaurant I'm going to – over there.

Wait a moment while I **pump up** my tyre.

I'll have to ask her to **pull up**. I'm feeling sick.

What a beautiful view! Can you just **pull over** and I'll take a photograph?

Thanks for the lift. See you later.

No problem. I'll be here at four o'clock to **pick** you **up**.

I'll just **pull in** at this petrol station and fill up before we get onto the motorway.

phrasal verb	meaning
draw up	If a vehicle, or someone in a vehicle, draws up, they arrive somewhere and stop.
drop off sb/sth or **drop** sb/sth **off**	take someone to a place that they want to go to, or deliver something to a place, usually in a car, often when you are going somewhere else
pump up	fill something with air using a pump
pull up	If a car pulls up, it stops, often for a short time.
pull over	move a vehicle to the side of the road in order to stop
pick up sb/sth or **pick** sb/sth **up**	collect someone who is waiting for you, or collect something you have left somewhere or that you have bought
pull in or **pull into** somewhere	If a car pulls in or pulls into a place, it moves to the side of the road or to another place where it can stop.

B Driving and cycling problems

Police said the cyclist had **pulled out**[1] to overtake a parked lorry when she lost control and was hit by a car coming in the opposite direction.

[1] driven out of the traffic lane she was in and entered a faster lane or the other side of the road

Two children were **knocked down**[2] by a drunken driver. Both children were seriously injured and police have arrested the driver.

[2] hit by a vehicle and injured or killed

An elderly man was **run over**[3] at the corner of Pierce Street and Welbourne Avenue. He was taken to Hughes Hospital suffering from head injuries.

[3] hit by a vehicle and driven over, injuring or killing him

A **pile-up**[4] involving twenty vehicles caused a 10-mile **tailback**[5] on the M12 motorway today. Police blamed fog and black ice.

[4] (noun) crash involving several vehicles
[5] (noun) long line of traffic that is moving very slowly

Exercises

63.1 **Complete these sentences using phrasal verbs from A. Write the verbs in the appropriate form.**

1 If you .... in the next lay-by, we can have a short break.
2 If you'd like a lift to the party, I could .... on my way there and then I can easily .... on my way home afterwards.
3 I had been waiting for at least half an hour before a bus eventually ....
4 I was looking out of the window when Rose's taxi .... outside our gate.

63.2 **Write the phrasal verb expressions presented on the opposite page into one of these categories.**

words relating to moving and stopping the car or bike	words relating to accidents and traffic problems	words relating to transporting other people

63.3 **Complete this letter with an appropriate particle from the box. Use each word once only.**

out   back   in   off   out   over   up

Dear Diana,

Thank you for the lovely day we had with you. It was so kind of you to let us bring Anna's friend, Gina. Unfortunately, the only problem was the journey home. There had been a terrible pile-................................. (1) on the motorway and, as a result, there was a tail................................. (2) for at least six miles. In the end, we pulled .... (3) at a service station and waited there until it cleared. In the car park there, Gina nearly got knocked .... (4) as a car pulled .... (5) far too quickly from behind a parked lorry. We were very relieved when we finally dropped Gina .... (6) at her parents' and made our own way home.

Much love,

Chloe

63.4 **Here are some more phrasal verbs and nouns connected with driving. Match the words in bold in 1–6 with the definitions a–f.**

1 To get to the farm, take the second **turn-off** on the left after the crossroads.
2 The cyclist left the main road and **turned off** down a narrow track.
3 The car was **written off** in the accident.
4 The insurance company agreed that the bike was a **write-off**.
5 You **get out** of the car here and I'll find a parking spot and then meet you in the café.
6 Sam **ran into** the car in front when the driver braked suddenly.

a) leave a vehicle
b) damage a vehicle so badly that it cannot be repaired
c) accidentally hit something while driving a vehicle
d) leave the road you are on to travel along another one
e) road that goes off another road
f) vehicle that is not worth repairing after an accident

A Setting up your device

Setting up[1] your new tablet couldn't be easier!

1 **Plug** it **in**[2] and charge the battery to 100%.
2 When the tablet is fully charged, **switch** it **on**[3] and follow the instructions to set up your account.
3 To receive email on your new tablet, open the email app and **sign in**[4] to your account.
4 If you get **locked out**[5] of your account, you can request an email to reset your password. After you have **put in**[6] a new password, you'll be able to log in again.
5 And finally, if you want to get more news and great offers from us, don't forget to **sign up**[7] for our newsletter!

[1] get something ready to use
[2] connect to an electrical supply
[3] make it start by pressing a switch or button (*opp* **switch off**)
[4] write your username and password to enter a page or system (*opp* **sign out**)
[5] unable to enter (for example if you enter the wrong password)
[6] typed in
[7] agree to receive something

B Using your device

Move your fingers together on the screen to **zoom in**[1]. Move them apart to **zoom out**[2].

To **bring up**[3] the photo that you've just taken, tap on the picture icon at the bottom of the screen.

Move your finger up or down on the screen to **scroll down**[4] or **scroll up**[5].

To **turn up**[6] the volume, use the button on the side of the phone.

[1] make something look bigger and closer
[2] make something look smaller and further away
[3] open onto the screen
[4] move text and images up on a screen
[5] move text and images down on a screen
[6] increase (*opp* **turn down**)

C Problems

If the phone signal is bad, the call might **break up**. [you cannot hear the other person's voice clearly]

If your phone **goes off** in the cinema, that can be really embarrassing! [makes a noise]

If you are talking and you get **cut off**, the connection is lost and the call ends.

If the battery **runs out**, then you need to charge it. [has no more power]

If you download a lot of videos, you might **use up** all your data for the month. [finish the amount you have]

Exercises

64.1 Complete the sentences using verbs from the box. Write the verbs in the correct form.

> break   bring   put   set   sign   zoom

1 Does Laura have her eyes closed in that photo? Can you .... in so I can check?
2 I've .... in the wrong password for my account three times and now I'm locked out.
3 Sorry, the train is just going through a tunnel. You're .... up – can you say that again?
4 I can't work out how to .... up my work email on my new phone.
5 If you can't .... in to your account, please check you're using the correct email address and password.
6 My computer's getting really slow. It takes ages to .... up documents or photos after I've clicked on them.

64.2 Use the correct form of phrasal verbs from C to complete the story of Nina's day.

You wouldn't believe all the problems I had with my phone yesterday!
First of all, I tried to call my friend at lunchtime, but we kept getting
(1) .... Then I went into my French lesson and my phone
(2) .... – it was my friend trying to ring me back! Later, I was
trying to download some music, but that didn't work because I'd
(3) .... all my data. Then the battery (4) ....
and I couldn't charge it until I got home. I think I need a new phone!

64.3 Choose the correct word to complete the sentence.

1 If you sign *in / up* for email updates, you'll receive a 10% discount on your next order.
2 If you're using a public computer, make sure you log *in / out* of all your accounts before you leave.
3 I kept turning *up / down* the volume, but I still couldn't hear anything. I think there's a problem with the speakers.
4
   A Where do I log in?

   B *Roll / Scroll* up to the top of the page and it says 'sign in' on the right.

5 My new phone is completely different from my old one. When I first got it, I couldn't even figure out how to switch it *on / over*!
6 A lot of coffee shops now have places where you can *put / plug* in your laptop.

64.4 Correct the mistakes in these sentences.

1 My phone went on in the job interview. I'd forgotten to switch it off!
2 If you write up to our newsletter, we'll send you all our latest offers.
3 I got locked into of my email account and had to phone the IT helpdesk to help me reset my password.
4 I can't really see what's happening in that picture. Can you scroll in at all?
5 I can't plug in to my emails. It says the password is wrong.
6 My phone is very old and the battery cuts out really quickly.

> ### Over to you
>
> Several of the phrasal verbs in this unit have other meanings. Use the Mini dictionary to help you find out the other meanings of *set up*, *bring up*, *go off*, *turn up*, *turn down* and *break up*.

A Working with systems, files and documents

Harry I've put a **back-up** [noun: extra copy for safety] of my essay on a memory stick, but it would be a disaster if I lost it after all the work I've done.

Laura Well, **back** your work **up** [make a copy of computer information so that you do not lose it] on my hard drive as well.

Sienna You've done an excellent job **keying in** [put information into a computer using a keyboard] all the figures. It's good to have the budget on the server.

Dan It did take me a long time to **type** the figures **in** [put information into a computer using a keyboard].

Sienna I am sorry about that. I'm afraid I've got one more request. Everyone at the meeting will need a **printout** [noun: printed copy of an electronic document] of the budget. Please could you **print out** [produce a printed copy of a document that has been written on a computer] six copies?

Holly I've **set up** [prepare or arrange something for use] a new system for accessing the photo selections that people upload to the website. That will **free up** [make something available to be used] space and **filter out** [pass information through a device to remove unwanted information] any spam. Do you want to try it out?

Rory OK. So I **click on** [carry out a computer operation by pressing a button on the mouse or keyboard] this icon to zoom in on the picture, and then on this one to zoom out.

Note that with the verbs *back up*, *type in*, *key in*, *print out*, *set up*, *free up* and *filter out,* the object can go either before or after the particle, e.g. *back a file up* or *back up a file*.

B Using a network and the Internet

phrasal verb	meaning	example
log in/on	put your name into a computer or website so that you can start using it	You can **log on/in** using my password if you want to use my computer.
log off/out	finish using a computer system or website	Don't forget to **log off/out** when you've finished.
pick up sth or **pick** sth **up**	connect to the Internet and access emails	I'll be able to **pick up** my emails on my phone while I'm away.

Tip

Many websites are in English. Next time you visit a website, note down any phrasal verbs that are used on the web pages, e.g. **check out** *our new products*.

Exercises

65.1 Imagine that you are writing a report on a computer in your office or college. Write the things from the box below in the order in which you would do them.

| back up your work | log off | type in your report | log on | print out your work |

65.2 Complete each of these sentences using a phrasal verb expression from the opposite page.

1 Although I'll be on holiday for a couple of weeks, I'll still be .... my emails every day.
2 Maxime has .... a brilliant website for his new company. Let me send you the link so that you can check it out.
3 On this memory stick you'll find a .... of all the data connected with the project.
4 I'll need a .... of that information for each person attending the meeting.

65.3 Choose the correct word to complete these sentences.

1 I need to find a more efficient way to filter .... unwanted emails.
   a) off   b) on   c) into   d) out
2 For security reasons, always log .... when you leave your computer unattended for any period of time.
   a) on   b) in   c) out   d) up
3 Esther is very quick at keying .... data.
   a) onto   b) on   c) into   d) in
4 It didn't take long to print the whole report ....
   a) out   b) down   c) up   d) in
5 The Internet service where she was staying was unreliable so she wasn't able to pick .... all her emails until she got home.
   a) out   b) on   c) off   d) up
6 I've deleted lots of old files to free .... space on my laptop.
   a) down   b) out   c) up   d) off

65.4 Explain what you would do with these computer accessories.

1

2

3

A

Violence **flared up**[1] again today in the troubled southern region when several bombs **went off**[2] in the centre of the capital. Support for the rebels is growing, and it is expected that the rebels will succeed in **bringing down**[3] a government that is increasingly unpopular. There are fears that a full-scale civil war may **break out**[4].

[1] suddenly happened and became serious (used about something negative like violence, anger or an argument)
[2] exploded

[3] causing people in power to lose their position
[4] suddenly start, usually used about something dangerous and unpleasant like war, fire or disease (noun = **outbreak**)

B

SLIMMING BREAKTHROUGH[1]

News **leaked out**[2] yesterday that a major US pharmaceutical laboratory is about to launch a dramatic new slimming drug. The lab was in discussions last year with a British company about the manufacture of the drug, but the British company **pulled out**[3] after a disagreement about safety procedures. A French company also **broke off**[4] talks with the lab last month.

[1] (noun) an important discovery or success that enables you to achieve or deal with something
[2] became public so that people who should not have known about something learn of it
[3] stopped being involved
[4] ended suddenly before they had been completed

C

80%   4:21PM

Sudden rise in traffic accidents

A survey published today reveals that the number of accidents caused by cars driving too fast has **shot up**[1] in the last couple of years. A government spokesperson said that they are determined to **crack down**[2] on any driver caught exceeding the speed limit. Police have been promised financial support to enable them to **step up**[3] all possible measures to make motorists reduce their speed.

[1] increased very quickly
[2] treat people more strictly in order to try to stop them doing things they should not do (noun = **crackdown**)

[3] do more of something, usually in order to improve a situation

D

BREAKING NEWS

Jail **breakout**[1] alarms villagers

A dangerous prisoner who escaped from Kenton Prison last night is causing alarm among local residents. It is thought that the escaped convict may have found a **hideaway**[2] not far from the prison and police have encouraged the inhabitants of nearby villages to **look out for**[3] anything suspicious.

[1] (noun) escape (from the verb **break out**)
[2] (noun) secret place where someone goes to be alone
[3] carefully watch people or things around you so that you will notice a particular person or thing

Exercises

66.1 Look at these news headlines. Then answer the questions below by ticking the correct box.

TOP SECRET DEFENCE REPORT LEAKS OUT

GOVERNMENT BROUGHT DOWN BY ARMS SCANDAL

POLICE TO CRACK DOWN ON CAR THIEVES

Violence flares up in Hirada

SWEDEN PULLS OUT OF TRADE AGREEMENT

TERRORIST HIDEAWAY RAIDED BY SPECIAL FORCES

1 There has been a huge fire in the city of Hirada.	true ☐	false ☐
2 A terrorist hiding place has been attacked by troops.	true ☐	false ☐
3 A government has collapsed because of a scandal.	true ☐	false ☐
4 A top secret report has been published.	true ☐	false ☐
5 Sweden has gained huge benefits from a trade agreement.	true ☐	false ☐
6 The police will take a hard attitude to car thieves.	true ☐	false ☐

66.2 In this unit there are a number of phrasal verbs which have noun forms. Complete the table below. Use a dictionary if necessary.

Cambridge Dictionary

tionary.cambridge.org

phrasal verb	noun form
	crackdown
break out (from prison)	
break out (war, disease, etc.)	
break through	
	hideaway
flare up	
look out for	

66.3 Here are some short extracts from newspapers. Complete what you would tell a friend who has not read the extract using phrasal verb expressions from the opposite page.

1 A bomb exploded in the capital last night, injuring six people.
You: Hey, did you read that? A bomb ....

2 Riots have erupted between the Northern tribes and the Southern League.
You: Did you read that? Riots ....

3 The rebels are beginning to increase their attacks on military bases.
You: Did you see that? The rebels ....

4 The teachers' union has suddenly ended talks with local government officials.
You: Have you heard? The teachers' ....

5 Villagers have been advised by police to keep their eyes open for anything suspicious.
You: The police are advising villagers to ....

6 Five prisoners have escaped from Gilston High Security Prison.
You: Wow! There's been a ....

A Crime reports in newspapers

Here are some people telling others about things they have just read in the newspaper. Look at the phrasal verbs they use to explain what happened.

SECURITY GUARD ATTACKED

A security guard at an electronics factory was attacked and badly injured by thieves last night. They punched him and kicked him ...

Gosh! A security guard was **beaten up** at that electronics factory last night. Terrible!

£300K JEWEL ROBBERY

Thieves entered a town-centre jewellery store by force last night and stole £300,000 worth of jewels and watches ...

Did you hear? Somebody **broke into** that jewellery shop in the town centre last night and stole £300,000 worth of stuff.

PRISONERS ESCAPE

Three prisoners escaped from the Holton Maximum Security Prison this morning. Police are searching a wide ...

Hey! Three prisoners have **broken out** of Holton Jail. We'd better lock all our doors tonight!

SCHOOL COMPUTERS STOLEN

Two men persuaded a teacher at Stanbridge School yesterday that they were collecting six computers for repair and maintenance. They took them away, but it later became clear they were thieves.

Wow! Did you hear that? Two guys **walked off with** six computers from a school yesterday in broad daylight!

B Other verbs connected with crime

If you ...	then you ...
hold up sth/sb or **hold** sth/sb **up**	steal money from a building, person or vehicle, by using violence or by threatening to use it
hack into sth	get into someone else's computer system without permission in order to look at information or do something illegal
tip off sb or **tip** sb **off**	warn someone secretly about something that will happen so that they can take action or prevent it from happening
put sb **up to** sth	encourage someone to do something stupid or wrong
take in sb or **take** sb **in**	deceive someone or make them believe something that is not true
lead on sb or **lead** sb **on**	make someone believe something that is not true, especially to make them do something they don't really want to do
let off sb or **let** sb **off**	do not punish someone who has committed a crime or done something wrong, or do not punish someone severely
lean on sb	try to make someone do something by threatening or persuading them (informal)
are or **get mixed up in** sth	are or become involved in an illegal or bad activity

Exercises

67.1 Match the beginning of each sentence with its ending.

1 An old man was beaten	into the house by a side window.
2 The thieves walked	up a local bank yesterday.
3 The burglars broke	into the computer system at work.
4 The prisoner managed to break	off with some priceless antique silver.
5 The thieves held	up in his own home yesterday.
6 Someone managed to hack	out in broad daylight.

67.2 Describe what each speaker is doing using one of the phrasal verbs from the opposite page.

1

OK, I'm going in. Bring the van round.

3

It was Rocky who broke into the bank, Sergeant Jones.

2

As this is your first offence, we shall not send you to prison this time.

4

If you don't give me that confidential report, I'll tell your boss about your criminal past.

67.3 Complete these dialogues using phrasal verbs.

Nadia   I suspect that young neighbour of ours has got (1) .... in something illegal.

Ethan   Yes, I was beginning to think that too. He spends a lot of time with rather suspicious-looking people and I think they may be (2) .... to doing some dishonest things.

Nadia   Well, I suppose they could (3) .... him by threatening him if he refuses to help them.

Ethan   Or he might just not realise what's happening. He was always very easily (4) .... by people.

Nadia   Well, if he does end up in court, I suppose they might (5) .... lightly as he's never been involved in crime before.

67.4 Here are some newspaper headlines using noun forms of phrasal verbs presented on the opposite page. Match each headline 1–4 to the first sentence of its article a–d.

1 HOLD-UP AT BANK – $10,000 STOLEN
2 **TIP-OFF LEADS TO ARREST**
3 TEN BREAK-INS IN ONE NIGHT
4 THIRD BREAKOUT THIS YEAR

a) Oddways Prison is clearly not as secure as it is supposed to be.
b) Police are extremely grateful to an anonymous caller who rang them last night.
c) Terrified staff were held at gunpoint at the National Bank on Brown Street yesterday.
d) A series of burglaries was reported in Brook Street and adjoining roads last night.

68 Power and authority

A The start of a political career

Interviewer Why did you decide to **stand for**[1] Parliament?

Politician Well, I'd been a social worker for a number of years and that had opened my eyes to the huge social divisions in this country. I firmly believed that these were wrong. I wanted to help **bring in**[2] laws that would lessen the divisions between the rich and the poor. I wanted to **do away with**[3] taxes for the poorest members of society and to **clamp down**[4] on rich people who were attempting to avoid paying tax. In short, I wanted to do everything I could to **stand up for**[5] the principles that I believed in.

1 compete in an election for an official position
2 introduce
3 abolish or get rid of
4 do something to stop or limit a particular activity (noun = **clampdown**)
5 defend something that you believe is important

B Life in Parliament

Interviewer So, once you were elected, how did you **go ahead**[1] with your plans for social change?

Politician Well, although some other Members of Parliament from my party **backed** me **up**[2], the more influential ones told me not to be too hasty. I learnt then that our party had **entered into**[3] an agreement with the country's top business leaders and had promised not to increase taxes for the wealthy for the time being.

Interviewer Did you **stand up to**[4] those influential MPs?

Politician Yes, I told them I was not in Parliament to **carry out**[5] the wishes of big business.

1 start to do something (noun = **go-ahead**: permission for something to start)
2 supported
3 officially agreed to do something
4 state opinions forcefully and refuse to change your mind or do what others want
5 do something you have been told to do

C Forming a new party

Interviewer Did other MPs in your party still **stand by**[1] you at this point?

Politician Not all of them, but a few very good people did **stick by**[2] me and we eventually decided to **break away**[3] and form our own new party.

Interviewer So, what happened next?

Politician Unfortunately, none of us were re-elected at the next election, but we have been continuing with our campaigns and hope that at some point in the not too distant future we may be able to **carry out**[4] our plans to make society a better and fairer place.

1 continue to support
2 continue to support
3 stop being part of a group because you disagree with them or do not want to be controlled by them
4 do something that you have said you will do

> ### Tip
> See if you can find any more phrasal verbs relating to this theme by looking at newspaper articles about political issues.

Exercises

68.1 Look at these short biographies of politicians. Complete the entries using verbs from the box. Write the verbs in the correct form.

break	enter	stand	carry	stick	clamp	bring	stand

●●● ‹ ›   C Q ⌂

Search

1 **Drummond, Antonia** First .... for Parliament in 2005 election but was defeated. Elected in 2010 as MP for Sandford East. In 2012, introduced a bill in Parliament to .... down on street crime. Hobbies: badminton and judo.

2 **Dursland, Julian** Elected to Parliament in 2001. MP for Hosely West. In 2006, with five other conservatives, he .... away from his party and formed the New Progressive Conservative Party (NPCP). In 2011, NPCP, under his leadership .... into discussions to merge with the Family Values Party (FVP). Hobbies: golf and fox-hunting.

3 **Randolph-Quincy-Brough, Theodore** Elected to Parliament in 1992. MP for Chingwhale and Mudsleighe. Member of the group which .... out the 1997 rebellion against party leader Hugh Nonwit. Has attempted three times to .... in legislation banning pigeon-racing. Hobbies: sailing and poetry.

4 **Entwhistle, Louisa** Elected to Parliament in 1992. MP for Mickly North. Famous for publicly .... up to party leader Kenneth Drake in 2007 and being suspended from the People's Labour Party for six months. Known for .... by her colleagues, whatever the price. Hobbies: rambling, painting and theatre.

68.2 Correct the mistakes with the phrasal verbs in these political interviews.

1   Interviewer   Will your party now change its mind about its tax plans?

     Politician   No, we are determined to go towards with our proposals.

2   Interviewer   So, what will happen to the present committee structure?

     Politician   We intend to do up with out-of-date committees and to modernise the whole committee structure to make it more efficient.

3   Interviewer   Do you think Ms Reiner should now resign?

     Politician   No, I do not. I and her many supporters are determined to stick on her in the face of these appalling and unfair attacks from the press.

4   Interviewer   Did Mr Carson's remarks yesterday represent party policy?

     Politician   Yes, the party fully backs Mr Carson across.

68.3 Rewrite each sentence, replacing the underlined word with a phrasal verb expression based on the word in brackets.

1 The People's Purple Party believes that the monarchy should be <u>abolished</u>. (DO)
2 The PPP aims to <u>introduce</u> legislation banning all hunting. (BRING)
3 The PPP is determined to <u>restrict</u> smoking in public open spaces. (CLAMP)
4 The leader of the PPP says nothing will stop the Party <u>fulfilling</u> its aims. (CARRY)
5 He swears he will do all he can to <u>defend</u> the principles the PPP supports. (STAND)
6 The PPP has got the <u>permission</u> to hold a demonstration next week. (GO)

69 American and Australian phrasal verbs

Most phrasal verbs are used in all the countries where English is the main language. However, as English has developed in different countries, some phrasal verbs have emerged with regional meanings. The distinctions between regional varieties of phrasal verbs are not clear-cut. In some parts of North America or Australia, UK phrasal verb equivalents are heard as frequently as their regional variations. Similarly, many phrasal verbs originating in the USA or Australia have spread to the UK through films and TV programmes.

A North America

Here are some phrasal verbs more frequently used in North American varieties of English.

US verb	UK equivalent	meaning	example
bawl out	tell off	speak angrily to someone	The boss **bawled** Jack **out** for losing the deal.
figure out	work out or suss out	find the solution to a problem or the answer to something	Let's try to **figure out** how much I owe you.
goof around/off	mess about/around	behave stupidly or waste time doing unimportant things	Tom spent too much time **goofing around** and failed his exams.
wash up	freshen up	clean your hands and face with soap and water (in UK English *wash up* means to wash the dishes)	I'm sure you'd like to **wash up** after your journey.

US English sometimes adds a particle where UK English would use the verb on its own. For example, an American might say **Wait up**! or **Listen up**! rather than **Wait**! or **Listen**! These are used mainly as imperatives and the *up* emphasises the idea that the speaker is giving a command. Americans can also **visit with** friends or **meet with** colleagues, whereas a British speaker would just **visit** or **meet** them.

B Australia

Here are some phrasal verbs which are typical of Australian English.

Australian verb	UK equivalent	meaning	example
barrack for	cheer for	give support to a team or person	I'll be **barracking for** you in the competition tomorrow.
belt into	throw yourself into	begin to do something quickly and with a lot of effort	We just **belted into** the job and got it finished in an hour.
get into	lay into	criticise	She really **got into** me. I didn't think I deserved so much criticism.
shoot through	do a runner	leave a place suddenly and often secretly	He's not here any more. He **shot through** a couple of days ago.

Exercises

69.1 Match the questions on the left with the most likely American English replies on the right.

1 Would you like to wash up?	Dunno. I can't figure out why it's not working.
2 What's wrong with the laptop?	To visit with some friends.
3 Why is she so upset?	Because I goofed around so much.
4 Where's Rachel gone?	Her parents have just bawled her out.
5 Why d'you think you failed the test?	Sure. Where's the restroom?

69.2 Complete these things an Australian might say using phrasal verbs from the opposite page.

1 Jack is very upset because Elsie has .... just before their wedding.
2 Carla really .... Ariana for leaving the flat in such a mess.
3 Hugo tends to .... a job without thinking it through first.
4 Have you decided who you're going to .... in the game tomorrow?

69.3 Here are some things that British people might say. Write what an American or an Australian might say instead.

1 I expect your grandmother will want to freshen up when she arrives.
American: ....

2 The teacher laid into me for doing such a bad essay.
Australian: ....

3 Will lost his job for messing around at work.
American: ....

4 Daria threw herself into the spring cleaning and the house was soon transformed.
Australian: ....

5 Could you phone around to find the cheapest place to rent a car?
American: ....

6 I can't work out why he's behaving so oddly.
American: ....

7 He did a runner last month and the police have been looking for him ever since.
Australian: ....

8 I'll be ready soon. Wait!
American: ....

9 I'm visiting my aunt at the weekend. Would you like to come too?
American: ....

Hi! Welcome to our Texas home! Would you like to wash up after your long journey?

A   Structuring your writing

At the beginning:

I will **start off by** outlining recent research into primary education in inner city areas. [begin]

The first section **sets out** the main points which will be covered in this essay. [explains in an organised way]

Changing topics or referencing:

Moving on, it is important to consider other aspects of this topic. [continuing to the next point]

Turning to another effect of climate change, we have clear evidence to show that sea levels have risen in recent years. [changing the topic to]

I would also like to **touch on** a research study led by Whitely and Proctor (2014). [mention briefly]

To **come back to** the previous point about air pollution, it is important to understand that there are a number of factors that contribute to the problem. [refer back to – *syn* **go back to**]

To **follow up on** a point mentioned in the first section: the long-term impact of a healthy diet is often forgotten. [give more information related to something mentioned before]

This **picks up on** a point raised by Dr Cohen's research. [connects to, gives more attention to]

In this section, we will explore the main arguments **relating to** the government's new pension scheme. [connected to]

The professor has **based** his theory **on** the results of two large research projects. [used ideas or information as a start for something else]

At the end / concluding:

To **sum up**, the key finding from this analysis is that the positive impact on the students lasted for at least five years. [summarise, conclude]

In conclusion, I want to **draw together** the main themes of this essay. [collect]

In this section, I would like to **bring together** the results from the three research studies. [collect]

Following these arguments, we **arrive at** a clear conclusion. [reach a result, *syn* **come to**]

> **Tip**
>
> **Start off by** is always followed by the *ing* form.
> *This report will start off by classifying the main features of the region.*

B   More phrasal verbs for writing

In his research, Dr Brukner **goes on** to suggest that this behaviour is not unusual. [continues]

In this section, I have **drawn** mainly **on** the findings of Ledd and Harbury (2016). [used information to help you do something]

It is important to **point out** that the computer simulations are not 100% accurate. [emphasise]

In this section, I want to **focus on** the economic situation at that time. [give a lot of attention to]

I believe that this factor **accounts for** many of the negative survey responses. [explains, is the reason for]

> **Tip**
>
> In academic writing, *go on to* is also often followed by *say/argue/describe*.
> *I will then go on to describe the main criteria used to evaluate the results.*

Exercises

70.1 **Choose the correct word to complete the sentence.**

1 The first part .... out the main arguments against a centralised system.
   a) starts   b) sets   c) touches
2 These results are .... on a sample of 500 full-time employees.
   a) based   b) arrived   c) set
3 This .... back to an earlier point about privatisation.
   a) moves   b) goes   c) turns
4 This section will .... together the most important similarities and differences between the two products.
   a) bring   b) relate   c) base
5 In the introduction, I will .... off by explaining the general principles of his theory.
   a) set   b) move   c) start
6 In the last section, I will .... up the main points that I have discussed in this essay.
   a) relate   b) sum   c) turn
7 With respect to the second group of cases, we .... at a completely different conclusion.
   a) draw   b) arrive   c) pick
8 In the next section, I would like to .... to another region of the country: the south.
   a) turn   b) come   c) bring

70.2 **Rewrite the underlined parts of these sentences using phrasal verbs from A and B opposite.**

1 I will <u>mention this area briefly</u> later. At this point, I'm concerned only with the major theories.
2 To <u>return to</u> the topic of pre-school education, this is clearly of growing importance to the government.
3 To <u>give more information on</u> the research conducted by Brukoff, I should now like to discuss the procedures he used in that study.
4 <u>Continuing to</u> the next section, I will describe the population changes in recent years.
5 To support my conclusion, I will <u>use</u> data collected from the last five years.

70.3 **Correct the mistakes with the phrasal verbs in this text. There are six mistakes in total.**

This essay starts out the main arguments about whether professional athletes are paid too much. I would like to set off by define 'professional' athletes: these are people who are paid to do the job. I believe that the amount they are paid should turn to their skills and ability. It is also important to point the fact that some sports are better paid than others. For example, if we focus to football, TV rights and sponsorship account for the higher levels of pay...

> ## Over to you
>
> Write the first paragraph of an essay about the topic in 70.3, or another topic which you are interested in, using some of the verbs from this unit.

Key

Unit 1

1.1
1 I <u>sent off</u> the order last week but the goods haven't <u>turned up</u> yet.
2 I <u>came across</u> an interesting book in the university library. I <u>noted down</u> the title.
3 The starter motor was <u>playing up</u> and the car <u>broke down</u> when we stopped at the service station.
4 I <u>brought up</u> this item at the last meeting. It's really time to <u>sort out</u> the problem.
5 I wish he'd stop <u>messing</u> us <u>about</u>! He's <u>put</u> the meeting <u>off</u> three times and now he wants to <u>call</u> it <u>off</u> altogether.

1.2
1 send off = mail   turn up = arrive
2 come across = find   note down = write
3 play up = not work properly   break down = stop working
4 bring up = mention   sort out = deal with
5 mess about = cause inconvenience   put off = postpone   call off = cancel

1.3
1 Correct
2 Incorrect: the object must come after the particle.
 She looked after the children when their mother was in hospital.
3 Correct
4 Incorrect: this verb is used without an object.
 We ate out and had a wonderful dinner last night.
5 Incorrect: the object must be human.
 It was a beautiful summer evening so I asked my new colleague out for a drink.

1.4
1 on   2 with   3 against   4 with   5 with

Unit 2

2.1
1 broke   2 get   3 keep   4 pick   5 turn   6 cut

2.2
The particle could be put in a different position in sentences 5 and 6:
5 Please **turn off** your phones. The performance is about to begin.
6 The heavy snow blocked the roads and **cut off** the farm completely.

2.3
1 Abstract   *Go against* here means oppose or defy.
2 Concrete   *Cut out* here means use scissors to remove the recipe from the magazine.
3 Abstract   *Cut out* here means stopped running.
 Abstract   *Broke down* here means stopped working altogether.
 Abstract   *Turned up* here means arrived.
4 Concrete   *Dress up* here means dress in formal clothes or your best clothes.
5 Abstract   *Went through* here means experienced.

2.4
1 They just **brushed aside** my complaints; it made me very angry. *Or* They just **brushed** my complaints **aside**.
2 I **fell for** his story about having lost all his money. How stupid I was!
3 I couldn't **make out** what he was saying with all the noise.
4 Could you **chase up** Emily's report? She promised it last week but I haven't seen it yet. *Or* Could you **chase** Emily's report **up**?
5 If you are phoning from outside the country, **leave out** the first zero in the city code. *Or* … **leave** the first zero in the city code **out.**

2.5
1 The government have issued a statement condemning the recent protests.
2 The union accepted the new pay deal and cancelled the strike.
3 The number of people not owning a smartphone nowadays has declined dramatically.
4 There was a disturbance in Blackmoor Prison yesterday and three prisoners escaped.
5 Could you organise lunch for our visitors? There will be four of them.

Unit 3

3.1
1 We don't know for sure.
2 No, she didn't go into Ruby's house.
3 George was in a higher position.
4 The speaker went to the Richardsons' house.
5 round

3.2
1 b   2 a   3 a   4 b

3.3
1 Incorrect. The object must come between the verb and the particle:
I **have** three important meetings **on** tomorrow.
2 Correct
3 Incorrect. The object must come between the verb and the particle:
Sue was only **having** her sisters **on** when she told them she was planning to become a model.
4 Incorrect. This meaning of the phrasal verb *have on* is never used in the continuous form:
I **have** a lot of work **on** today.
5 Correct
6 Incorrect. The object must come before the particle because it is a pronoun:
Lola was wearing new jeans this morning and she **had** them **on** yesterday.

3.4
1 Can you move over to make room for your sister?
2 When Daisy finished her essay, she asked Harry to read it over.
3 Luke has invited me back to his house tomorrow.
4 Max was only having his parents on when he told them he'd failed his driving test.
5 What do you have on tomorrow?
6 Eva had the light on in her bedroom, so I knew she was at home.
Or Eva had on the light in her bedroom, so I knew she was at home.

Unit 4

4.1

phrasal verb	verb + particle noun
show off	show-off
warm up	warm-up
hold on	none
hide out	hideout
turn over	turnover
tear down	none

4.2
1 pile-up   2 cutbacks   3 outcry   4 bystanders
5 breakthrough

4.3
1 getaway   2 off-putting   3 throwaway   4 outgoing
5 bygone

4.4
1 get away   2 put off   3 throw away   4 go out   5 go by

4.5
1 I was looking for a way to turn off the air conditioning – The on/off switch is in the hall.
2 Have your heard about the scandal in the office? – Mm, amazing goings-on!
3 The economy's not doing so well these days. – Yes, there's been a downturn.
4 A database can organise all the information you type into it. – Yes, but I don't understand the input.
5 You have to consider how much you spend each month. – I know, I need to watch my outgoings.

Unit 5

5.1
1 d   2 f   3 e   4 a   5 c   6 b

5.2 1 a) I put my feet in a puddle of water and my feet are soaking now.
  b) She intervened or became involved to stop the argument from becoming more serious.
  The connection between the meanings is the sense of going into the middle of something.

  2 a) This music is rubbish. I wish you'd turn off the radio.
  b) The lecture was so boring that I stopped paying attention.
  The connection between the meanings is the sense of a break in continuity.

  3 a) There's a hole in my bag. I think my pen must have fallen from the bag onto the ground or floor.
  b) He stopped going to college before the end of his course and became a mechanic.
  The connection between the meanings is the sense of leaving a place or environment.

  4 a) We fixed the boxes to the roof of the car by using ropes.
  b) Marcos dreams of travelling, but he doesn't feel free to do it because he is trapped by his family and work responsibilities.
  The connection between the meanings is the sense of being unable to move or being restricted.

5.3 1 What are you really trying to say? I wish you would say exactly what you mean!
  2 The teacher did all she could to repeat the vocabulary so frequently that her pupils knew it well before the exam.
  3 The old education system used to remove the best pupils and teach them in separate schools.
  4 The noise of the children playing made it impossible for me to hear his speech.

5.4 *Suggested answer:*
  As the rain didn't **stop**, the football game was **cancelled**. So the team **began** discussing its strategy for the next match instead. We didn't **leave** the clubhouse until the cleaners **arrived** in the evening.

Unit 6

6.1 1 apart   5 along
  2 out   6 out
  3 around/round   7 out
  4 out

6.2 *Suggested answers:*
  1 Ben: Really? How did that come about?
  2 Ivan: Huh! Do you think it will ever come off?
  3 Bella: When do you think you'll come to a decision?
  4 Katie: Yes, I was intending to, but right at the last minute something came up.

6.3 I know that you are **coming up against** a lot of problems at work every day at the moment, but don't worry, they're only temporary, and I've heard that a new job opportunity is going to **come up/along**, which could change things completely. Whenever your name **comes up** in conversation, everyone always speaks very highly of you.

  You think you have **come across someone** who seems to share the same world view as you, but be careful, I don't think she is what she seems to be. Don't forget that, in the end, true love **comes down to** finding someone you can trust.

Unit 7

7.1 1 b   2 c   3 d   4 b   5 a   6 a   7 d

7.2 *Suggested answers:*
  1 How do you and Joseph get on? – We're great friends.
  2 What exactly are you getting at? – Let me put it another way for you.
  3 How do you get by on a student loan? – I manage somehow, though it isn't easy.
  4 How did you get so behind? – I just wasn't organised enough.
  5 When are you going to get round to it? – Soon, I promise.

6 Shall we get together this evening? – Sure, that would be nice.

7 Will you manage to get away soon? – I certainly hope so.

7.3 1 I've been planning to sort out my files but I haven't **got around/round to it** yet.

2 I **can't get over** how much money they spent on their New Year's party.

3 Don't try to **get away with not** paying your train fare – an inspector might come on and want to see your ticket.

4 The teachers in the school often **get together** after work on Fridays in a café near the school.

5 They **got around/round** the problem of offending anyone and just invited all their friends to the wedding.

6 I usually find it quite hard to understand what Professor Mactoft is **getting at** in his lectures.

7 I hope **I can get away with not sending** any Christmas cards this year.

8 Emily has **got terribly/very behind with her thesis**.

Unit 8

8.1 1 through   2 off/on   3 through   4 without   5 on   6 about

8.2 *Suggested answers:*

1 I'm thinking of going in for the New York Marathon next year.

2 My father went through some difficult times in his life.

3 Unemployment and high crime levels often go together.

4 He decided to go through with the operation even though there were risks.

5 I refused to go along with their decision to close the youth club.

6 I didn't realise how late it was and I went on studying till after midnight.

7 We had to go without hot water for 24 hours while they were repairing the pipes.

8 Do you think I should go in for the advanced level exam? It might be too difficult.

9 She just went off without saying goodbye. I wonder if I offended her?

10 What was going on in the staffroom at lunchtime? I heard someone shouting.

8.3 1 b   2 c   3 c   4 c

Unit 9

9.1 1 b   2 c   3 a   4 c   5 b

9.2 1 forward

2 around/round (*out* is also possible here)

3 after

4 ahead or forward

5 down

6 at (*over* is also possible here)

9.3

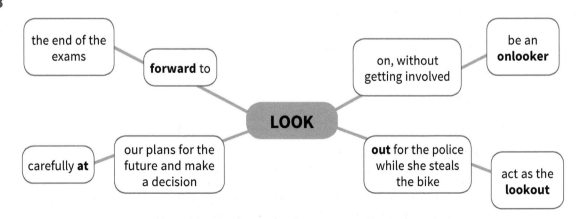

9.4 1 find the new words in a dictionary
2 visited an old friend who I hadn't seen for a long time (when you go to the town or country where that person lives)
3 the situation is improving
4 quickly examined the report
5 examined the report (rather more carefully than *looking over* it)
6 investigating the murder

Unit 10

10.1 1 Logan   2 Zara   3 Theo   4 Lars   5 Martha

10.2 1 As soon as we had checked in at the hotel, we made straight for the beach.
2 She made up some story about the bus being late, but I'm sure she just overslept.
3 Nobody could make out why the camera was not working properly. (The sentence is now in the active voice because *make out* cannot be used in the passive.)
4 Harry is very good at making up stories for the children; they love his tales.
5 Can you make out what that white thing on the horizon is? (Verb and particle cannot be separated.)
6 The report is made up of three sections. (In this sense of *make up* the verb and particle cannot be separated.)

Unit 11

11.1 1 I like sleeping in tents but I don't like putting them up. (When the object is a pronoun, it must go before the particle.)
2 Correct
3 We put a new dishwasher in last week. It's wonderful. *Or* We put in a new dishwasher last week. It's wonderful.
4 Correct
5 That light is too strong. Shall we put it out? (When the object is a pronoun, it must go before the particle.)

11.2 1 up   2 on   3 up   4 off   5 out   6 onto *or* on to

11.3 *Suggested answers:*
1 Could you **put** the light **out** please? You don't need it on. *Or* Could you **put out** the light …
2 They're **putting up** some new buildings near the railway station. *Or* They're **putting** some new buildings **up** …
3 The Scouts **put** their tent **up** very quickly and then started unpacking their things. *Or* The Scouts **put** their tent **up** …
4 Could we possibly **put** our meeting **back** to 10 o'clock? *Or* Could we possibly **put back** our meeting …
5 When we moved into our new house, we decided to **put in** a new, more attractive fireplace. *Or* … we decided to **put** a new, more attractive fireplace **in**.
6 Can you **put** some music **on**, please? I work better with music in the background.

11.4 1 b   2 e   3 d   4 a   5 c

Unit 12

12.1 I bought a new jacket but it had a mark on it so I took it back.

The shop assistant took me ~~offside~~ so that other people could be served.

She said that if I was prepared to keep the jacket she would take ~~away~~

ten per cent. I didn't really take in what she was saying at

first, but once I understood, I decided to take her ~~over~~ on the offer.

✓
aside
off
✓
up

12.2
1 **Hugo:** OK, OK. Sorry, I shouldn't have said it. I **take it back**. *Or* I **take back** what I said.
2 **Clare:** Yes, she's really **taken to** it. She's so **taken up** with it that she's stopped going to the swimming pool.
3 **Matthew:** Well, I'm not surprised! I warned you not to **take it apart** in the first place. (not ~~take apart it~~)
4 **Julia:** Well, why don't you **take up** golf? *Or* … **take** golf **up**?
5 **Ryan:** It's what you get when you **take** £15 **away** from £45. *Or* It's what you get when you **take away** £15 from £45.
6 **Daniel:** Yes, teaching 28 hours a week really **takes it out of** me.
7 **Layla:** Yes, he just **took off** without even saying goodbye.

Unit 13

13.1 *Possible answers:*
1 She needs to tidy up the kitchen.
2 She needs to sweep up the food the child has dropped on the floor. *Or* She needs to sweep up the rubbish from the floor.
3 She must hang up the coat.
4 Toys are jumbled up on the floor.
5 When she has cleared everything up, she might feel tired but happy.

13.2
1 turned *or* showed
2 liven
3 chop
4 shows *or* turns
5 opened

13.3 1 b   2 a *or* d   3 c   4 a *or* b   5 c   6 d   7 b *or* d   8 b

13.4
1 The *up* can be left out of the following sentences:

I spent all morning yesterday **clearing (up)** my study.
After that I tried to **tidy (up)** my bedroom.
There were dirty clothes all **jumbled (up)** in a pile on the floor.
… I **loaded (up)** the washing machine.
Then I discovered the washbasin was **clogged (up)** in the bathroom, so I had to clear that.
By that time I'd **used (up)** all my energy …
Eat (up) your vegetables!
Drink (up) your juice!
Seth's used (up) all the milk.
She's just **opened (up)** a restaurant serving exotic food from different countries.
No, she has a business partner and they **divide (up)** the work – and the profits!
She spends half the day **chopping (up)** food and cleaning the kitchen.

In the other example sentences on the opposite page, the *up* is essential.

2 In the sentences where the word *up* is not essential, using it seems to add a meaning of:
– either something being done completely (tidy up, clear up, jumble up, load up, clog up, eat up, drink up, use up).
– or something being made into lots of small pieces (divide up, chop up). This meaning can be seen in verbs such as smash up, cut up, tear up.

Unit 14

14.1
1 I'll show you out, if you like.
2 For some reason my name was left out of the guest list.
3 I've locked myself out of my car.
4 He can see/show himself out – there's no need to take him there.
5 She cut out advertisements from the magazines that would give her money off her shopping.
6 The security guard let us out of the building site.

14.2 1 lost
2 try
3 help
4 locked
5 cut
6 show *or* see, see, let

14.3 1 He's locked himself out of his car.
2 She's left out the letter E. *Or* She's left the letter E out.
3 The DVD of *Star Lords* is coming out soon. *Or Star Lords* is coming out on DVD soon.

14.4 1 c   2 e   3 a   4 d   5 b

Unit 15

15.1 1 sold
2 broke
3 clear *or* slip *or* run (*Clear* suggests that the speaker is more annoyed.)
4 see
5 head *or* slip (*Slip* emphasises the idea of leaving discreetly. *Clear* would sound too abrupt and informal in this context.)
6 dozed
7 send
8 lift *or* lifting

15.2 1 It won't take him long to **run off** the letters you asked him to do.
2 I often **doze off** in boring lectures.
3 Let's try and **slip off** before the others wake up.
4 In the middle of a long speech, the actor suddenly **broke off** and ran off the stage.
5 I've **sent** all the Christmas presents for abroad **off**. *Or* I've **sent off** all the Christmas presents for abroad.
6 The school disco has **put** her **off** discos in general. *Or* The school disco has **turned** her **off** discos in general.
7 Tell that boy in our front garden to **clear off** – he's annoying the dog.
8 Fortunately, he **laughed off** the criticism of his acting. *Or* He **laughed** the criticism of his acting **off**.
9 I'll **run off** a copy of the report for you.

15.3 *Author's answers:*
1 I think I'd probably just laugh it off.
2 I'd be most likely to doze off in front of a political discussion.
3 My husband, son and dog usually see me off if I go on a journey on my own.
4 I can usually run off an English essay quickly as long as the subject is not too difficult.
5 A lecturer might break off in the middle of a talk if someone raised their hand to ask a question.
6 If you plan to slip off during a party, you're intending to go quietly without letting anyone know that you have gone.
7 If someone tells some young people to 'clear off', they probably feel cross or annoyed with them.
8 I might be put off eating my dinner if I saw a hair on the plate.

15.4 1 I'm going to **see** Artem **off** at the airport tomorrow. *Or* I'm going to **see off** Artem at the airport tomorrow.
2 I've just **sent off** a letter to Elizabeth. *Or* I've **sent** a letter to Elizabeth **off**.
3 The rocket is due to **lift off** tomorrow at noon. (Note that there is also a noun **lift-off**: The **lift-off** is due at noon tomorrow.)
4 I hope I've managed to **turn** him **off** the idea of redecorating the house. *Or* I hope I've managed to **put** him **off** the idea of redecorating the house.
5 I **dozed off** when all the others went off to play tennis.
6 We're planning to **head off** in the early evening.

Unit 16

16.1
1 I read the gardening article you gave me and then **passed** it **on** to a friend who's also interested in plants.
2 Do you think she's really angry, or do you think she's just **putting it on**?
3 He looks very pale and tired. Something is clearly **weighing on** him.
   Or Something is clearly **weighing on** his mind.
4 It's a lovely jacket. **Try it on.**
5 I'm **going to keep on** working until I've finished this report.
6 You can **rely/depend/count on** William.

16.2
1 False, because *keep on* means to continue to do something, and Anwar has decided to tell Oscar the news tomorrow.
2 False, because *take in* means to reduce the width of a piece of clothing, and Alice's skirt was too loose.
3 True
4 True
5 False, because *count on* means rely on, and Edward has been able to rely on his parents' support.
6 True

16.3
1 Hey, that man just pushed **in** – that taxi should have been ours!
2 Heidi's bad news has been weighing **on my mind** all day.
3 I need time for **the news to sink in**.
4 I couldn't leave the room because someone had locked me **in**. (You are locked *out* of a room if you cannot get in.)
5 Phrasal verbs may seem hard but you must keep **on** trying.
6 You'll never guess who called **in at the office** today!

Over to you
Possible answers:

pass on = die
e.g. I'm so sorry to hear that your dad has passed on.

take in = let someone stay in your house
e.g. She took me in for a month while the building work was done on my house.

rub sth in (informal) = talk to someone about something which you know they want
to forget because they feel bad about it
e.g. I know I shouldn't have failed the exams, but there's no need to keep rubbing it in.

Unit 17

17.1
1 We know that Jamie's luggage is heavy and/or that there is a lot of it.
2 Yes, but she's trying to eat less chocolate than she used to. Though she would probably be quite happy if she could **cut** it **out** totally. [stop eating it completely]
3 He wrote it rather than remembered it.
4 No, it has closed permanently, not just for the evening.
5 Perhaps they did it because the bushes were so big that they were blocking the light or blocking the path.

17.2 1 shut   2 cut   3 hand   4 chopped   5 keep   6 go

17.3
1 *Read through, look through* and *go through* are all possible. Using *through* perhaps suggests more thoroughness than *over*, which can be quite superficial. However, the difference is very slight.
2 They all share an idea of change or of moving from one state or time to another:
   stay over = staying from one day to the next
   get over = change from feeling bad to feeling better
   fall over = change from a vertical to a horizontal position
3 a) heaviness which causes difficulty
   b) put on paper or on an electronic device

c) move in the direction of the ground
d) stop an activity
e) reduce a number or amount, or not let it rise
4 a) communicating or expressing clearly
b) move to make more room for someone else
c) examine to make sure they are correct
d) hit it with their foot so that it spills
e) flow over the side of the pan

Unit 18

18.1
1 mess about/(a)round   behave stupidly or waste time
2 hang about/(a)round   spend time somewhere not doing very much
3 lie about/(a)round   lie down doing very little
4 sit about/(a)round   spend time sitting down and doing very little
5 laze about/(a)round   relax, enjoy yourself and do very little

18.2   1 lies *or* lazes   2 hanging   3 sitting   4 lazing *or* lying   5 messing

18.3   *Suggested answers:*
1 Do you want to **wait/stick around** after the meeting? I finish work at 5 p.m. and I could **show/take you (a)round** the old town.
2 Nothing much happened at the demonstration. We just **stood about/(a)round** and held our banners up.
3 They spend most weekends just **hanging/messing about/(a)round** in their boat; they don't really sail it seriously.
4 On my first day, the boss **showed/took me (a)round** the workshop and introduced me to various people I'd be working with.
5 At the drinks party people were just **milling about/(a)round** hoping to find someone they knew.
6 Look, I'm sorry, I don't want to **mess you about/around**, but I wonder if we could postpone our meeting till next week?

18.4
1 I've got to leave now, but I'll see you somewhere or other.
2 Don't tell me what to do.
3 My suitcase got a bit damaged on the plane.
4 He told the kids to stop behaving so badly.
5 I'm just looking to see what you have in the gallery.

Unit 19

19.1   1 b   2 c   3 a   4 f   5 d   6 e

19.2
1 sent   5 put
2 lives   6 could do
3 go   7 stick
4 couldn't ask   8 catching

19.3
1 go, with
2 call for
3 dying for
4 dealt with
5 catch up with

19.4
1 I couldn't **put up with** such noisy neighbours as yours.
2 It's been such a busy week. I'm **dying for** the weekend.
3 Evelyn's shoes **go** perfectly **with** her handbag. *Or* Evelyn's shoes **go with** her handbag perfectly.
4 All the students at his university were **rooting for** Austin in the golf championship.
5 I **couldn't ask for** a better job.
6 Stella **lives for** her grandson.

Unit 20

20.1 *Possible answers:*
1 Let me take you through the way we do things here.
2 Don't worry, I saw through Leo the first moment I met him.
3 I'm so sorry. I set my alarm but slept through it.
4 Could you go through these figures and see if you can find any mistakes?
5 You don't need to read it in detail. Just flick/look through it.
6 Well, she has lived through some terrible things over the last few years.

20.2
1 take *or* took, take	4 bite	7 cashback
2 bite	5 go	8 bounced
3 send	6 answer	

20.3 *Suggested answers:*
1 James rang while you were out. Please could you call/phone/ring him back.
(not ~~call/phone/ring back him~~)
2 I don't like these trousers I bought today. I think I'll take them back.
(not ~~take back them~~)
3 Harry missed his train this morning because he slept through his alarm. (not ~~he slept his alarm through~~)
4 Ella isn't really reading the magazine; she's just flicking through it.
(not ~~flicking it through~~)
5 I wanted to tell her how upset I was, but I managed to bite it back. (not ~~bite back it~~)

Unit 21

21.1
1 At the supermarket yesterday, Julia ran into Jake.
2 Harvey is getting over his broken heart by throwing himself into his studies.
3 When she saw me dressed up as a pirate, she burst into laughter.
4 He doesn't think before he speaks, so don't read too much into his words.
5 In your essay you should have gone more fully into the causes of the war.
6 We were disagreeing about the film and then Robyn entered into the argument.
7 The police are doing all they can to look into what happened.
8 I don't really buy into all that alternative medicine stuff.

21.2
1 running away
2 tidy away *or* pack away *or* put away
3 stay away from
4 locked herself away
5 turn away
6 tear yourself away

21.3 *Suggested answers:*
1 I was very surprised when Claudia burst into tears/laughter/song.
2 It makes sense to stay away from dangerous parts of town at night.
3 My best friend always throws himself into everything he does.
4 Sometimes I'd really like to run away from all my problems and go and live on an island.
5 I find this job so stressful. I really should look into other possible careers.
6 When I went to the town centre last week, I ran into my old headmistress.
7 Before moving house I spent weeks packing away all my personal belongings.
8 Whenever visitors are coming, I usually tidy away anything that is lying around.

21.4   1 c   2 e   3 a   4 d   5 b

21.5 *Suggested answers:*
A number of the phrasal verbs with *into* are connected with going into something in detail: look into sth, read sth into sth, go into sth, throw yourself into sth.

Other phrasal verbs with *into* are connected with starting something: burst into sth, enter into sth, launch into sth.

Others are connected with meeting someone or something: run into sth/sb, bump into sth/sb, bang into sth.

The phrasal verbs with *away* are all connected with separation, keeping something at a distance or putting something in a separate place.

Unit 22

22.1
1	pushed	4	bring, fit
2	run	5	press
3	clock, clock	6	take

22.2 *Suggested questions:*
1 What do you usually do at weekends? *Or* How do you spend your evenings?
2 How did he fail the exam? *Or* Why did he drop out of the course?
3 Is that girl a friend of yours?
4 Why do you always carry your laptop? *Or* Why have you got your tablet with you?
5 Shall we leave now?

22.3
1 We had to wait an hour for the next train, so we went for a walk to **while away** the time.
2 A young French woman **latched on to** me at the party last night. I think she wanted to practise her English.
3 I **clock on** at 7.30 a.m. every morning. *Or* I **clock on at** work at 7.30 a.m. every morning.
4 We have to finish this job by six o'clock. We'd better **press on** with it.
5 I just don't know how we're going to **fit** three meetings **in** before the summer break.
  Or I just don't know how we're going to **fit in** three meetings before the summer break.

Unit 23

23.1 1 b   2 c   3 a   4 d   5 a

23.2
1 In (a) the lecture simply went on for longer than expected. In (b) the person found it slow and boring.
2 In (a) Ethan delayed us, whereas in (b) he made us move or work faster.
3 In (a) the song reminds the speaker of their childhood, whereas in (b) the speaker simply says that the song was written when he was a child.
4 In (a) the children were walking much more quickly than the speaker, whereas in (b) the speaker was trying to make the children walk faster.

23.3
1 Time seems to pass more quickly as you get older.
2 Music and smells have great powers to remind you of the past.
3 Mr Jones looks or behaves like people used to look or behave in the past; in other words, he is very old-fashioned in some way.
4 We should forget what happened in the past. (The implication is that there have been problems, arguments or conflicts in the past, but that you now want to make peace.)
5 You never know what the future holds for you.

23.4 *Suggested answers:*
1 The old oil lamps in my grandfather's house looked like leftovers from a bygone era.
2 The smell of marker pens always takes me back to my schooldays.
3 There was a hold-up on the motorway because of an accident.
4 Sometimes, if the textbook is boring, the lesson seems to drag on.
5 We can never know what lies ahead.
6 There are some leftover pizzas from the party. Would you like one?

Unit 24

24.1 *Suggested answers:*
1 The fields stretch away to the horizon.
2 The house is tucked away in the forest.
3 There are small houses dotted around the landscape.
4 The house on the island is cut off from the mainland.
5 The room opens onto a balcony.

24.2
1 stay in
2 stay out
3 leave something behind
4 stay behind *or* stay on
5 brighten up
6 stay on
7 call back

24.3
1 I **left** my memory stick **behind** at the computer class. I'll have to go back and see if it's still in the machine.
2 When you were a teenager, did your parents allow you to **stay out** late?
3 Assistant: I'm afraid the report isn't ready yet. It will be another couple of hours.
  Customer: OK. I'll **call back** tomorrow.
4 We've decided to paint the kitchen to **brighten** it **up** a bit. It's so gloomy and dull at the moment.
5 I'm really tired. I think I'll **stay in** tonight and not go to the party after all, sorry.
6 The teacher asked the two badly behaved girls to **stay behind** after the lesson.
7 We loved the resort so much we decided to **stay on** another week, even though our friends had gone home.

Unit 25

25.1
1 brings back
2 spring from *or* sprang from
3 lies behind
4 stir up
5 sparked off
6 set, off

25.2
1 off
2 set
3 bring
4 off
5 ruled
6 off
7 stir
8 pay

25.3
1 suspects
2 violence
3 memories
4 reforms
5 feelings
6 fireworks

25.4
1 stir up
2 pay him back
3 triggered off *or* sparked off
4 sparked off *or* triggered off
5 ruled out
6 sprang from

Unit 26

26.1 1 picked up *or* gone up   2 heating up   3 going up   4 filling up

26.2 1 woke up   2 looking up

26.3

		⁶P			⁷G		⁸W
	⁵P		A		I		O
¹C	H	A	N	G	E	O	V	E	R
	A				E		N
	²S	T	U	C	K		
	E			³G	E	T	
	⁴B	L	O	W			

26.4
1 The **changeover** to the new accounting system has caused endless problems.
2 There was a lot of trouble in the office last month, but it's all **blown over** now and things are back to normal.
3 Shall I **heat up** that pizza for you? I expect it's gone cold by now.
4 All these computers will be **phased out** over the next year and we'll get new laptops.

Unit 27

27.1
1 fall through	4 take off *or* catch on
2 take over	5 bring off *or* pull off
3 downfall	6 come off

27.2
1 S	4 S	7 S
2 S	5 S	8 F
3 F *or* S*	6 S	9 S

*If you are muddling through, you are managing, even if not very well, so it could be S as well as F.

27.3
History   muddle through
Maths   build on
English   catch up
Geography   stay ahead
Physics   pay off

27.4   *Suggested answers:*
1 Beatrice walked into a job in London.
2 Aaron's hard work eventually paid off.
3 The company is hoping to pull off an important deal this week.
4 Ruby never expected her singing career to take off so quickly.
5 The project may well fall through because of a lack of funds.
6 Harper finds it hard to keep up with the other kids in her class.
7 The new mobile phone design has caught on almost overnight.
8 Top software companies are finding it increasingly difficult to stay ahead (of their competitors).

Unit 28

28.1
1 started, outset, packed
2 set, polish *or* finish, broke, finish *or* polish
3 give, cut, fizzled
4 drying, call

28.2   *Author's answers:*
1 I should set about filling in my annual tax forms.
2 I was planning on going to Spain at New Year but had to call off the trip because I was ill.
3 Playing the guitar helps me to wind down.
4 I eat too much chocolate and should cut down on that.
5 I once started tennis lessons but gave them up after a few weeks.

Over to you
Possible answers:
start on sth = begin to deal with something
start over (American English) = start doing something from the beginning because you did not do it well the first time
start up = start to work (of a vehicle or engine)

Unit 29

29.1
1 It is probably on a high shelf or in a high cupboard.
2 No, she's only gone for a short time, or at least that is what the speaker is implying.

3 He has to move closer to someone.
4 Emily has to move more because she has to actually change seats rather than just move a little bit further along.
5 No, the speaker expects you to use your hands to tear it.
6 She's probably about to go outside because she is putting her coat on.

29.2
1 The children helped me to **wrap up** the parcel. *Or* The children helped me to **wrap** the parcel **up**.
2 Can you **tie up** Albert's shoe laces for him? *Or* Can you **tie** Albert's shoe laces **up** for him?
3 **Pick up** the ball at once. *Or* **Pick** the ball **up** at once.
4 **Slow down** – it's beginning to snow and there's ice on the road.
5 Annabelle loves **blowing up** balloons! *Or* Annabelle loves **blowing** balloons **up**!

29.3 *Suggested answers:*
1 The tree has fallen down.
2 She's reaching out to put money in the machine.
3 He's blowing up a balloon. *Or* He's blowing a balloon up.
4 He's picking up a ball. *Or* He's picking a ball up.
5 She's tearing up a photo. *Or* She's tearing a photo up.
6 She's wrapping up a present. *Or* She's wrapping a present up.

29.4
1 slowed   2 reached   3 pop   4 blow

Unit 30

30.1
1 stamp   2 root   3 falling   4 screwed *or* tore   5 knocked

30.2
1 tear apart   The lions are tearing a dead animal apart. *Or* The lions are tearing apart a dead animal.
2 put out   The firefighters are putting out a fire. *Or* The firefighters are putting a fire out.
3 pull down *or* tear down   He is pulling/tearing the building down. *Or* He is pulling/tearing down the building.

30.3
1 Gisela: Yes, well, it was a bit of **a setback**, but I've applied for a different grant and hope I'll get that.
2 Dan: Well, my parents have lent me some money to **see me through** while I'm studying. Note that: 'see through me' is not possible here. 'See through somebody' means to become aware that they are deceiving you; see Unit 20.
3 Eloise: Yes, but they **are fighting back** now and their union is much stronger.
4 Dominic: Oh yes, he **bent over backwards** to help me.
5 Jayden: Yes, I made an innocent comment and she just **turned on me**. Note that 'turned me on' is not possible here. 'Turn somebody on' means to excite them; see Unit 52.
6 Cameron: OK, don't worry, I'll **see to it**.

Unit 31

31.1
1 Connor   2 Oscar   3 Sara and Alice   4 Gabriel

31.2
1 turn down
2 ordering, about *or* around
3 leave, aside
4 get on to
5 turn to
6 bubbling over
7 deal with
8 keep to
9 pass on

31.3
1 speak up = speak more loudly
2 get through to someone = make someone understand
3 speak up = publicly express your opinions about something or someone, especially in order to support them
4 get across something or get something across = successfully communicate an idea to other people
5 butt in (informal) = interrupt a conversation or discussion, often stopping someone who is talking
6 dry up = stop speaking because you forget what to say next

Unit 32

32.1
1 freshen up
2 dress up
3 (to) do up *or* (to) do my dress up
4 wrap up, put on *or* put a scarf on

32.2
1 I don't want to wear my new jacket tonight. You can **put it on** if you like.
Note that pronouns always go before the particle.
2 Although the house looked rundown from the outside, it was very **smart/clean/ well-maintained** inside.
3 If you're going out in the snow, make sure you **wrap up** well.
4 Do you think this scarf and coat **go together** OK?
5 He hates the way his ears **stick out**.
6 It takes me a long time to get the kids ready in the morning because Sam and Layla can't **do up** their own shoes yet. Or .... **put** their own shoes **on** yet.
7 Joseph and his brother are so alike – I can't **tell** one **from** the other.
8 It's a very formal party, so you **need to / should** dress up.

32.3
1 rundown 2 in 3 stands* 4 stick 5 set

sticks is also possible but sounds less formal.

32.4
1 There are many examples.
2 The speaker thinks the performance was special, and probably better than the performances of the other actors in the film.
3 Daisy's writing is better.
4 Yes, it does.
5 The speaker thinks this will improve the series.

Unit 33

33.1
1 If a performance is booked up, you can't get tickets for it.
2 If people are said to pour into (a place), you know that there are a lot of people.
3 If people cram into a room, the room is then very crowded.
4 Events like poetry readings or poetry competitions might be put on to tie in with National Poetry Week.
5 A comedian is more likely to send up celebrities than post office workers.
6 An actor would need someone to stand in for them if they lost their voice or were sick.

33.2
1 b 2 c 3 a 4 b 5 c

33.3
1 called off   4 taking off *or* sending up*
2 standing in   5 packed out
3 put on   6 tie in
*If the imitation is very humorous, then *send up* is more appropriate.

33.4
1 putting on   5 sending up
2 ties in   6 taking off *or* sending up
3 was booked up   7 walked out
4 cram into   8 put off *or* put back

Unit 34

34.1
1 I know, but I'm sure everything will turn out all right in the end.
2 I must have mixed/muddled them up. Sorry.
3 I've run up against that problem too.
4 OK. I'll see if I can get out of my trip to London.
5 I wouldn't bank on it.
6 I know, but try to rise above it.

34.2   1 revolves   2 mix-up   3 back   4 crop   5 turns

34.3   *Suggested answers:*
1 hot up   4 calmed down
2 caught up   5 to back off
3 were thrown together   6 bank on his help

Unit 35

35.1   1 track down   3 turns to   5 come under
2 drawn on/upon   4 points out   6 check up on

35.2   Hannah and Ben were playing a game. Hannah had thought of a famous football player and Ben was trying to **find out who it was**. He **turned to his mother** but she **pointed out** that she knew absolutely nothing about football. He would have to try to **track the answer down himself** (*or* **track down the answer himself**) and to **watch out for any clues** that Hannah might deliberately give. After ten minutes Ben still hadn't **latched on** to who she was talking about, so he **gave up** and Hannah told him the answer.

35.3   *Suggested answers:*
1 You might check up on a person, facts or something you've been told.
2 You might point out an important fact, a mistake or a connection between two things.
3 Someone might find out some information, a secret or someone's date of birth.
4 You might take in something you're told, good or bad news, or the implications of a situation.
5 A secret, a rude remark or a taboo word might slip out.

35.4   1 make someone notice something by showing it with your finger
2 try to see
3 find by using physical senses
4 leave quickly and quietly
5 turn your body to face

Unit 36

36.1   1 c   2 d   3 a   4 e   5 b

36.2   It's time you **sorted** yourself **out**. You're 27 now and you still haven't got a job! You've got to **face up to** reality. It's about time you realised that the secret of success **lies in** taking positive action. Over the next couple of days, I will expect you to **come up with** a few ideas about how you're going to improve your situation. Why don't you go and **see about** that job Uncle Robert offered you at his factory? I've offered to help **talk** things **over** with you, but you never seem to want my help. Yet you don't **deal with** things yourself!

36.3   it's just dawned on me: I've suddenly realised or understood something
rules out: makes something impossible or unsuitable
the answer jumps out at you: the answer can immediately be seen
work through things: deal with a problem by talking about it in detail
sort things out: make a decision by discussing it with someone else or thinking about it carefully

Unit 37

37.1   1 over *or* through   2 weigh   3 by   4 ahead   5 think   6 sleep

37.2   *Possible answers:*
1 I probably would run an important decision by my parents first, especially one concerning my professional life.
2 I usually try to make myself sleep on it first as things often seem better after a good night's sleep.
3 I'd prefer to do without a car. My holidays are really important to me.

4 When planning ahead for their retirement, people might contribute to a pension or they might try to save money regularly.

5 People might chicken out of giving a speech, or going paragliding, or asking someone to go out with them on a date.

37.3 *Suggested answers:*

1 We should allow for the fact that he is still only young. (not ~~We should allow the fact for that he is still only young.~~)

2 I really can't help you as I have a lot of things on today. (not ~~I have on a lot of things today.~~)

3 He wants to opt out of art classes at school next year so he can do extra music. (not ~~He wants to opt of art classes out~~ …)

4 We didn't bargain for Max turning up at the party with a lot of his friends. (not ~~We didn't bargain Max for turning up~~ …)

5 My son is set against going to university. (not ~~My son is set going to university against.~~)

6 I could do without people coming for dinner this evening. (not ~~I could do people without~~ …)

37.4

1 I was going to do the parachute jump, but I chickened **out** in the end.

2 I have a lot of things **on** this weekend.

3 In judging her work, you should really allow **for** her inexperience.

4 If we buy the flat, we'll have to **do** without holidays for a few years.

5 Let's run our plan **by** Sarah before we make our final decision.

6 I could **do** without having to go to a conference this weekend.

7 In deciding how much holiday money we need, we should allow **for** the fact that food is very expensive there.

Unit 38

38.1   1 spoken   2 stick   3 back   4 outcry   5 stay   6 give

38.2 *Suggested answers:*

1 Yes, he backed him up. (not ~~He backed up him.~~)

2 Yes, it seems they've fallen out.

3 Yes, she always sticks up for her. (not ~~Yes, she always sticks her up for.~~)

4 Yes, I agree. I think we should back out.

5 Yes, she's always putting him down. (not ~~Yes, she's always putting down him.~~)

6 No, we shouldn't hold it/that against her. (not ~~No, we shouldn't hold against her it/that.~~)

7 Yes, I think it's really getting to her. (not ~~Yes, I think it's really getting her to.~~)
Or Yes, I think it's really beginning to get to her.

38.3
1 give in *or* back down   4 stuck together
2 fallen out   5 getting to
3 back out

Unit 39

39.1   1 b   2 c   3 a   4 a   5 c   6 b

39.2

presenting an opinion or trying to persuade	successfully persuading	people's reactions to persuasion
put across/over	talk around/round	fall for
put forward	bring round	brush aside
put sth to sb	rope in	
call for	have on	
press for	talk into	
	talk out of	

39.3
1. She didn't take it seriously and refused to think about it seriously.
2. We don't know, but we know that it's not the USA because she was just teasing Daniel.
3. No, they didn't have much choice in the matter.
4. We know she wasn't robbed and that she isn't always truthful because she was trying to trick Harry by inventing the story.
5. Yes, it does want reform.

39.4
1. pressing for *or* calling for
2. bring; round *or* talk; around/round
3. putting forward
4. call for *or* press for
5. rope in
6. talk, into

Unit 40

40.1
stand out and outstanding
An outstanding person is someone who stands out or is noticeable because of special, positive characteristics.
show off and a show-off
A show-off is a person who shows off or tries to impress others in an annoying way.

40.2
1. Ahmed   2. Paula   3. Logan   4. Laura   5. Imogen

40.3
Suggested answers:
1. Dan won the prize as his short story stood out (as the best). *Or* Dan won the prize as his short story stood out from all the others.
2. Molly got the sack because her work just didn't measure up.
3. What on earth does Phoebe think she's playing at? She's behaving so oddly.
4. I wish Ed wouldn't show off all the time! *Or* I wish Ed wasn't/weren't such a show-off all the time.
5. If you screw up again, you'll lose your job.
6. I know I was stupid but please don't rub it in.
7. Seth's father laid into him for scratching his new car.
8. Why does everyone always pick on me?

Unit 41

41.1
Suggested answers:
a) Mind out!   Hold on!   Hang on!
   Watch out!   Look out!   Keep it up!
b) Lighten up!   Steady on!   Come off it!   Spit it out!
   Come on!   Go on!   Hurry up!   Fire away!

Depending on the situation and your relationship with your boss or teacher, you might feel it is appropriate to use these expressions: Steady on! Hurry up! Go on! Come on!

41.2
1. Come off it!
2. Hold on!
3. Come on! Spit it out!
4. Lighten up!
5. Mind out!
6. Steady on!
7. Keep it up!

41.3
1. Fire away!   2. Spit it out!

41.4
Hang on! and *Hold on!* both mean wait a minute.
Possible situation: Someone is talking at great length and you want to interrupt to ask something.
Mind out! and *Watch out!* both mean be careful.
Possible situation: Someone is about to step in front of a car.
Hurry up! and *Go on!* both mean do something faster.
Possible situation: Someone has paused in the middle of an interesting story and you want to encourage the storyteller to continue.

Unit 42

42.1   *Suggested answers:*
1 She's rubbing out what was written on the board.
2 He's crossing a word out.
3 She's handing out some books to the class.
4 He's handing in a worksheet.
5 She's working out the sum/answer.

42.2   1 not pleased   2 not pleased   3 pleased   4 pleased   5 not pleased
6 not pleased

42.3   1 fell behind   2 catch up   3 work out   4 missed out   5 messed up

42.4   1 At the end of the lesson we have to **put away** our books in our bags. *Or* At the end of each lesson we have to **put** our books **away** …
2 Students often **play up** when they are bored in class.
3 The teacher **rubbed out** the new words from the board and then tested us. *Or* The teacher **rubbed** the new words **out** …
4 We have to **hand in** our registration forms for the exam on Friday. *Or* We have to **hand** our registration forms **in** …
5 I usually **leave out** my middle name when I am filling in forms. *Or* I usually **leave** my middle name **out** …
6 Some people were **handing out** leaflets about a demonstration in the town centre. *Or* Some people were **handing** leaflets **out** …
7 My partner and I had to **act out** our dialogue in front of the whole class. *Or* My partner and I had to **act** our dialogue **out** …

42.5   *Possible answers:*
1 You are often asked to cross out rough work in an exam so that the examiner knows which work needs to be marked.
2 If a teacher gives out a sheet listing all the kings and queens of Britain, it is a handout. It would only be a worksheet if it also included some exercises or activities relating to the information.
3 Most students carry an eraser in their pencil cases in order to rub out mistakes that they make.
4 It would be quite easy for me to work out how many euros are equal to 250 US dollars if I had a calculator.
5 I think some pupils may play up in class if they find the class too easy, too difficult or too dull for them.

Unit 43

43.1   *Suggested answers:*
1 I'm going to sign up for a course in statistics next year. (not ~~I'm going to sign for a course up~~ …)
2 Several students dropped out of the Moral Philosophy course.
3 We break up on 20 June. (not ~~We break on 20 June up.~~)
4 He was thrown out of university after one term. He'd done no work at all.
5 I can't come out tonight. I have to write up my essay for tomorrow.
   Or I can't come out tonight. I have to write my essay up for tomorrow.
6 I go back to college on 12 September. (not ~~I go on 12 September back to college.~~)

43.2   Only *breaking up* would make most students happy.
Swotting up and *mugging up* both involve hard work.
Scraping through means only just passing an exam (but perhaps a student who had not worked hard would be happy!).
Being thrown out and *dropping out* show that you have not made a success of student life.

43.3   1 mug up *or* swot up
2 kept up
3 brush up on *or* mug up on *or* swot up on *or* polish up (on)

4 come up
5 scraped through
6 write up
7 break up
8 go back

43.4 Alfie hardly **swotted/mugged** up at all for his exams. He brushed **up** on the history of the French Revolution, but no questions on the French Revolution **came** up in the exam. He was afraid that he would be thrown **out of** university for failing his exams. However, he did just manage to **scrape** through them and so he will be in college when we **go** back next term. He has promised to try to keep **up** with work next year as he is planning to sign **up** for a couple of quite difficult courses, including business studies. He'll have to polish **up*** his French because the business studies course involves spending a term in France working in a business. He thinks he can just **pick** up** the language when he gets there, but I think he should study it before he goes because he only has school French.

* We can also say: He'll have to polish his French up …

** We can also say: He thinks he can just pick the language up when he gets there …

Over to you

Included in the Mini dictionary are:
break away   break down   break in(to)   break off   break out   break up
While they each have different meanings, *break* seems to suggest a sudden, sometimes violent or negative event which changes a situation; for example, a marriage *breaks up*, a disease/epidemic *breaks out*, a group of people *break away* from another group.

Unit 44

44.1 1 e, h, i   2 g   3 e, h, i   4 e, i   5 d   6 a   7 b   8 f   9 c

44.2 1 read out
2 dipped into
3 scribble down *or* jot down *or* note down
4 write it out
5 fill in *or* fill out
6 note down (*or*, if you are in a hurry, jot down *or* scribble down)
7 read up on
8 turn over
9 jot down *or* note down *or* scribble down

44.3 1 cut it out   2 touch on   3 tone down   4 cropped up   5 sum up

Unit 45

45.1 a) stand down, step down, knock off, lay off
b) fix up, pencil in

45.2 1 taking   6 pull
2 on   7 ahead
3 carry   8 stands *or* steps
4 left   9 hand
5 in

45.3 *Possible answers:*
1 Yes, please fill me in. (not ~~Yes, please fill in me.~~)
2 Certainly, I'll follow them up later today. (not ~~Certainly, I'll follow up them later today.~~)
3 Yes, I'll fix something up for you for next week. *Or* Yes, I'll fix up something for next week.
   Note that 'pencil in something' *or* 'pencil something in for next week' is also possible, but means that the arrangement is not yet definite.
4 Well, I've been doing it for years and I thought it was time to hand over to someone else.

Or … I thought it was time to step/stand down.

5 Sure, why don't we pencil it in for next Tuesday afternoon? (not ~~Sure, why don't we pencil in it for next Tuesday afternoon.~~)

45.4 *Author's answers:*

1 These are some of the tasks I have to carry out each day – reading and answering emails, filing and making phone calls.

2 I usually knock off at about 5 p.m.

3 Yes, most of the teachers at the language school where I used to work were laid off a few years ago.

4 I think you have to be well organised and good at getting on with other people in order to get ahead.

5 I filled in an application form and then had an interview with my current boss.

Unit 46

46.1 1 pile up   2 be snowed under   3 be tied up   4 catch up with

46.2 *Suggested answers:*

1 I've been trying to catch up with all the work I couldn't do when I was ill.

2 Sorry, I was tied up all last week, so I couldn't go to any of the meetings.

3 Paperwork has just piled up recently. I don't know where to start.

4 I'm sorry I can't do the report this week. I'm just snowed under.

46.3 1 on   2 out of   3 away   4 in   5 up with

46.4

I need to chase ~~out~~ Austin's report so that we can

keep things moving ~~away~~ with the European sales

campaign. I know he's been working ~~in~~ it and I

know he's been working ~~upwards~~ the same goals

as all of us to branch ~~up~~ into new markets in Europe,

but he's not good at sticking ~~for~~ things and you

need to keep ~~in~~ it with campaigns like this one.

| up |
| along |
| on |
| towards |
| out |
| at |
| at |

Unit 47

47.1 *Suggested answers:*

1 The suspected criminal took out all the money from his bank account and has not been seen since.

2 As Sebastian's girlfriend has been working in Australia for the past two years, they have run up huge debts because of travel costs.

3 The bill for the books we ordered came to $70.85.

4 I lent him €500 a year ago and he still hasn't paid me back. (not … ~~paid back me.~~)

5 Now that I've lost my job, we're going to have to cut back (on) what we spend on our weekly trip to the supermarket.

6 If you pay the restaurant bill with your credit card, I'll settle up with you later.

47.2 1 up   2 off   3 back   4 aside   5 down (Note that knockdown is written as one word.)

47.3 1 b   2 c   3 c   4 a   5 d

47.4 *Author's answers:*
1 I'm saving up for a new mountain bike.
2 I usually take €200 out.
3 I'd expect it to come to about €150.
4 My mortgage is my biggest debt and I won't pay that off for years.
5 I might pick up second-hand books and CDs.

Unit 48

48.1 1 beat   2 fork   3 skimp   4 picked *or* snapped   5 sell

48.2 *Suggested answers:*
1 I could stock up on important foods such as bread, milk, fruit, vegetables and meat to take with me.
2 I could splash out on some new furniture.
3 I could ask him/her to knock something off the price.
4 I should shop around to find the best price.
5 I could suggest that we club together to buy her some flowers.

48.3 1 She became addicted to online shopping and ran **up** huge credit card bills.
2 We were ripped **off** in that restaurant. They charged us for four desserts when we only had two.
3 He sold **off** his share in the business and went travelling round the world.
4 When he offered me his tennis racket for only $100, I snapped it **up** because it was still in excellent condition.
5 We had to fork **out** for a new washing machine because our old one broke down.

48.4 1 rip off someone or rip someone off: a rip-off
2 These verbs have noun forms:
pick up something/someone or pick something/someone up: a pick-up
Examples: It's an 8.30 a.m. pick-up tomorrow, so we'll have to get up at seven.
[a car/taxi/bus will be coming to collect us]
He drives an old pickup and wears a cowboy hat. [small truck with an open back]
Economists are expecting a pick-up in house sales later this year. [an increase or improvement]
I thought she was just being friendly, but then I realised it was a pick-up. [informal: attempt to form a sexual relationship with me]

sell off something or sell something off: a sell-off
Example: The company sell-off raised millions of pounds. [a sale of all or part of a business]

sell out something: a sell-out
Examples: The concert was a sell-out. [all the tickets were sold]
The workers were disappointed that the union had agreed to end the strike, and they called it a sell-out. [a betrayal of principles]

Unit 49

49.1 1 d   2 f   3 e   4 b   5 a   6 c

49.2 *Suggested answers:*
1 Henry: Yes, they've been pouring money into farming.
2 Elise: Yes, you're right. He started up around ten years ago. *Or* He set up his business about ten years ago.
3 Jamie: Yes, I'd put it at three million (euros). *Or* Yes, I'd say it runs to three …
Or Yes, I'd say their losses run into three …
4 Alicia: Yes, they're setting up a branch there. *Or* Yes, they're starting up a branch there. (Note that *set up* sounds better than *start up*.)
5 Connor: Yes, the upkeep is very expensive.

49.3   1 take over   2 hire out   3 turnover   4 outlet   5 set-up   6 run to

Unit 50

50.1   1 Why don't you **call around** several different companies to get the information you need?
2 It's difficult to **get through** to the customer helpline in the mornings.
3 I'm sorry, he's out right now. Can you **call back** (*or* **ring/phone back**) at about five o'clock?
4 Maryam **called in** to say she's not feeling well.
5 Jack: Hi! Fine thanks. Just a minute, I'll **put you on to your aunt** so you can tell her all the news. (*or* I'll **put your aunt on** so you …)
6 I'll **get back to you** in a few days.
7 Is it OK if I **put you on speakerphone** so that everyone can hear your news?

50.2

```
             [1]C
       [5]U [2]P              [3]R
       [6]T  H   R   O   U   G  [4]H
             O               N      U
[7]L  I  S   T   E   N   I   N   G
             E                      N
                                    G
```

50.3   speak up = speak more loudly
hold on = wait a moment
break up = If someone who is talking on a phone is breaking up, their voice cannot fully be heard.
switch on = turn an electrical device on
switch off = turn an electrical device off

50.4   *Suggested answers:*
1 Sorry, my phone was switched off. *Or* Sorry, I'd switched off my phone.
2 Sorry, you're breaking up and I can't hear what you're saying.
3 Sorry, could you speak up? There's a lot of background noise.
4 Sorry, I only got your message when I switched my phone on after the concert.
5 Sorry, can you hold on just a minute?

Unit 51

51.1   Positive feelings – George, Theo and Anna
Negative feelings – Jude, Faith, Henry, Mary and Thomas

51.2   1 The news that I didn't have to do the exam after all **cheered me up**.
2 Look, Dominic. **Calm/cool down!** Getting angry won't solve the problem.
3 When she heard of her friend's death, she **broke down** and wept.
4 She's **(so) hung up** about silly little problems at work.
5 I wish you'd **brighten up**! You're making me feel depressed! (You can also say: I wish you'd **cheer up**! using *cheer up* without an object.)

51.3   1 Yes, I'm beginning to warm to it too.
2 Sure, I'd jump at the chance.
3 I know – I do feel for them both.
4 Yes, I hope he pulls himself together before his next attempt.
5 Don't get carried away!
6 What more can we do to cheer her up?

51.4   1 broke   2 tear   3 pull   4 up   5 to
6 felt   7 down   8 hung   9 cheer

Unit 52

52.1   1 fallen   2 falling-out   3 chat–   4 paired off   5 chat … up   6 go for
7 fallen   8 fit   9 ask   10 hit it off *or* get along

52.2   1 My friend and I fell **out** last week because she thinks I'm in love with her boyfriend.
2 The new student was finding it difficult to fit **in**, as he was older than the other students.
3 When George met his new colleague, he really fell **for** her and now he talks about her all the time.
4 Ethan and David hit it **off** immediately when they were introduced.
5 That girl over there was trying to **chat** me up.

52.3   Annie: So what did you think of the film?

Jade: It was so romantic! I loved it, especially at the end where Chris finally **asked Lara out**.

Annie: That was sweet. But I didn't like it when Julie and Raul **paired off**. She said at the beginning that she didn't normally **go for** men who spend a lot of time at the gym. So it wasn't very realistic when she immediately **fell for** him.

Jade: But it was because they **hit it off** online first. She didn't know what he looked like! And then he **fitted in well with** her group of friends, which always helps.

Annie: Yes, I suppose so. But my favourite storyline was Lena and Seth. The ones who were **going out** at the start but then had a big argument. It was so funny when he started **chatting her up** at the carnival and she didn't know it was him - until he took off the lion costume!

Jade: Ha ha! Yes, that was definitely the funniest bit.

Unit 53

53.1   1 c   2 f   3 e   4 a   5 b   6 d

53.2   1 My sister and her husband **split up** last year.
2 Millie was very upset when her boyfriend **finished with** her.
3 We had been **growing apart** for a long time, so it was better to separate properly.

53.3
1 make up
2 ran off with
3 settle down
4 let, down
5 live, down
6 miss out
7 settle for
8 break off

Unit 54

54.1   1 Jason   2 Gina   3 George   4 Michael   5 Eleanor   6 Rebecca

54.2   1 keeping, let
2 shut, keep
3 pin
4 talks
5 poured, opened, outpouring

54.3   1 let on   2 gone back   3 keeping   4 owned up   5 have it out with

Unit 55

55.1
1 carry on
2 takes after
3 drop out
4 handed down
5 live up to
6 become of
7 bringing up
8 pass for

55.2   *Author's answers:*
1 I was named after a character in a book.
2 I think I take after my mother in appearance.
3 I probably take after my father in character.

4 I think that children should be treated as children when they are growing up. They need to play and learn new things.

5 Someone might drop out of university because of ill health or because they were not enjoying their studies.

6 A girl I know is only 15, but she could easily pass for 20 in both appearance and behaviour.

7 I have a tea service that has been handed down from my great-grandparents.

8 I think that both parents have an equally important role to play in bringing up their children.

9 I would like to carry on working for as long as possible as I enjoy working.

55.3
1	named	6	become
2	take	7	turn
3	brought	8	ended *or* wound
4	live	9	ended *or* wound
5	dropping	10	carried

Unit 56

56.1   1 down   2 off   3 up   4 up   5 up   6 off

56.2
1 I've had a sore throat for a week now – I just can't **shake it off**.
2 Megan hadn't eaten anything for 48 hours, and so it wasn't surprising that she **passed out** in the middle of her gym lesson.
3 The doctors were afraid that the 102-year-old man wouldn't survive the attack of pneumonia, but amazingly he **pulled through** and was soon on his feet again.
4 I think **I'm coming down with** a cold – I feel a bit shivery.
5 My thumb **swelled up** after I accidentally hit it with a hammer.
6 The sea was so rough that many people **were throwing up** over the side of the ship.
7 People usually write letters of condolence to the relatives of someone who has **passed away/on**.
8 My grandmother is in great pain because she **has put her hip out**.
9 After the operation, her sister **cared for** her until she was completely recovered.
10 How do you think you **came down with** (*or* **went down with**) chickenpox?

56.3
1 Andrew's uncle passed away last year.
2 Beth is fighting off a bout of flu.
3 Erica is kept very busy caring for her elderly mother.
4 Flora's ankles swelled up during the long flight.
5 Most people usually slow down a bit as they get older.
6 I think Gabriel is going down with flu.

56.4   *Possible answers:*
1 When her great-aunt passed away, Carla felt very sad.
2 Jack broke down when he failed his final exams.
3 The last time I threw up was after a party where I'd eaten too much.
4 You can get a blocked-up nose if you have a cold or an allergy.
5 Kate's finger swelled up after it was hit by a hockey ball.
6 The best way to fight off a cold is to stay in bed and drink a lot.

Unit 57

57.1
1 join in = participate
2 give in = surrender
3 go for = attempt to achieve
4 pull ahead = overtake
5 knock out = defeat

57.2
1 warm-up
2 knockout
3 burn off (*Work off* would also be possible in this context.)

4 work off
5 warm up
6 cool down

57.3 *Author's answers:*
1 I work out about four times a month. Usually I go to an aerobics class.
2 I might warm up by doing some gentle stretches and by running on the spot.
3 I'd be pleased because if I pulled ahead of the other runners, it means that I am winning.
4 Tennis is better than table tennis at burning off calories because it is more energetic than table tennis.
5 I'd prefer to join in a snooker game as I'm not very good at football.
6 A top athlete would go for the gold medal.

57.4 *Suggested answers:*
1 The player or the team is kicking off. *Or* It is the kick-off.
2 The woman is burning off calories. *Or* The woman is working out on an exercise bike.
3 The athlete is warming up or is doing a warm-up. *Or* (if he has just done some sport) The athlete is cooling down.

57.5 1 told to leave   2 was / were defeated by   3 progressed

Unit 58

58.1 1 d   2 e   3 a   4 c   5 b   6 f

58.2
1 up
2 stay
3 lie-
4 up, up
5 sleeping *or* lying
6 over
7 oversleep

58.3
1 waiting up *or* staying up
2 put her up *or* let her sleep over
3 oversleeping *or* sleeping in
4 moved out
5 moved in together

Unit 59

59.1
1 He said I could **bring** Alice **along** if I liked.
2 He **asked** us **over/round** after the film. *Or* He **invited** us **around/round/over** after the film.
3 He said he would **pop in/into** the shop for some biscuits on the way home.
4 He said he loved **having** people **around/round/over**.
5 He said I could borrow the DVD if his friend **brought** it **round** before my party.

59.2
1 My parents are always asking **after** you, so I'll tell them your news next time I see them.
2 Do drop **in/round** some time when you're passing our house and have a cup of coffee.
3 My uncle has invited me and a friend **out** to a smart restaurant to celebrate my birthday.
4 Of course you can bring your brother **along** when you come to our place tomorrow.
5 I often call **round** and see my grandmother on my way home from work.
6 I hope I'm not in trouble. The boss has just asked me to pop **in** to her office (*or* pop **into** her office).

59.3
1 a) The speaker has to go upstairs to Owen's office.
   b) The speaker has to go downstairs to Owen's office.
2 a) The speaker plans to invite Alex and Ella to a meal at his or her home.
   b) The speaker plans to take Alex and Ella for a meal in a restaurant.

3 a) This visit sounds a little more formal than the visit in (b) and the visitors may ring Daisy first to check that the time is convenient.

b) This visit sounds more informal than the one suggested in (a) and Daisy is unlikely to know about it in advance.

4 a) The speaker is going to bring their niece to visit someone and may not stay during the visit.

b) The speaker's niece is going to accompany the speaker on a visit.

59.4 *Possible answers:*
Do call round and see me any time you are in the area.
Pop in and have some supper with me one evening.
Please come over and have dinner with me next weekend.
Do come round this weekend. It'd be great to see you.

59.5 stand someone up = fail to meet someone on purpose, especially someone with whom you were starting to have a romantic relationship
tag along = go somewhere with a person, especially when they have not asked you to go with them
run across someone = meet someone you know when you are not expecting to meet them

Unit 60

60.1 1 top   2 heat   3 thaw   4 pour   5 hand   6 measure

60.2 *Suggested answers:*
1 Jake: Yes, I think it's gone off.
2 Harry: Yes, we need something that will go (nicely) with it.
3 Lily: OK, I'll put them on.
4 Oliver: Yes, we'll have to make sure it doesn't boil over.
5 David: Good idea. It's ages since we last ate out.

60.3 1 be left over; noun: leftovers (Note that this noun is always plural.)
take away; noun: takeaway
top up; noun: top-up
2 hand round
3 live on *or* live off

60.4 1 leftovers   2 live on *or* live off   3 hand round *or* pass round   4 top-up
5 take it away   6 takeaway   7 was left over

60.5 *You can separate the verb and particle in the following sentences:*
1 Would you hand the peanuts round, please?
3 Don't forget to thaw the gateau out.

Unit 61

61.1 1 to cloud over   4 warmed up
2 cool down   5 clears up
3 has picked up *or* is picking up   6 brightens up *or* clears up

61.2 1 We were snowed in. We couldn't even open the front door.
2 We were flooded out. All our carpets were ruined.
3 The rain didn't let up. We ate our picnic in the car.
4 It cleared up later on. We went for a walk in the evening.
5 A strong wind picked up. Some trees got blown down.
6 The match was rained off. The teams were very disappointed.

61.3 1 downpour   5 were rained off
2 let up *or* clear up *or* brighten up   6 brightens up *or* clears up
3 flooded out   7 cool down
4 had blown over   8 warm up

61.4
1 more cheerful
2 angry
3 finish
4 better
5 more enjoyable
6 worried

Unit 62

62.1
1 Khalfan set off last Sunday. *Or* Khalfan set out last Sunday.
2 Harriet got on the plane in Dubai.
3 My journey started off in a very exciting way.

62.2
1 start
2 takes
3 touch
4 gets
5 check
6 check
7 stop
8 stop
9 carry-on
10 get

62.3

phrasal verb	noun/adjective form	example
touch down	touchdown	The plane burst into flames on touchdown.
check in	check-in	There was a long queue at the check-in.
get away	getaway	Police are trying to trace the getaway car.
take off	take-off	Please fasten your seatbelts for take-off.
stop over	stopover	We had a stopover in New York.

62.4 I **set off** for St Pancras station at 11 a.m. and there I **got on** the midday Eurostar train to Paris. It **pulled out** exactly on time and soon we were in the Channel Tunnel. After a couple of hours, we **pulled in** at Paris Gare du Nord station. Next day I **checked out of** my hotel and flew back. We **touched down** at Heathrow Airport at 11 a.m.

Unit 63

63.1
1 pull up *or* pull over
2 pick you up, drop you off
3 drew up *or* pulled up *or* pulled in
4 pulled up *or* drew up

63.2

words relating to moving and stopping the car or bike	words relating to accidents and traffic problems	words relating to transporting other people
draw up	knock down	drop off
pull up	run over	pick up
pull over	pile-up	
pull in	tailback	
pull into		
pull out		
pump up		

63.3 1 up   2 back   3 in   4 over   5 out   6 off

63.4 1 e   2 d   3 b   4 f   5 a   6 c

Unit 64

64.1 1 zoom   2 put   3 breaking   4 set   5 sign   6 bring

64.2 1 cut off   2 went off   3 used up   4 ran out

64.3 1 up   2 out   3 up   4 Scroll   5 on   6 plug

64.4 1 My phone went **off** in the job interview. I'd forgotten to switch it off!
2 If you **sign** up to our newsletter, we'll send you all our latest offers.
3 I got locked **out** of my email account and had to phone the IT helpdesk to help me reset my password.
4 I can't really see what's happening in that picture. Can you **zoom** in at all?
5 I can't **sign** in to my emails. It says the password is wrong.
6 My phone is very old and the battery **runs** out really quickly.

Unit 65

65.1 *Suggested answers:*
log on
type in your report
back up your work (Note that some people may choose to print out their work before they back it up.)
print out your work
log off

65.2 1 picking up   2 set up
3 back-up   4 printout

65.3 1 d   2 c   3 d   4 a   5 d   6 c

65.4 You'd use these computer accessories to:
1 key in some figures
2 print out a document
3 back up a report

Unit 66

66.1 1 False. Although to *flare up* can be used of fires or violence, here the context clearly means it is violence which has suddenly occurred.
2 True
3 True
4 False. It has not been published, but people have discovered what the report contains because someone has unofficially or illegally released the information.
5 False. They have withdrawn from the trade agreement.
6 True

66.2

phrasal verb	noun form
crack down	crackdown
break out (from prison)	breakout
break out (war, disease, etc.)	outbreak
break through	breakthrough
hide away	hideaway
flare up	flare-up
look out for	lookout*

*A lookout can be either a person or a place.

There is also a noun *outlook*, which means prospect or view, but it comes from a different sense of the phrasal verb *look out*, namely have a view over, e.g.
Our hotel room **looked out** over a park.
The **outlook** for the economy is very bad.

66.3 *Suggested answers:*

1 Hey, did you read that? A bomb **went off** in the capital last night, injuring six people.
2 Did you read that? Riots have **broken out** between the Northern tribes and the Southern League.
3 Did you see that? The rebels are beginning to **step up** their attacks on military bases.
  Or The rebels are beginning to **step** their attacks on military bases **up**.
  (Note that this sounds more awkward than the first version.)
4 Have you heard? The teachers' union has **broken off** talks with local government officials.
  Or The teachers' union has **broken** talks **off** with local government officials.
  (Note that this sounds more awkward than the first version.)
5 The police are advising villagers to **look out for** anything suspicious.
6 Wow! There's been a **breakout** at (*or* from) Gilston High Security Prison.

Unit 67

67.1
1 An old man was beaten up in his own home yesterday.
2 The thieves walked off with some priceless antique silver.
3 The burglars broke into the house by a side window.
4 The prisoner managed to break out in broad daylight.
5 The thieves held up a local bank yesterday.
6 Someone managed to hack into the computer system at work.

67.2
1 The man is breaking into a shop.
2 The judge is letting a criminal off. *Or* The judge is letting off a criminal.
3 He's tipping off the police. *Or* He's tipping the police off.
4 She's leaning on someone. *Or* She's putting someone up to something.

67.3
1 mixed up
2 putting him up
3 lean on *or* be leaning on
4 taken in *or* led on
5 let him off

67.4 1 c   2 b   3 d   4 a

Unit 68

68.1
1 stood, clamp
2 broke, entered
3 carried, bring
4 standing, sticking

68.2
1 Politician: No, we are determined to **go ahead** with our proposals.
2 Politician: We intend to **do away** with out-of-date committees and to modernise the whole committee structure to make it more efficient.
3 Politician: No, I do not. I and her many supporters are determined to **stick by** her in the face of these appalling and unfair attacks from the press.
4 Politician: Yes, the party fully backs Mr Carson **up**.

68.3
1 The People's Purple Party believes that the monarchy should be **done away with**.
2 The PPP aims to **bring in** legislation banning all hunting.
  Or The PPP aims to **bring** legislation **in** banning all hunting.
3 The PPP is determined to **clamp down on** smoking in public open spaces.
4 The leader of the PPP says nothing will stop the Party **carrying out** its aims.
  Or The leader of the PPP says nothing will stop the Party **carrying** its aims **out**.
5 He swears he will do all he can to **stand up for** the principles the PPP supports.
6 The PPP has got the **go-ahead** to hold a demonstration next week.

Unit 69

69.1
1 Would you like to wash up?   Sure. Where's the restroom?
2 What's wrong with the laptop?   Dunno. I can't figure out why it's not working.
3 Why is she so upset?   Her parents have just bawled her out.
4 Where's Rachel gone?   To visit with some friends.
5 Why d'you think you failed the test?   Because I goofed around so much.

69.2
1 shot through   2 got into   3 belt into   4 barrack for

69.3
1 I expect your grandmother will want to wash up when she arrives.
2 The teacher got into me for doing such a bad essay.
3 Will lost his job for goofing around at work.
4 Daria belted into the spring cleaning and the house was soon transformed.
5 Could you call around to find the cheapest place to rent a car?
6 I can't figure out why he's behaving so oddly.
7 He shot through last month and the police have been looking for him ever since.
8 I'll be ready soon. Wait up!
9 I'm visiting with my aunt at the weekend. Would you like to come too?

Unit 70

70.1
1 b   2 a   3 b   4 a   5 c   6 b   7 b   8 a

70.2
1 I will **touch on this area** later. At this point, I'm concerned only with the major theories.
2 To **go/come back to** the topic of pre-school education, this is clearly of growing importance to the government.
3 To **follow up on** the research conducted by Brukoff, I think that some of his conclusions require further investigation.
4 **Moving on to** the next section, I will describe the population changes in recent years.
5 To support my conclusion, I will **draw on** data collected from the last five years.

70.3
This essay **sets** out the main arguments about whether professional athletes are paid too much. I would like to **start** off by **defining** 'professional' athletes: these are people who are paid to do the job. I believe that the amount they are paid should **relate** to their skills and ability. It is also important to point **out** the fact that some sports are better paid than others. For example, if we focus **on** football, TV rights and sponsorship account for the higher levels of pay…

Mini dictionary

The numbers in the Mini dictionary are Unit numbers not page numbers.

act out sth to perform the actions and say the words of a situation or story *42*

allow for sth to consider or include something when you are making plans or judging a situation *37*

answer (sb) back if someone, especially a child, answers back, or answers someone back, they reply rudely to someone they should be polite to *20*

arrive at reach a result *70*

ask after sb/sth to ask for information about someone, especially about their health *59*

ask out sb or ask sb out to invite someone to come with you to a place such as the cinema or a restaurant, especially as a way of starting a romantic relationship *1, 52*

ask sb over/round to invite someone to come to your house *59*

back down to admit that you are wrong or that you have been defeated, often because you are forced to *38*

back off to stop being involved in a situation, especially in order to allow other people to deal with it themselves *34*

back out to decide not to do something that you were going to do or that you had agreed to do *38*

back up (sth) or back (sth) up to make a copy of computer information so that you do not lose it *65*

back up sb or back sb up to say that someone is telling the truth *38*

back up sb or back sb up to support or help someone *68*

back-up *n* an extra copy of computer information *65*

bang into sth to knock against something, usually by accident *21*

bank on sth to depend on something happening *34*

bargain for/on sth to expect something to happen and be prepared for it *37*

barrack for sb *informal, American & Australian* to shout encouragement to the players in a football team *69*

base on use ideas or information as a starting point for something else *70*

bash sth/sb about to treat something or someone in a rough way *18*

bawl out sb or bawl sb out *informal, American & Australian* to tell someone angrily that something they have done is wrong *69*

be booked up if an event, person, or place is booked up, they have no space or time available for someone *33*

be caught up in sth to be involved in a situation, often when you do not want to be *34*

be cut off to be a long way from other places and people *24*

be dying for sth *informal* to want something very much, especially food or drink *19*

be getting at sth *informal* if you ask someone what they are getting at, you are asking them what they mean, usually because they have expressed something indirectly *7*

be hung up *informal* to be very worried about something and spend a lot of time thinking about it *51*

be left over if an amount of money or food is left over, it remains when the rest has been used or eaten *60*

be left over to exist from an earlier time *23*

be littered with sth if something is littered with a particular type of thing, it has or contains a lot of that thing *32*

be mixed up in sth *informal* to be involved in an illegal or unpleasant activity *67*

be playing at sth if you ask what someone is playing at, you ask what they are doing, in a way which shows that you are surprised and angry *40*

be put out to be annoyed, often because of something that someone has done or said to you *11*

be rained off if a sport or other outside activity is rained off, it cannot start or continue because it is raining *61*

be set against sth/doing sth to be opposed to doing or having something *37*

be snowed in if a person or place is snowed in, there is so much snow that it is impossible to travel anywhere or leave that place *61*

be snowed under *informal* to have so much work that you have problems dealing with it *46*

be taken up with sth to be very busy doing something *12*

be thrown together if people are thrown together in a situation, that situation causes them to meet each other and to get to know each other *34*

be tied up *informal* to be busy so that you are unable to see or speak to anyone else or go anywhere *46*

be tucked away to be in a quiet or hidden place which not many people see or go to *24*

beat down sb/sth or beat sb/ sth down to force someone to reduce the price of something *48*

beat up sb or beat sb up to hurt someone badly by hitting or kicking them again and again *67*

become of sb/sth if you ask what became of someone or something, you want to know where they are and what happened to them *55*

belt into sth *Australian* to begin to do something quickly and with a lot of effort *69*

bend over backwards to do sth to try extremely hard to do something to help or please someone *30*

bite back to do something bad to someone because they have done something bad to you *20*

bite back sth or **bite sth back** to stop yourself from saying something that shows your real feelings or thoughts *20*

blend in or **blend into sth** if something or someone blends in, they look or seem the same as the things or people around them and so you do not notice them *32*

blocked-up *adj* filled with something so that nothing can pass through [used of a narrow space] *4, 56*

blow down (sth) or **blow (sth) down** if something blows down, or if the wind blows something down, that thing falls to the ground because the wind blows it *17*

blow over if a storm blows over, it becomes less strong and then ends *61*

blow over if an unpleasant situation [e.g. argument] blows over, it gradually becomes less important and is then forgotten *26*

blow up *informal* to suddenly become very angry *5*

blow up (sth/sb) or **blow (sth/ sb) up** to destroy something or kill someone with a bomb, or to be destroyed or killed with a bomb *5*

blow up sth or **blow sth up** to fill something [e.g. balloon, tyre] with air *5, 29*

boil over if a liquid that is being heated boils over, it flows over the side of the pan *17, 60*

booked up if an event, person, or place is booked up, they have no space or time available for someone *33*

bottle out *informal, British* to suddenly decide not to do something because you are afraid *36*

bottle up sth or **bottle sth up** *informal* to not allow yourself to show or talk about your feelings, especially feelings of anger and sadness *51*

bounce back if an e-mail bounces back, it comes back to you because the address is wrong or there is a computer problem *20*

branch out to start to do something different from what you usually do, especially in your job *46*

break away to stop being part of a group because you disagree with them or because you do not want to be controlled by them *68*

break down if a machine or vehicle breaks down, it stops working *1, 2*

break down to be unable to control your feelings and to start to cry *51*

break down to become mentally or physically ill because of an unpleasant experience *56*

break in to get into a building or car by using force, usually in order to steal something *4*

break-in *n* when someone forces their way into a building or car, usually to steal something *4, 67*

break into sth to get into a building or car by using force, usually in order to steal something *67*

break off to suddenly stop speaking *15*

break off (sth) or **break (sth) off** to stop doing something *28*

break off (sth) or **break (sth) off** if discussions between two groups of people break off, or if someone breaks them off, they end suddenly, before they have been completed *66*

break off sth or **break sth off** to end a relationship *53*

break off with sb to end a romantic relationship with someone *53*

break out if something dangerous and unpleasant [e.g. war, disease, fire] breaks out, it suddenly starts *66*

outbreak *n* when something unpleasant or difficult to control starts, such as war or disease *66*

break out to escape from prison *67*

breakout *n* an escape *66, 67*

break through sth to succeed in dealing with a problem or difficult situation *66*

breakthrough *n* an important discovery or success that helps you achieve or deal with something *4, 66*

break up if a marriage breaks up, or if two people who have a romantic relationship break up, their marriage or relationship ends *53*

break up if schools or universities, or the people who study or work in them break up, classes end and the holidays start *43*

break up if someone who is talking on a mobile phone is breaking up, their voice cannot be heard *50, 64*

break-up *n* the act or event of breaking up *53*

brighten up to suddenly look or feel happier *51*

brighten up if the weather brightens up, the sky becomes lighter and the sun starts to shine *61*

brighten up sth or **brighten sth up** to make somewhere more attractive, often by adding colours *24*

bring about sth or **bring sth about** try extremely hard to do something to help or please someone to make something happen *25*

bring along sb/sth or **bring sb/ sth along** to bring someone or something somewhere *59*

bring around/round sb/sth or **bring sb/sth around/round** to bring someone or something somewhere, especially to someone's house *59*

bring sb around/round to persuade someone to agree with you or to do what you want them to do *39*

bring back sth or bring sth back to make someone remember or think about something from the past *1, 25*

bring down sb or bring sb down to cause people in positions of power [e.g. government, president] to lose their position *66*

bring forward sth or bring sth forward to change the date or time of an event so that it happens earlier than planned *22*

bring in sth or bring sth in if a government or organisation brings in something new [e.g. law, rule], they make it exist for the first time *68*

bring off sth or bring sth off to succeed in doing something difficult *27*

bring round/around sb/sth or bring sb/sth round/around see **bring around/round bring up sb or bring sb up** to look after a child and educate them until they are old enough to look after themselves *55*

bring together collect *70*

bring up sth or bring sth up to start to talk about a particular subject, or open something on a screen *1, 31, 64*

brush aside sb/sth or brush sb/sth aside to refuse to listen to what someone says, or to refuse to think about something seriously *2, 39*

brush up (on) sth to practise and improve your skills or your knowledge of something that you learned in the past but have partly forgotten *43*

bubble over to be very excited and enthusiastic *31*

build on sth to use a success or achievement as a base from which to achieve more success *27*

bump into sb to meet someone you know when you had not planned to meet them *21*

burn off sth or burn sth off to use or get rid of energy or something which provides energy [e.g. calories, fat], by doing a lot of physical exercise *57*

burnout *n* illness or extreme tiredness because you have been working too hard *14*

burst into sth to suddenly start to make a noise, especially to start crying, laughing or singing *21*

butt in to interrupt a conversation or discussion or someone who is talking *31*

buy into sth *informal* to completely believe in a set of ideas *21*

bygone *adj* from the past *23*

bystander *n* a person who sees something happening but who is not involved *4*

call around/round (sb) to call several people, often in order to find out information *50*

call back to go back to a place in order to visit someone or collect something that you were unable to visit or collect earlier *24*

call back/round (sb) or call (sb) back to call someone for the second time or to call someone who called you earlier *20, 50*

call for sb to visit a place in order to collect someone *19*

call for sth to need or deserve a particular action or quality *36*

call for sth to say that you think a particular thing should be done, usually in order to change or improve a situation *39*

call in *British & American* to visit a place or person for a short time, usually while you are going somewhere else *16*

call in to call someone at your place of work, usually to explain why you are not there *50*

call off sth or call sth off to decide that a planned event or activity will not happen, especially because it is no longer possible or useful *1, 2, 33*

call off sth or call sth off to decide to stop an activity that has already started *5, 28*

call round *British & American* to visit someone who lives near to you for a short time *59*

call up (sb) or call (sb) up to call someone *50*

calm down (sb) or calm (sb) down to stop feeling upset, angry, or excited, or to make someone stop feeling this way *51*

calm down (sth) or calm (sth) down if a situation calms down, or if you calm it down, it becomes more peaceful *34*

can't/couldn't get over sth if someone can't get over something, they are very surprised or shocked that something has happened or that something is true *7*

care for sb to look after someone who is too young, too old, or too ill to look after themselves *56*

carried away to become so excited about something that you do not control what you say or do and you forget about everything else *51*

carry on to continue doing something *55*

carry-on *n* a small case or bag that you take on a plane with you *62*

carry out sth or carry sth out to do or complete something, especially something important *45*

carry out sth or carry sth out if you carry out something that you said you would do, or that you have been told to do [e.g. instructions, order, threat], you do it *68*

cashback *n* money from your bank account that you can get from a shop when you buy goods with a debit card *20*

catch on to become popular *27*

catch up to reach the same quality or standard as someone or something else *27, 42*

catch up on/with sth to do something you did not have time to do earlier *46*

catch up with sb to meet someone you know, after not seeing them for a period of time *19*

caught up in sth to be involved in a situation, often when you do not want to be *34*

changeover *n* a complete change from one system or method to another *4, 26*

chase up sb or chase sb up to ask someone to do something that they said they would do but that they have not done yet *46*

chase up sth or chase sth up to try to get something that belongs to you or that you need, or to try to discover more information about something *2*

chat up sb or chat sb up *informal, British & Australian* to talk to someone in a way that shows them that you are sexually attracted to them and to try to make them attracted to you *52*

chat-up *n informal* a way of talking which suggests you are sexually attracted to someone and want them to be attracted to you *52*

check in to show your ticket at an airport so that you can be told where you are sitting and so that your bags can be put on the aircraft *62*

check in or check into sth to arrive at a hotel and say who you are so that you can be given a key for your room *62*

check-in *n* the place at an airport where you go to say that you have arrived for your flight *4, 62*

check out to leave a hotel after paying and giving back the key of your room *62*

checkout *n* the place where you pay for things in a big shop *4*

check over sth/sb or check sth/sb over to examine something or someone to make sure that they are correct, healthy or working properly *17*

check up on sb to discover what someone is doing in order to be certain that they are doing what they should be doing or what they said they would do *35*

cheer up (sb) or cheer (sb) up if someone cheers up, or if someone or something cheers them up, they start to feel happier *51*

chicken out *informal* to decide not to do something you had planned to do because you are too frightened *37*

chop down sth or chop sth down to cut through a tree or a group of trees so that they fall to the ground *17*

chop up sth or chop sth up to cut something, especially food, into small pieces *13*

clamp down if someone in authority clamps down, they do something in order to stop or limit a particular activity *68*

clampdown *n* a sudden action taken by a government or people in authority to stop or limit a particular activity *68*

clean off to remove writing from something by cleaning it with a cloth *42*

clear off *informal* to leave a place quickly *15*

clear out sth or clear sth out to make a place tidy by removing things that are unwanted *14*

clear up if the weather clears up, it improves *61*

clear up (sth) or clear (sth) up to make a place tidy and clean, especially by putting things where they usually belong *5, 13*

click on sth to carry out a computer operation by pressing a button on the mouse or keyboard *65*

clock in/on to record the time you arrive at work, usually on a machine with a clock *22*

clock off/out to record the time you leave work, usually on a machine with a clock *22*

clog up (sth) or clog (sth) up if something [e.g. road, pipe] clogs up, or if something clogs it up, it becomes blocked and nothing in it is able to move *13*

close down (sth) or close (sth) down if a business or organisation closes down, or if someone or something closes it down, it stops doing business *17*

cloud over if the sky clouds over, it becomes covered with clouds *61*

club together if a group of people club together, they share the cost of something between them *48*

come about when you say how or why something comes about, especially something which is not planned, you explain how or why it happens *6*

come across sth/sb to discover something by chance, or to meet someone by chance *1, 6*

come along to arrive at a place *6*

come apart if something comes apart, it separates into pieces *6*

come around/round to become conscious again *2, 6*

come around/round to visit someone at their house *2, 59*

come back to sth to start talking about a particular subject again *31, 70*

come down to sth if a situation or decision comes down to something, that is the thing that will influence it most *6*

come down with sth to become ill, usually with a disease that is not very serious *56*

come off to happen successfully or as planned *6, 27*

Come off it! *informal* something that you say in order to tell someone that you do not believe them or that you disagree with them *41*

Come on! something that you say to someone in order to encourage them to do something you want them to do, especially to hurry up, to try harder, or to tell you something *41*

come out if dirt or colour comes out of something, especially clothing or cloth, it disappears or becomes less strong after being in water *6*

come out if someone who has been in prison or hospital comes out, they leave *6*

come out if the truth about something comes out, it becomes known publicly after it has been kept secret *6*

come out if results or information come out, they are given to people *6*

come out if something that is published [e.g. book, newspaper], a musical recording [e.g. single, album], or a film comes out, it becomes available for people to buy or see it *14*

come over to visit someone at their house *59*

come round/around see **come around/round come to sth** if you come to a decision or a conclusion, you make a decision about something, or you decide what you think about something *6*

come to sth to be a particular total when amounts or numbers are added together, or reach a result *47, 70*

come under sth if a piece of information comes under a particular part of a list, book, or collection of things, you can find it in that part *35*

come up if a subject [e.g. issue, name] comes up in a conversation, it is discussed or mentioned *6*

come up if a job or opportunity comes up, it becomes available *6*

come up if a problem or difficult situation comes up, it happens when you do not expect it *6*

come up if a question or a subject comes up in an exam, that question is asked or questions about that subject are asked in the exam *43*

come up against sth/sb to have to deal with a difficult situation or someone who disagrees with you or tries to stop you doing what you want to do *1, 6*

come up with sth to think of or to suggest a plan or idea, a solution to a problem, or an answer to a question *36*

cool down (sb/sth) or cool (sb/ sth) down to become cooler, or to make someone or something become cooler *57, 61*

cool down/off (sb/sth) or cool (sb/ sth) down/off to become calmer, or to make someone or something become calmer *51, 61*

could do with sth/sb to need or want something or someone *45*

could do without sth *informal* something you say when something is annoying you or causing problems for you, because your situation at that time makes it difficult for you to deal with it *37*

couldn't ask for sb/sth if you say that you couldn't ask for someone or something better, you mean that that person or thing is the best of their kind *19*

count on sb to have confidence in someone because you know that they will do what you want *16*

cover-up *n* an attempt to stop people discovering the truth about something bad *4*

crack down if someone in authority [e.g. police, government] cracks down, they start treating people much more strictly in order to try to stop them from doing things they should not do *17, 66*

crackdown *n* when bad or illegal behaviour is dealt with in a very severe way, in order to stop it happening *66*

cram in/into if a lot of people or animals cram in or cram into a place, they all go into it even though it is too small for all of them and becomes very full *33*

crop up if a problem crops up, it suddenly happens, often when it is not expected *34*

crop up if something, especially a word, crops up, it appears, often in something that you read, hear, or see *44*

cross out sth or cross sth out to draw a line through something that you have written, usually because it is wrong *42*

cut back (sth) or cut (sth) back to reduce the amount of money that is being spent on something *47*

cutback *n* a reduction in the amount of money that is being spent on something *4*

cut down to eat or drink less of a particular thing, usually in order to improve your health *17*

cut down sth or cut sth down if you cut down a tree or a bush, you make it fall to the ground by cutting it near the bottom *17*

cut down sth or cut sth down to reduce the amount or number of something *28*

cut off sb or cut sb off to stop people from continuing a phone or Internet conversation by breaking the connection *50*

cut off sb/sth or cut sb/sth off to prevent people from reaching a place or leaving a place *2*

cut off to be a long way from other places and people *24*

cut out if an engine, machine or piece of equipment cuts out, it suddenly stops working *2*

cut out sth or cut sth out to remove something by cutting, especially something made of paper or cloth *2, 14*

cut out sth or cut sth out to remove part of a piece of writing *44*

date back to have existed since a particular time *23*

dawn on sb if a fact dawns on you, you realise or understand something after a period of time when you did not realise or understand it *36*

deal with sth if something [e.g. book, film, article] deals with a particular subject or idea, it is about that subject or idea *19*

deal with sth to take action in order to achieve something, or in order to solve a problem *31, 36*

depend on sb/sth to trust someone or something and know that they will help you or do what you expect them to do *16*

die for sth *informal* see **be dying for sth** *19*

dip into sth to read small parts of a book or magazine *44*

divide up (sth) or divide (sth) up to separate something into smaller parts or groups, or to form smaller parts or groups *13*

do away with sth to get rid of something, or to stop using something *1, 68*

do up sth or do sth up to fasten something *32*

do with see **could do with sth/sb** to need or want something or someone *45*

do without (sth/sb) to manage without something or someone *37* see **could do without sth/sb**

dotted around if people or things are dotted around, they are in different parts of an area and are not close together *24*

downfall *n* the sudden failure of a person or organisation, or something that causes this *4, 27*

downpour *n* a sudden, heavy fall of rain *61*

doze off *informal* to gradually start to sleep, especially during the day *15*

drag on if an unpleasant or difficult situation or process drags on, it continues for too long *23*

draw on sth to use information or your knowledge or experience

of something to help you do something *35*

draw together collect *70*

draw up if a vehicle, or someone in a vehicle, draws up, they arrive somewhere and stop *63*

dress up (sb) or dress (sb) up to put on formal or special clothes for a special occasion, or to put them on someone else *2, 32*

drift apart if two friends drift apart, they gradually become less friendly and their relationship ends *53*

drink up (sth) or drink (sth) up to completely finish your drink *13*

drop around/round *informal* to make a short visit to someone in their home, usually without arranging it before *59*

drop around/round sth or drop sth around/round *informal* to deliver something, usually something small *59*

drop in to make a short visit to someone in their home, usually without arranging it before *59*

drop off sb/sth or drop sb/sth off to take someone to a place that they want to go to, or to deliver something to a place, usually in a car, often when you are going somewhere else *1, 63*

drop out if a student drops out, they stop going to classes before they have finished their course *4, 43, 55*

dropout *n* a person who leaves school or college before finishing a course *4*

drop round/around see **drop around/round**

dry up if a supply of something dries up, it ends *28*

dry up to stop speaking when you are acting or making a speech, especially because you suddenly forget what to say next *31*

dying for sth *informal* to want something very much, especially food or drink *19*

eat out to eat a meal in a restaurant, not at home *1, 60*

eat up sth or eat sth up to eat all the food you have been given *13*

email back (sb) or email (sb) back to send a reply to someone by email, usually a reply to an email someone has sent you *20*

end up to finally be in a particular place, state, or situation, especially without having planned it *55*

end up doing sth to finally do something, especially without having planned to *55*

enter into sth to start to become involved in something, especially a discussion *21*

enter into sth if you enter into an agreement, you officially agree to something *68*

face up to sth to accept that a difficult or unpleasant situation exists *36*

fall apart if something falls apart, it breaks or breaks into pieces because it is old or weak *30*

fall behind (sth/sb) to fail to develop at the same rate as something else, or to fail to achieve a standard reached by other people *42*

fall down to fail because of not being satisfactory for a particular purpose *4*

fall down to fall to the ground *29*

fall for sb/sth *informal* to be attracted to someone or something *52*

fall for sth to be tricked into believing something that is not true *2, 39*

fall out to argue with someone and stop being friendly with them *38, 52*

falling-out *n informal* an argument *52*

fall over if someone falls over, they fall to the ground *3, 17*

fall through if a plan or agreement falls through, it fails to happen *27*

feel for sb to feel sorry for someone because they are very unhappy or in a difficult situation *51*

fight back to defend yourself when someone or something attacks you or causes problems for you *30*

fight off sth or fight sth off to try hard to get rid of something unpleasant or unwanted, especially an illness or bad emotions *56*

figure out sth or figure sth out *American* to understand something or someone, or to find the answer to something by thinking carefully *69*

fill in sb or fill sb in to tell someone about the things that have happened while they have not been there, or to give someone the information they need in order to do something *45*

fill in sth or fill sth in to write or record the necessary information on an official document [e.g. form, questionnaire] *44*

fill out sth or fill sth out to write or record the necessary information on an official document [e.g. form, questionnaire] *44*

fill up (sth) or fill (sth) up to become full, or to make something become full *26*

filter out to pass information through a device to remove unwanted information *65*

find out (sth) or find (sth) out to get information about something because you want to know more about it, or to learn a fact or piece of information for the first time *35*

finish off sth or finish sth off to complete the last part of something that you are doing *28*

finish with sb *informal, British & Australian* to end a romantic relationship with someone *53*

Fire away! *informal* something that you say in order to tell someone that you are ready for them to start asking you questions, or to start speaking *41*

fit in to feel happy in a group of people because you are similar to them *52*

fit in sb/sth or fit sb/sth in to find time to do something or see someone *22*

fix up sb/sth or fix sb/sth up to provide or arrange something for someone *45*

fizzle out to gradually end or disappear, especially in a disappointing way *28*

flare up if something [e.g. violence, argument, anger] flares up, it suddenly happens and becomes very serious *66*

flick through sth to look briefly at the pages of something [e.g. book, magazine] *20*

flood out sb or flood sb out to force someone to leave their home because of floods *61*

follow up sth or follow sth up to do something in order to make the effect of an earlier action or thing stronger or more certain *45*

follow up on sth give more information about something mentioned before *70*

fool around to spend time having fun or behaving in a silly way *18*

fork out sth or fork sth out *informal* to pay or give money for something, especially when you do not want to *48*

free up to make something available to be used *65*

freshen up to quickly wash yourself so that you feel clean *32, 69*

get across sth or get sth across to successfully communicate an idea to other people *31*

get ahead to be successful in the work that you do *45*

get along if two or more people get along, they like each other and are friendly to each other *52*

get around/round sth to find a way of dealing with or avoiding a problem *7*

get around/round to sth/doing sth to do something that you have intended to do for a long time *7*

get at sth see **be getting at sth** *7*

get away to leave a place or person, often when the situation makes it difficult for you to do this *2, 7*

get away to go somewhere to have a holiday, especially because you need to rest *62*

getaway *adj* used to escape something or someone *62*

get away with sth/doing sth to do something successfully even though it is not the best way of doing it *1, 7*

get away with sth/doing sth to succeed in not being criticised or punished for something wrong that you have done *7*

get sth back or get back sth if you get something back, something that you had before is given to you again *47*

get back to sb if you get back to someone, you communicate with them, usually to give them information that you were not able to give them before *50*

get behind if you get behind with work or with payments, you have not done as much work or paid as much money as you should by a particular time *7*

get by to have just enough money to pay for the things that you need, but nothing more *7*

get carried away to become so excited about something that you do not control what you say or do and you forget about everything else *51*

get cut off (during a phone call) lose the connection *64*

get down sth or get sth down to get something that is above your head by reaching with your hand *29*

get down to sth/doing sth to start doing something seriously and with a lot of your attention and effort *5*

get in if a train, plane, or other vehicle gets in at a particular time, that is when it arrives *62*

get into sb *informal, Australian* to criticise someone *69*

get locked out (of an account) be unable to enter it *64*

get mixed up in sth to become involved in an illegal or bad activity *67*

get off (sth) to leave a bus, train, aircraft, or boat *62*

get on if two or more people get on, they like each other and are friendly to each other *2, 5, 7*

get on to continue doing something, especially work *5, 7*

get on (sth) to go onto a bus, train, aircraft, or boat *2, 5, 62*

get on to/onto sth to start talking about a subject after discussing something else *31*

get out to move out of a vehicle *63*

get out of sth/doing sth to avoid doing something that you should do, often by giving an excuse *34*

get over sth to begin to feel better after an experience that has made you unhappy *17, 26* see **can't/couldn't get over sth get sth over with** to do and complete something difficult or unpleasant that must be done *7*

get round/around see **get around/round get through** to manage to talk to someone on the phone or Internet *50*

get through to sb to succeed in making someone understand or believe something *31*

get to sb *informal* to make someone feel upset or angry *38*

get together (sb) or get (sb) together if two or more people get together, or if someone gets two or more people together, they meet in order to do something or spend time together *7*

get (sb) up to wake up and get out of bed, or to make someone do this *58*

getting at sth *informal* if you ask someone what they are getting at, you are asking them what they mean, usually because they have expressed something indirectly *7*

give away sth or give sth away to give something to someone without asking for payment *47*

give in to finally agree to what someone wants after a period when you refuse to agree *2, 38*

give in to accept that you have been defeated and agree to stop competing or fighting *57*

give in sth or give sth in to give a piece of written work or a document to someone for them to read, judge, or deal with *2, 42*

give out sth or give sth out to give something to a large number of people *42*

give up to stop trying to think of the answer to a joke or question *35*

give up (sth) or give (sth) up if you give up a habit [e.g. smoking, drinking] or give up something unhealthy [e.g. cigarettes, alcohol], you stop doing it or having it *26, 28*

give up sth or give sth up to stop doing a regular activity or a job *28*

give up (sth/doing sth) or give (sth) up to stop doing an activity or piece of work before you have completed it, usually because it is too difficult *28*

go about doing sth if someone goes about doing something for a long time, they spend their time behaving badly or doing something that is unpleasant for other people *8*

go about sth/doing sth to start to do something or deal with something *8*

go against sth/sb to do the opposite of what someone has asked or advised you to do *2*

go ahead to start to do something *68*

go-ahead *n* permission for something to start *68*

go along with sth/sb to support an idea, or to agree with someone's opinion *8*

go back if schools or students go back, the schools are open and the students start going to lessons again after the holidays *43*

go back sth *informal* if people go back a number of years, they have been friends for that many years or since that time *20*

go back on sth to not do something that you promised or said you would do *54*

go back to refer back to *70*

go by if time goes by, it passes *23*

bygone *adj* from the past *23*

go down to become lower in level *2*

go down with sth *informal, British* to become ill, usually with a disease that is not very serious *56*

go for sth to choose something *8*

go for sth to try to get or achieve something *19, 57*

go for sth/sb to like a particular type of thing or person *52*

go forward to win one stage of a competition and compete in another stage *57*

go in for sth to compete in a competition, or to do an exam *8*

go into sth to describe, discuss, or examine something in a detailed way *21*

go off to leave a place and go somewhere else *8*

go off if food or drink goes off, it is not good to eat or drink any more because it is too old *8, 60*

go off if a warning device [e.g. alarm] goes off, it suddenly makes a loud noise *64*

go off if a bomb or gun goes off, it explodes or fires *66*

go on to continue to exist or happen *8*

go on to continue doing something *8*

go on to happen *8*

go on to talk in an annoying way about something for a long time *8*

Go on! *informal* something that you say to encourage someone to do something *8, 41*

goings-on *n* strange or amusing events *4*

go out if a light goes out, it stops giving light 8

go out *British* to lose when you are playing in a sports competition, so that you must stop playing in the competition 57

go out with sb to have a romantic relationship with someone 52

go over sth to talk or think about something in order to explain it or make sure that it is correct 17

go through sth to experience an unpleasant or difficult situation or event 2, 8

go through sth to carefully examine the contents of something or a collection of things in order to find something 8

go through sth to carefully read or discuss every part of something in order to make sure that it is correct or acceptable 17, 20

go through with sth to do something unpleasant or difficult which you have planned or promised to do 8

go together if two types of thing or people go together, they are usually found with each other 8

go together if two pieces of clothing or two types of food go together, they look or taste good when you wear or eat them at the same time 32

go under if a company or business goes under, it fails financially 49

go up if an amount, rate, or standard goes up, it rises 26

go with sth if one thing goes with another, they suit each other or they look or taste good together 19, 60

go without (sth) to not have something which you usually have 8

goings-on *n* strange or amusing events 4

goof around/off *informal, American* to avoid doing any work 69

grow apart if people who are good friends grow apart, they gradually become less friendly, often because they do not have the same interests and opinions any more 53

grow on sb *informal* if something or someone grows on you, you like them more and more, although you did not like them at first 51

grow up to gradually change from being a child to being an adult 55

hack into sth to get into someone else's computer system without permission in order to look at information or do something illegal 67

hand down sth or hand sth down to give or teach something to someone who will be alive after you have died 55

hand in sth or hand sth in to give a piece of written work [e.g. essay] to a teacher 42

hand out sth or hand sth out to give something to each person in a group of people 42

handout *n* a piece of paper that is given to people who go to a talk or class and which has information on it about the subject dealt with in the talk or class 4, 42

hand over sth or hand sth over to give something to someone else 17

hand over (sth/sb) or hand (sth/sb) over to give someone else responsibility for or control of something or someone 45

hand round sth or hand sth round to offer something, especially food or drink, to each person in a group of people 60

hang about/around/round (swh) *informal* to spend time somewhere, usually without doing very much 18

hang on *informal* to wait, especially for a short time 22

Hang on! *informal* something that you say when you are confused or surprised by something and you need to think 41

hang out/around/round swh or with sb *informal* to spend a lot of time in a particular place, or to spend a lot of time with someone 22

hang up to end a telephone conversation, often suddenly, by putting the part of the phone call 50

hang up *informal* see **hung up** 51

hang up sth or hang sth up to hang something, especially clothes, on a hook 13

hang-up *n informal* a feeling of embarrassment or fear about something, often when it is not necessary to feel that way 51

have it out with sb *informal* to talk to someone about something that they have said or done that has made you angry in order to improve the situation 54

have sb around/round if you have someone around, they come to your house for a social visit 59

have sb on to persuade someone that something is true when it is not, usually as a joke 39

have sth on to have an arrangement to do something 37

have sb over if you have someone over, they come to your house to visit you 59

head off to start a journey or leave a place 15

heat up (sth) or heat (sth) up to become warm or hot, or to make something warmer or hotter 26

heat up sth or heat sth up to make food hot so that it can be eaten 60

help out (sb) or help (sb) out to help someone, especially by giving them money or by doing work for them 14

help sb off with sth to help someone remove a piece of outer clothing [e.g. coat] 29

help sb on with sth to help someone to put on a piece of clothing 29

hide away to go to a place

where other people will not find you 66

hideaway n a place where someone goes to be alone 66

hire out sth or **hire sth out** British & Australian to allow someone to use something for a short period of time after they have paid you money 49

hit back to criticise or attack someone who has criticised or attacked you 40

hit it off if two or more people hit it off, they like each other and become friendly immediately 52

hold sth against sb to like or respect someone less because they have done something wrong or behaved badly 38

hold down sth or **hold sth down** to control the level of something [e.g. prices, costs, inflation] and to prevent it from increasing 17

hold off (sth/doing sth) to delay something or doing something 15

hold on to wait for a short time 41, 50

Hold on! something you say to show that you are surprised or confused about something and that you need time to think about it for a short time 41

hold up sth/sb or **hold sth/sb up** to delay something or someone 23

hold up sth/sb or **hold sth/sb up** to steal money from a building [e.g. bank], a person, or a vehicle, by using violence or by threatening to use violence 67

hold-up n a delay 23

hold-up n when someone steals from someone else using violence or the threat of violence 67

hot up informal if an event or situation hots up, it becomes more exciting and there is a lot more activity 34

hung up informal to be very worried about something and spend a lot of time thinking about it 51

hurry up to do something more quickly 41

hurry up sb/sth or **hurry sb/ sth up** to make someone do something more quickly, or to make something happen sooner 23

invite along sb or **invite sb along** to ask someone if they would like to go with you to an event or activity 3

invite around/round sb or **invite sb around/round** to ask someone to come to your home 3, 59

invite back sb or **invite sb back** to ask someone to come to your home after you have been out somewhere together 3

invite in sb or **invite sb in** to ask someone if they would like to come into your house 3

invite out sb or **invite sb out** to ask someone to go with you to a place, for example a restaurant or the cinema 3, 59

invite over sb or **invite sb over** to ask someone to come to your home 3, 59

invite up sb or **invite sb up** to ask someone if they would like to come upstairs 3

join in (sth) to become involved in an activity with other people 57

jot down sth or **jot sth down** to write or record something quickly on a piece of paper or an electronic device so that you remember it 44

jumble up sth or **jumble sth up** to mix things together in an untidy way 13

jump at sth to eagerly accept a chance to do or have something 51

jump out at sb if something jumps out at you, you notice it immediately 36

keep (sb) at sth to continue working hard at something difficult or something which takes a long time, or to make someone continue to work hard 46

keep away (sb/sth) or **keep (sb/ sth) away** to not go somewhere or near something, or to prevent someone or something from going somewhere or near something 21

keep down sth or **keep sth down** to stop the number, level, or size of something from increasing 17

keep on at sb to talk to someone about something many times, usually because you want to complain about something they have done or not done 54

keep on doing sth to continue to do something, or to do something again and again 2, 16

keep sth from sb to not tell someone about something 54

keep to sth to do what you have promised or planned to do 31

keep up to go at the same speed as someone or something that is moving forward, so that you stay level with them 23

keep up to increase or to make progress at the same speed as something or someone else so that you stay at the same level as them 27

keep up sth or **keep sth up** to practise a skill that you learned in the past so that you continue to be good at it 43

keep it up to continue to do something, especially to work hard or to do good work 41

key in sth or **key sth in** to put information into a computer using a keyboard 65

kick-off n the time when a football match begins 57

knock down sb or **knock sb down** to hit someone with a vehicle and injure or kill them 63

knockdown adj very low (in price) 47

knock off (sth) informal to stop working, usually at the end of a day 45

knock off sth or knock sth off (sth) to take a particular amount away from something, especially a price *48*

knock out to defeat a person or team in a competition so that they have to stop taking part in it *57*

knockout *n* a competition in which only the winners of each stage play in the next stage, until one person or team is the final winner *57*

knock over sth/sb or knock sth/sb over to hit or push something or someone, especially accidentally, so that they fall to the ground or onto their side *17, 30*

latch on *informal, British & Australian* to understand something *35*

latch on to/onto sb to spend time with someone, especially when they do not want you with them *22*

laugh off sth or laugh sth off to laugh about something unpleasant in order to make it seem less important or serious *15*

launch into sth to start doing or saying something [e.g. speech, story] in a very enthusiastic way *21*

lay into sb to attack or criticise someone in an angry way *40, 69*

lay off sb or lay sb off to stop employing someone because there is no work for them to do *45*

laze about/around to relax and enjoy yourself by doing very little *18*

lead on sb or lead sb on to make someone believe something that is not true *67*

leak out if secret information leaks out, people who should not know this information find out about it *66*

lean on sb *informal* to try to make someone do what you want by threatening or persuading them *67*

leave aside sth or leave sth aside to not discuss or consider a particular subject so that you can discuss a different subject *31*

leave behind sth/sb or leave sth/ sb behind to leave a place without taking something or someone with you, either because you have forgotten them or because you cannot take them with you *24*

leave out sb/sth or leave sb/sth out to not include someone or something *2, 14*

leave sb to sth *informal* to go away from someone so that they do something by themselves or so they can continue what they are doing *45*

left over if an amount of money or food is left over, it remains when the rest has been used or eaten *60*

left over to exist from an earlier time *23*

leftover *adj* existing from an earlier time *23*

leftovers *n* food that was prepared for a meal but not eaten *4, 60*

let down sb or let sb down to disappoint someone by failing to do what you agreed to do or what you were expected to do *53*

let off sb or let sb off to not punish someone who has committed a crime or done something wrong, or to not punish someone severely *67*

let on to tell someone about something which was supposed to be a secret *54*

let out sb/sth or let sb/sth out to allow a person or animal to leave somewhere, especially by opening a locked or closed door *14*

let-out *n* an excuse or way of avoiding doing something you agreed to do *36*

let up *informal* if bad weather or an unpleasant situation lets up, it stops or improves *5, 61*

lie about/around *informal* to spend time lying down and doing very little *18*

lie ahead if an event or situation that will cause problems lies ahead, it will happen in the future *23*

lie behind sth to be the real reason for something *25*

lie in *British & Australian* to stay in bed in the morning later than you usually do *58*

lie in sth to exist or be found in something *36*

lie-in *n British & Australian* when you stay in bed in the morning longer than usual *58*

lift off if a spacecraft or aircraft lifts off, it leaves the ground *15*

lift-off *n* the moment when a spacecraft leaves the ground *15*

lighten up to become more relaxed and less serious *41*

Lighten up! *informal* something you say to tell someone to stop being so serious or annoyed *41*

listen in to secretly listen to a conversation, especially a phone or Internet conversation *50*

Listen up! *informal, American* something you say to tell people to listen to what you are going to say *69*

littered with sth if something is littered with a particular type of thing, it has or contains a lot of that thing *32*

live down sth or live sth down to stop feeling embarrassed about something you have done by waiting until people forget about it *53*

live for sth/sb to believe that something or someone is the most important thing or person in your life *19*

live off sth to only eat a particular type of food *60*

live off sth/sb to have enough money for the things you need by taking it from a supply of money or from another person *58*

live on sth to have a particular amount of money in order to buy the things you need 58

live on sth to only eat a particular type of food 60

live through sth to experience a difficult situation or event 20

live up to sth if someone or something lives up to people's expectations or a particular standard, they are as good as they were expected to be 55

liven up (sth) or liven (sth) up to become more interesting and exciting, or to make something become like this 13

load down sb or load sb down to give someone too many things to carry 17

load up (sth) or load (sth) up to put a lot of things into a vehicle or machine 13

lock yourself away to go to a room or building where you can be alone, usually so that you can work 21

lock in sb or lock sb in to prevent someone from leaving a room or building by locking the door 16

lock out sb or lock sb out to prevent someone from entering a building by locking the door 14

lock yourself out to accidentally prevent yourself from getting into a building or vehicle by leaving the keys inside when you shut the door 14

log in to connect a computer to a system of computers by typing your name, usually so that you can start working 65

log off (sth) to stop a computer being connected to a computer system, usually when you want to stop working 65

log on to connect a computer to a system of computers by typing your name, usually so that you can start working 65

log out to stop a computer being connected to a computer system, usually when you want to stop working 65

look after sb/sth to take care of someone or something by doing what is needed to keep them well or in good condition 1, 9

look ahead to think about what will happen in the future and plan for these events 9

look around/round to try to find something you want [e.g. job] by asking different people or by looking in different places 9

look around/round (swh) to walk through a building or around a place and look at the things in it 18

look at sth to consider a subject carefully in order to make a decision about it 9

look at sth to read something quickly and not very carefully 9

look back to think about or remember something that happened in the past 2

look down on sb/sth to think that someone is less important than you, or to think that something is not good enough quality for you to use 1, 9

look for sth/sb to try to find something or someone, either because you have lost them or because you need them 3

look forward to sth/doing sth to feel pleased and excited about something that is going to happen 1, 9

look into sth to discover and examine the facts about a problem or situation 9, 21

look on to watch an activity or event without becoming involved in it 4, 9

onlooker n a person who watches an activity or event without becoming involved in it 4, 9

look out for sb/sth to carefully watch the people or things around you so that you will notice a particular person or thing 9, 66

Look out! something you say or shout in order to tell someone that they are in danger 41

lookout n a person who is watching for danger 9, 66

look over sth/sb or look sth/ sb over to quickly examine something or someone 3, 9, 17

look round/around see **look around/round look through sth** to read something quickly and not very carefully 9, 17, 20

look up if a situation is looking up, it is improving 1, 9, 26

look up sb or look sb up to visit someone who you have not seen for a long time when you are visiting the place where they live 1, 9

look up sth or look sth up to look at a book or computer in order to find a piece of information 1, 9

look up to sb to respect and admire someone 9

lose out to not have an advantage that other people have 14

make for swh to go in the direction of a place 10

make out sb or make sb out to understand why someone behaves in the way that they do 1, 10

make out sth or make sth out to understand something, especially the reason why something has happened 10

make out sth/sb or make sth/ sb out to be able to see or hear something or someone, usually with difficulty 2, 10

make up to forgive someone who you have argued with and to become friendly with them again 53

make up sth or make sth up to say or write something that is not true [e.g. excuse, report, story] in order to deceive someone 10

make up sth or make sth up to invent something [e.g. story, game] 10

make up sth to form the whole of something 10

make-up n the combination of things which form something 10

make up for sth to replace something that has been lost, or to provide something good in order to make a bad situation better *10*

make it up to sb to do something good for someone who you have done something bad to in the past, or to someone who has done something good for you *10*

match up if two pieces of information match up, they are the same and this shows that the information is likely to be correct *35*

measure out sth or measure sth out to take a small amount of something from a larger amount, first weighing or measuring it in order to make sure that it is the right amount *60*

measure up to be good enough *40*

meet with sb *American* to have a meeting with someone in order to discuss or arrange something *69*

mess about/around to spend time playing or doing things with no particular purpose *18*

mess about/around to behave stupidly or to waste time doing unimportant things *18, 69*

mess sb about/around *informal* to treat someone badly, especially by changing your mind a lot or not doing what you have promised *1, 18*

mess up (sth) or mess (sth) up to spoil or damage something, or to do something badly *42*

mill about/around (swh) to walk around a particular place or area, usually while waiting for something *18*

Mind out! *British & American* something that you say in order to tell someone to be careful or to warn someone of a danger *41*

miss out to not do or get something that you would enjoy or that would be good for you, or to not have something that other people have *53*

miss out sb/sth or miss sb/sth out *British & American* to fail to include someone or something *42*

mix up sb/sth or mix sb/sth up to confuse two people or things by thinking that one person or thing is the other person or thing *34*

mix-up *n* a mistake caused by confusion which prevents something from being done or causes something to be done incorrectly *4, 34*

mixed up in sth *informal* to be involved in an illegal or unpleasant activity *67*

mouth off *informal* to talk about a subject as if you know more than everyone else, or to complain a lot about something *54*

move (sth) along if a process moves along, or if you move a process along, it develops in a satisfactory way *46*

move in to begin living in a new house or area *58*

move in together to start living in the same house as someone you are having a romantic relationship with *58*

move on continue to the next point *64*

move out to stop living in a particular house *58*

move over to change the place where you are sitting or standing so that there is space for someone else to sit or stand *3, 17, 29*

move up *British & Australian* to move slightly so that there is enough space for someone else *29*

muck about/around *informal* to waste time doing silly things *22*

muddle through to succeed in doing something even though you have difficulties because you do not really know how to do it *27*

muddle up sb/sth or muddle sb/sth up to confuse two people or things in your mind *34*

mug up (sth) or mug (sth) up *informal, British* to quickly try to learn the main facts about a subject, especially before an exam *43*

name sb/sth after sb/sth to give someone or something the same name as someone or something else *55*

narrow down sth or narrow sth down to make something [e.g. list, choice, option] smaller and clearer by removing the things that are less important *36*

note down sth or note sth down to write or type words or numbers, often so that you do not forget them *1, 17, 44*

off-putting *adj* unattractive or unpleasant *15*

onlooker *n* a person who watches an activity or event without becoming involved in it *9*

open onto sth if a room, window, or door opens onto a place, it opens in the direction of that place or has a view of it *24*

open up (sth) or open (sth) up to start a new shop or business *13*

open up to start to talk more about yourself and your feelings *54*

opt out to choose not to be part of an activity or arrangement, or to stop being involved with it *37*

order sb about/around to tell someone what they should do all the time *18, 31*

outbreak *n* when something unpleasant or difficult to control starts, such as war or disease *66*

outcry *n* a public expression of anger or disapproval *4, 38*

outlet *n* a shop that is one of many owned by a particular company and that sells the company's goods *49*

outpouring *n* a strong expression of emotion *54*

outset *n* the beginning of something *4, 28*

outstanding *adj* extremely good, or of a very high standard *40*

oversleep to sleep longer than you had intended *58*

own up to admit that you have done something wrong, especially something that is not important *54*

pack away sth or pack sth away to put something into a bag or container, or to put something in the place where it is usually kept *21*

packed out *adj* very full of people *33*

pack up (sth) or pack (sth) up to collect your things together and put them into bags or boxes, especially when you have finished doing something *28*

pair off if two people pair off, they start a romantic relationship *52*

pan out to develop or happen in a particular way *26*

pass away to die *56*

pass by if time or a period of time [e.g. week] passes by, it goes past *23*

pass for sb/sth if someone or something passes for someone or something else, they appear like that person or thing *55*

pass off *British & American* if an event passes off in a good way, it happens in that way *33*

pass on to die *56*

pass on sth or pass sth on to give something to someone else *16*

pass on sth or pass sth on to tell someone something that someone else has told you *31*

pass round sth or pass sth round to offer something to each person in a group of people *60*

pass out to become unconscious *56*

pay back sb or pay sb back to do something unpleasant to someone because they have done something unpleasant to you *25*

pay back sb/sth or pay sb/sth back to pay someone the money that you owe them *47*

pay off if something that you have done to try to achieve something pays off, it is successful *27*

pay off sth or pay sth off if you pay off a debt [e.g. loan, mortgage, overdraft], you pay back all the money you owe *47*

pay up *informal* to give someone the money that you owe them, especially when you do not want to *47*

pencil in sth/sb or pencil sth/sb in to arrange for something to happen or for someone to do something on a particular date, knowing that the arrangement might be changed later *45*

phase in sth or phase sth in to make a new system, process, or law gradually begin to happen or exist *26*

phase out sth or phase sth out to gradually stop using or supplying something *26*

phone around/round (sb) to call several people, often in order to find out information *50*

phone (sb) back to call someone for the second time or to call someone who rang you earlier *20*

phone up (sb) or phone (sb) up to call someone *50*

pick on sb to choose one person from a group of people to criticise or treat unfairly, especially when they are smaller or weaker than you *40*

pick up if something [e.g. business, economy, trade] picks up, it improves or increases after a bad period *26*

pick up if the wind picks up, it becomes stronger *61*

pick up sb/sth or pick sb/sth up to collect someone who is waiting for you, or to collect something that you have left somewhere or that you have bought *2, 63*

pick up sth/sb or pick sth/sb up to lift something or someone by using your hands *29*

pick up sth or pick sth up to learn a new skill or language by practising it rather than being taught it *43*

pick up sth or pick sth up to get or buy something when you have gone to a place to do something else *47*

pick up sth or pick sth up to buy something cheaply *48*

pick up sth or pick sth up to collect something you have left somewhere *65*

pick up on connect or give more attention to *70*

pick-up *n* an increase or improvement *48*

pick-up *n informal* when you start talking to someone you do not know because you want to have a sexual relationship with them *48*

pick-up *n* when a car, taxi, etc. collects you *48*

pickup *n* small truck with an open back *48*

pile up (sth) or pile (sth) up if something unpleasant [e.g. work, bills, losses] piles up, or if you pile it up, you get more and more of it *46*

pile-up *n* an accident involving several cars *4, 63*

pin down sb or pin sb down to make someone give you exact details or a decision about something *54*

plan ahead to make decisions or plans about something you will do or something that might happen in the future *37*

play down sth or play sth down to try to make people believe that something is not very important, or that it is unlikely to happen *54*

playing at sth if you ask what someone is playing at, you ask what they are doing, in a way which shows that you are surprised and angry *40*

play-off *n* a game between two teams that have equal points in order to decide which is the winner *57*

play up *British & Australian* if a machine or part of a machine plays up, it does not work as it should *1*

play up *British & American* if someone, especially a child, plays up, they behave badly *42*

plug in sth or plug sth in or plug sth into sth to connect a piece of electrical equipment to a supply of electricity or to another piece of electrical equipment *64*

point out sb/sth or point sb/sth out to make a person notice someone or something, usually by telling them where they are or by holding up one of your fingers towards them *35*

point out sth or point sth out to tell someone a fact that they did not already know, especially one that is important in the present discussion or situation *35*

polish off sth or polish sth off *informal* to finish something quickly and easily, especially a large amount of food or a piece of work *28*

polish up sth or polish sth up to practise and improve your skills or your knowledge of something that you learned in the past but have partly forgotten *43*

pop in/into *informal* to go into a place, especially a friend's house, just for a short time *59*

pop out *informal* to leave the place where you are and go somewhere for a short time *29*

pour down to rain heavily *61*
downpour *n* a sudden, heavy fall of rain *61*

pour in to arrive or enter somewhere in very large numbers *33*

pour sth into sth to provide a lot of money for something over a long period *49*

pour out to leave a place in large numbers *33*

pour out sth or pour sth out if you pour out your feelings or thoughts, you talk very honestly about what is making you sad *54*

outpouring *n* a strong expression of emotion *54*

pour out sth or pour sth out to fill a glass, cup etc. with a drink *60*

press (sb) for sth to try to persuade someone, usually someone in authority, to give you something or to allow something to happen *39*

press on to continue doing something in a determined way *22*

print out (sth) or print (sth) out to produce a printed copy of a document that has been written on a computer *65*

printout *n* information or a document that is printed from a computer *65*

pull ahead to suddenly get in front of another car or person that was previously driving or running at the same speed as you *57*

pull down sth or pull sth down to destroy a building or other structure because it is not being used or it is not wanted any more *30*

pull in if a train pulls in or pulls into a station, it arrives there *62*

pull in or pull into swh if a car pulls in or pulls into a place, it moves to the side of the road or to another place where it can stop *63*

pull off sth or pull sth off to succeed in doing or achieving something difficult *27*

pull out if a train pulls out, it starts to leave a station *62*

pull out to drive onto a road, either from another road or from the side of the road where you have stopped *63*

pull out (sb/sth) or pull (sb/sth) out to stop being involved in an activity or agreement *66*

pull over to drive a car to the side of the road in order to stop *3, 63*

pull (sb) through to recover from a serious illness, or to help someone to do this *56*

pull together to work as a group in order to achieve something *45*

pull yourself together to become calm after being so angry or upset that you were unable to behave in a sensible way *51*

pull up if a car pulls up, it stops, often for a short time *63*

pump up sth or pump sth up to fill something with air by using a pump *63*

pushed for sth to have very little or not enough of something, especially time or money *22*

push in *informal, British & American* to rudely join a line of people who are waiting for something by moving in front of some of the people who are already there *16*

put across sth or put sth across to explain or express something clearly so that people understand it easily *11, 39*

put sth at sth to roughly calculate that something will cost a particular amount or that something is a particular size or amount *49*

put away sth or put sth away to store things where they are usually stored *42*

put back sth or put sth back if you put a watch or clock back, you make it show an earlier time *11*

put back sth or put sth back to change the date or time of an event so that it happens later than planned *11, 33*

put down (sth) or put (sth) down to land in an aircraft, or to make an aircraft land *11*

put down sb or put sb down to make someone feel stupid or unimportant by criticising them *38*

put-down *n* an unkind remark that makes someone seem foolish *4*

put forward to change the date or time of an event so that it happens earlier than planned *33*

put forward sth or put sth forward if you put forward a clock or watch, you make it show a later time *11*

put forward sth or put sth forward to state an idea or opinion, or to suggest a plan, so that it can be considered or discussed *39*

put in sth or put sth in to fix new equipment or a new system in the correct place in a room or building, or to type (data) into a computer *11, 64*

put off sb or put sb off to tell someone that you cannot see them or do something for them until a later time *11*

put off sb or put sb off (sb/ sth/ doing sth) to make someone not like someone or something, or not want to do something *15*

off- putting *adj* unattractive or unpleasant *15*

put off sth/doing sth or put sth off to decide or arrange to do something at a later time *1, 2, 11, 33*

put on sb or put sb on (sth) to give someone the phone so that they can speak to the person who is on it *50*

put on sth or put sth on to make a device [e.g. light, fire] work by pressing a switch *11*

put on sth or put sth on to put something that sounds or pictures are recorded onto [e.g. CD, video] into a machine which makes you able to hear or see the recording *11*

put on sth or put sth on to put a piece of clothing onto your body *11, 32*

put on sth or put sth on to pretend to have a particular feeling, or to behave in a way which is not real or natural for you *16*

put on sth or put sth on to organise a play, show, or competition *33*

put on sth or put sth on to begin to cook food *60*

put-on *adj* pretend or not genuine *16*

put sb on speakerphone to turn on a loudspeaker on the phone so that everyone can hear the caller *50*

put sb on to/onto sth to tell someone about something or someone that could help them, often something or someone they did not know about before *11*

put out to be annoyed, often because of something that someone has done or said to you *11*

put out sth or put sth out to produce information [e.g. statement, warning, press release] and make it available for everyone to read or hear *2*

put out sth or put sth out to make a light stop shining by pressing a switch *11*

put out sth or put sth out to make something that is burning [e.g. fire, cigarette] stop burning *11, 30*

put out sth or put sth out to injure a part of your body [e.g. back, shoulder] by making a bone move from its usual place *56*

put over sth or put sth over to express an idea clearly so that people understand it *17, 39*

put through sb or put sb through to connect a phone or Internet caller to the person they want to speak to *50*

put up sb or put sb up to let someone stay in your home for a short period *58*

put sth to sb to suggest an idea or plan to someone so that they can consider it or discuss it *39*

put up sth or put sth up to build a structure [e.g. wall, building, statue] *11*

put up sth or put sth up to stick or fasten a piece of paper [e.g. notice, poster] to a wall so that it can be seen *11*

put up sth or put sth up to open something that is folded or rolled up [e.g. tent, umbrella] so that it is ready to be used *11*

put sb up to sth to encourage someone to do something stupid or wrong *67*

put up with sth/sb to accept unpleasant behaviour or an unpleasant situation, even though you do not like it *1, 11, 19*

rained off if a sport or other outside activity is rained off, it cannot start or continue because it is raining *61*

reach out (sth) or reach (sth) out to stretch your arm in front of your body, usually in order to get or touch something *29*

read sth into sth to believe that an action, remark, or situation has a particular importance or meaning, often when this is not true *21*

read out sth or read sth out to read something and say the words aloud so that other people can hear *44*

read over/through sth or read sth over/through to read something from the beginning to the end in order to find any mistakes or to understand it better *3, 17*

read through to read something from the beginning to the end in order to find any mistakes or to understand it better *17*

read up on sth to read a lot about a particular subject in order to learn about it *44*

relate to connect to *70*

rely on sb/sth to trust someone or something to do what you need them to do *16*

revolve around/round sth/sb if an activity or conversation revolves around something or someone, that thing or person is the main reason for the activity, or the main subject of the conversation *34*

ring (sb) back to call someone for the second time, or to call someone who rang you earlier *20, 50*

ring in *British & Australian* to phone someone at your place of work, usually to explain why you are not there *50*

ring off *British & Australian* to end a phone call *50*

rip off sb or **rip sb off** *informal* to cheat someone by making them pay too much money for something *4, 48*

rip-off *n informal* something that costs far too much money *4, 48*

rise above sth to not allow something bad that is happening or being done to you to upset you or to affect your behaviour *34*

root for sb *informal* to show support for someone in a competition, or to hope that someone will succeed in doing something difficult *19*

root out sth/sb or **root sth/sb out** to find and get rid of the thing or person that is causing a problem *30*

rope in sb or **rope sb in** *informal* to persuade someone to help you with something, especially when they do not want to *39*

rub in sth or **rub sth in** to put a substance [e.g. ointment] onto the surface of something and to rub it so that it goes into the surface *16*

rub sth in *informal* to talk to someone about something which you know they want to forget because they feel bad about it *40*

rub out sth or **rub sth out** to remove writing from something by rubbing it with a piece of rubber or with a cloth *42*

rule out sth/sb or **rule sth/sb out** to decide that something or someone is not suitable for a particular purpose, or to decide that something is impossible *25, 36*

run across sb to meet someone you know when you are not expecting to meet them *59*

run away to secretly leave a place because you are unhappy there *21*

run sth by sb *informal* to repeat something, or to tell someone about something, so that they can give their opinion of it or hear it again *37*

rundown *adj* in poor condition or shabby *32*

run into sb to meet someone that you know when you did not expect to meet them *21*

run into sth if the amount or cost of something runs into thousands, millions etc., it reaches that level *49*

run off sth or **run sth off** to print several copies of something *15*

run off sth or **run sth off** to quickly and easily write something that is usually difficult to write [e.g. poem, speech] *15*

run off with sb to secretly leave a place with someone in order to live with them or marry them, especially when other people think this is wrong *53*

run on to continue for longer than expected *23*

run out (of) to use all of something so that there is none left *14, 64*

run out if a document or official agreement runs out, the period of time it lasts for comes to an end *22*

run over sb/sth or **run sb/sth over** to hit someone or something with a vehicle and drive over them, injuring or killing them *63*

run through sth to repeat something in order to practise it or to make sure that it is correct *31*

run-through *n* a practice or rehearsal *4, 31*

run to sth to reach a particular amount, usually a large amount *49*

run up against sth if you run up against problems or difficulties, you begin to experience them *34*

run up sth or **run sth up** if you run up a debt [e.g. bill, deficit], you do things which cause you to owe a large amount of money *47, 48*

save up (sth) or **save (sth) up** to keep money so that you can buy something with it in the future *47*

scare away sb/sth or **scare sb/sth away** to make a person or animal so frightened that they go away *21*

scrape through (sth) to manage with a lot of difficulty to succeed in something [e.g. exam] *43*

screw up (sth) or **screw (sth) up** *informal* to make a mistake, or to damage or spoil something *40*

screw up sth or **screw sth up** to twist and crush paper or material with your hands *30*

scribble down sth or **scribble sth down** to write something very quickly on a piece of paper *44*

scroll across/down/up (sth) to move text or other information across/down/up a computer screen in order to view a different part of it *64*

see about sth to deal with something, or to arrange for something to be done *36*

see sb about/around to see someone in the places you usually see them *18*

see off sb or **see sb off** to go to the place that someone is leaving from in order to say goodbye *15*

see out sb or **see sb out** to go with someone to the door of a room or building when they are leaving *14*

see through sb/sth if you see through someone who is trying to deceive you, or if you see through someone's behaviour, you realise what they are really like and what they are trying to do *20*

see sb through (sth) to help or support someone during a difficult period in their life *30*

see to sth/sb to deal with something that needs doing or to help someone who needs your help *2, 30*

sell off sth or **sell sth off** to sell all or part of a business *15*

sell off sth or sell sth off to sell something at a low price because you do not want it or because you need some money *48*

sell-off *n* a sale of all or part of a business *48*

sell out if a shop sells out, it has no more of a particular product available to buy *48*

sell-out *n* when all the tickets for an event have been sold *48*

sell up (sth) or sell (sth) up to sell your house or business in order to go somewhere else or do something else *49*

send back sth or send sth back to return something to the company you bought it from because it is unsuitable or damaged *20*

send for sb to send someone a message asking them to come to see you *19*

send off sb or send sb off *British & Australian* to order a sports player to leave the playing area during a game because they have done something wrong *57*

send off sth or send sth off to send a letter, document, or parcel by post *1, 15*

send up sb/sth or send sb/sth up *informal* to make someone or something seem stupid by copying them in a funny way *33*

set about sth/doing sth to start doing something, especially something that uses a lot of time or energy *28*

set against sth/doing sth to be opposed to doing or having something *37*

set apart sb/sth or set sb/sth apart if a quality sets someone or something apart, it makes them different from and usually better than others of the same type *32*

set aside sth or set sth aside to use something, especially time or money, for one purpose and no other purpose *47*

setback *n* a problem that makes something happen later or more slowly than it should *30*

set off to start a journey *62*

set off sth or set sth off to cause a loud noise or explosion [e.g. bomb, firework, alarm] to begin or happen *25*

set off sth or set sth off to cause a series of events or a lot of activity, often without intending to do this *25*

set sb off (doing sth) to make someone start to laugh, cry, or talk about something that they often talk about *25*

set out to start an activity, especially when you have already decided what you want to achieve, or to explain something in an organised way *4, 70*

outset *n* the beginning of something *4, 28*

set out to start a journey *28, 62*

set out sth or set sth out to give all the details of something, or to explain something clearly, especially in writing *44*

set up sth or set sth up to start a company or organisation, or to get something ready to use *13, 49, 64*

set up sth or set sth up to prepare or arrange something for use *65*

set-up *n* the way in which things are organised or arranged *13, 49*

settle down to start living in a place where you intend to stay for a long time, usually with the same partner, especially after a period in which you have travelled a lot or changed partners *53*

settle for sth to accept something, often something that is not exactly what you want, or is not the best *53*

settle up to pay someone the money that you owe them *47*

shake off sth or shake sth off to get rid of an illness or something that is causing you problems *56*

shoot through *informal, Australian* to leave a place suddenly and often secretly, especially to avoid something *69*

shoot up if the number, amount, or rate of something shoots up, it increases very quickly *66*

shop around to compare the price and quality of the same item or service from different shops or companies before deciding which one to buy *48*

show sb around/round (swh) to go with someone to a place that they have not visited before and show them the interesting parts *18*

show off to try to make people admire your abilities or achievements in a way which other people find annoying *40*

show-off *n* someone who tries to make people admire them in a way other people find annoying *4, 40*

show out sb or show sb out to lead a visitor who is leaving to the door of a room or building *14*

show up to arrive, especially at a place where people are expecting you *13*

shut down (sth) or shut (sth) down if a factory or business shuts down, or if someone shuts it down, it closes and stops working *17*

shut (sb) up to stop talking or making a noise, or to make someone do this *54*

sign in to connect a computer to a series of computers, usually so that you can start working *64*

sign up to arrange to take part in an activity, or agree to receive something *43, 64*

sink in if a fact or idea, especially a surprising or unpleasant one, sinks in, you gradually start to believe it or realise what effect it will have on you *16*

sit about/around (swh) to spend time sitting down and doing very little *18*

skimp on sth to not spend enough time or money on something, or not use enough of something *48*

slave away to work very hard with little or no rest *46*

sleep in to sleep longer in the morning than you normally do *58*

sleep on sth if someone sleeps on a decision or problem, they wait until the next day before they decide what to do about it *37*

sleep over *informal* to sleep in someone else's home for a night *58*

sleepover *n* a party at which several young people sleep at a friend's house for a night *58*

sleep through sth if someone sleeps through a noise or an activity, the noise or activity does not wake them *20*

slip off to leave a place quietly so that other people do not notice you going *15*

slip out if a piece of information slips out while you are talking to someone, you tell it to them without intending to *35*

slip out to leave a place quietly so that other people do not notice you going *35*

slip up *informal* to make a mistake *5*

slow down to become less physically active than you were before *56*

slow down (sth/sb) or slow (sth/sb) down to become slower, or to make something or someone slower *29*

slow up (sth/sb) or slow (sth/ sb) up to become slower, or to make something or someone slower *29*

snap up sth or snap sth up to buy or get something quickly because it is very cheap or because it is exactly what you want *48*

snowed in if a person or place is snowed in, there is so much snow that it is impossible to travel anywhere or leave that place *61*

snowed under *informal* to have so much work that you have problems dealing with it *46*

sort out sth or sort sth out to make a decision about something by discussing it with someone else or by considering it carefully *1, 36*

sort out sth or sort sth out to arrange or organise things which are untidy *14*

sort yourself out *informal, British & Australian* to spend time dealing with your personal problems or organising your things *36*

spark off sth or spark sth off if something sparks off an activity [e.g. fighting, violence] or a state, it causes it to suddenly happen or exist *25*

speak out to publicly express your opinions, especially in order to criticise or oppose someone or something *38*

speak up to publicly express your opinions about something or someone, especially in order to support them *31*

speak up to begin to speak more loudly *31, 50*

spell out sth or spell sth out to explain something in detail and in a clear way *31*

spin-off *n* a product that develops from another more important product *49*

Spit it out! *informal* something you say to encourage someone to tell you something which they do not want to tell you *41*

splash out *informal* to spend a lot of money on something which is very pleasant but which you do not need *48*

split up if two people who are married or who have a romantic relationship split up, they end their marriage or relationship *53*

spread out arrange on a flat surface *14*

spread out sth or spread sth out to open something that is folded [e.g. map, towel] and put it down flat on a surface *42*

spring from sth to be caused by something *25*

squeeze in sth/sb or squeeze sth/ sb in to manage to do something or see someone when you are very busy and do not have much time available *46*

stamp out sth or stamp sth out to get rid of something that is considered wrong or harmful *30*

stand about/around/round to spend time standing in a place waiting for someone or doing very little *18*

stand by sb to continue to support or help someone when they are in a difficult situation *68*

stand down *British & Australian* to leave an important job or official position so that someone else can do it instead *45*

stand for sth if a letter stands for a word or name, it is the first letter of that word or name and it is used to represent it *19*

stand for sth *British & Australian* to compete in an election for an official position, or to try to be elected as a member of an organisation [e.g. parliament] *68*

stand in to do someone else's job for a short period of time, or to take someone else's place at an event, because that person cannot be there *33*

stand out if someone or something stands out, they are very noticeable because they look different or behave differently from other people or things *32*

stand out to be much better than other similar things or people *40*

outstanding *adj* extremely good, or of a very high standard *40*

stand round see **stand about**

stand up sb or stand sb up to fail to meet someone on purpose, especially someone with whom you were starting to have a romantic relationship *59*

stand up for sth/sb to defend something that you believe is important [e.g. principle, right], or to defend a person who is being criticised *68*

stand up to sb if you stand up to a powerful person or organisation, you state your opinions forcefully and refuse to agree with them or do what they want *68*

start off to start a life, existence, or profession in a particular way *28*

start off to start a journey or to begin something *62, 70*

start out to start a life, existence, or profession in a particular way *28*

start up (sth) or start (sth) up if a business or other organisation starts up, or if someone starts one up, it is created and starts to operate *49*

stay ahead to continue to be more advanced and successful than other people *27*

stay away from sth to avoid something that has a bad effect on you *21*

stay behind to not leave a place when other people leave it *24*

stay in to remain at home, especially in the evening *24*

stay on to stay in a place longer than you planned or after other people have left it *24*

stay out to not come home at night, or to come home late *24*

stay out of sth to not become involved in a discussion or an argument *38*

stay over to spend the night somewhere instead of returning to your home or continuing your journey *17*

stay up to go to bed later than usual *58*

Steady on! *British & Australian* something that you say in order to tell someone that you think what they are saying is too extreme *41*

step down to leave your job, especially so that someone else can do it *45*

step up sth or step sth up to do more of an activity or to increase the speed of a process, usually in order to improve a situation *66*

stick around *informal* to stay somewhere for a period of time *18*

stick at sth to continue to work hard at something even though it is difficult or tiring *46*

stick by sb to continue to support someone when they are having problems *68*

stick out if part of something sticks out, it comes out beyond the edge or surface of something *32*

stick out if a quality or characteristic of someone or something sticks out, it is very easy to notice *32*

stick together *informal* if two or more people stick together, they support each other, especially when they are in a difficult situation *38*

stick up for sb *informal* to defend a person when they are being criticised *38*

stick with sth to do or use something as you had planned and not change to something else, or to continue doing something even though it is difficult *26*

stick with it *informal* to continue doing something even though it is difficult *19*

stir up sth or stir sth up to cause arguments or bad feeling between people, usually on purpose *25*

stock up to buy a lot of something, often food or drink *48*

stop off to visit a place for a short time when you are going somewhere else *62*

stop over to stop somewhere for a period of time when you are on a long journey *62*

stopover *n* a short stay in a place that you make while you are on a longer journey somewhere else *62*

stressed-out *adj* very worried and anxious *14*

stretch away if an area of land stretches away, it continues over a long distance *24*

sum up (sth/sb) or sum (sth/ sb) up to describe briefly the most important facts or characteristics of something or someone *44, 70*

suss out sb/sth or suss sb/ sth out *informal, British & Australian* to discover what someone or something is really like, or to find out how a machine or piece of equipment works *69*

sweep up (sth) or sweep (sth) up to remove rubbish or dirt, usually from the floor, using a brush *13*

swell up if a part of your body swells up, it becomes larger or rounder than usual, often because of an illness or injury *56*

switch off (sth) or switch (sth) off to turn off an electrical device [e.g. light, radio] or an engine by using a switch *50, 64*

switch on (sth) or switch (sth) on to turn on an electrical device [e.g. light, radio] or an engine by using a switch *50, 64*

swot up (sth) or swot (sth) up *informal, British & Australian* to learn as much as you can about something, especially before an exam *43*

tag along to go somewhere with a person, especially when they have not asked you to go with them *59*

tailback *n* a long line of traffic that is moving very slowly *63*

take after sb to have a similar appearance or character as an older member of your family *55*

take apart sth or take sth apart to separate something into its different parts *12*

take around/round sb or take sb around/round (swh) to walk through a building or to visit a place with someone, showing them the most interesting or important parts *18*

take aside sb or take sb aside to separate someone from a group of people so that you can speak to them privately *12*

take away sth or take sth away if you take one number away from another one, you subtract the first number from the second *12*

take away sth or take sth away *British & Australian* to buy food in a shop or restaurant and eat it somewhere else *60*

takeaway *n* a meal that you can buy and take somewhere else to eat, or a shop where you can buy this food *60*

take back sth or take sth back to return something to the person or organisation that you borrowed or bought it from *12*

take back sth or take sth back to admit that something you said was wrong *12*

take back sth or take sth back if a shop takes back goods that it has sold to you, it agrees to give you money or goods for them because they are damaged or unsuitable *20*

take back sb or take sb back if something takes you back, it makes you remember a period or an event in the past *23*

take down sth or take sth down to write or type something, especially something that someone says *17*

take in sb or take sb in to let someone stay in your house *5*

take in sb or take sb in to deceive someone, or to make someone believe something that is not true *5, 67*

take in sth or take sth in if a boat takes in water, water enters the boat through a hole *5*

take in sth or take sth in to look at something carefully, noticing all the details *5, 12*

take in sth or take sth in to make a piece of clothing narrower by removing the sewing from the edges and sewing closer to the middle of the material *5, 16*

take in sth or take sth in to understand the meaning or importance of news or information, or to understand and remember facts *5, 35*

take off to suddenly leave somewhere, especially without telling anyone that you are going *12*

take off to suddenly become successful or popular *27*

take off if an aircraft, bird, or insect takes off, it moves from the ground and begins to fly *62*

take off sb/sth or take sb/sth off to copy the way a person behaves, or to copy the way something is done, often in order to make people laugh *33*

take off sth or take sth off to remove something, especially something that you are wearing *2*

take off sth or take sth off (sth) to subtract a particular amount from a total *12*

take off sth or take sth off to spend time away from your work *22*

take-off *n* when an aircraft leaves the ground and begins to fly *62*

take on sb or take sb on to begin to employ someone *45*

take on sth or take sth on to accept a particular job or responsibility and begin to do what is needed *45*

take out sth or take sth out to arrange to get an official document [e.g. insurance policy] from an organisation or court of law *12*

take out sth or take sth out to get money from a bank *47*

take out sth on sb or take sth out on sb to treat someone badly because you are upset or angry, even though they have done nothing wrong *40*

take sth out of sb to make someone feel very tired *12*

take over to become more successful or powerful than something or someone else that is involved in the same type of activity *27*

take over (sth) or take (sth) over to start doing a job or being responsible for something that someone else was doing or was responsible for before you *45*

take over sth or take sth over to get control of a company by buying most of its shares (= the equal parts into which the ownership of the company is divided) *49*

takeover *n* an act of gaining control of a company *49*

take round see **take around**

take sb through sth to explain something to someone, or to show someone how to do something *20*

take to sb/sth to start to like someone or something *51*

take to sth/doing sth to start to do something often *12*

take up sth or take sth up to start doing a particular job or activity *12*

take sb up on sth to accept an offer that someone has made *12*

taken up with sth to be very busy doing something *12*

talk down to sb to talk to someone as if they were less clever than you *54*

talk sb around/round to persuade someone to agree with you or to do what you want them to do *39*

talk sb into sth/doing sth to persuade someone to do something *39*

talk sb out of sth/doing sth to persuade someone not to do something *39*

talk over sth or talk sth over to discuss a problem or situation, especially before making a decision about it *3, 36*

tear apart sth or tear sth apart to pull something violently so that it breaks into two or more pieces *30*

tear sb apart to make someone feel very unhappy *51*

tear sb away to force someone to stop doing something that they enjoy in order to do something else *21*

tear down sth or tear sth down to destroy a building or other structure because it is not being used or it is not wanted any more *4, 30*

tear up sth or tear sth up to tear something, especially paper or cloth, into a lot of small pieces *29*

tell sth/sb apart to be able to see the differences between two similar things or people and judge which is which *32*

tell sb/sth from sb/sth if you can tell one person or thing from a similar person or thing, you are able to say which of them is which because you can see the differences between them *32*

tell off sb or tell sb off to speak angrily to someone because they have done something wrong *69*

text back sb or text sb back to send a text message in reply to someone *20*

thaw out (sth) or thaw (sth) out if frozen food thaws out, or if you thaw it out, it is taken out of a freezer so that it gradually becomes warmer and is not frozen any more *60*

think ahead to think carefully about what might happen in the future, or to make plans for things you want to do in the future *37*

think back to think about things that happened in the past *23*

think over sth or think sth over to think carefully about an idea or plan before making a decision *3, 37*

think through sth or think sth through to think carefully about something you are planning to do and to consider the possible results of it *37*

throw yourself into sth to start doing something with a lot of enthusiasm and energy *21, 69*

throw out sb or throw sb out to force someone to leave a college, school, house or organisation *43*

throw up (sth) or throw (sth) up to vomit *56*

thrown together if people are thrown together in a situation, that situation causes them to meet each other and to get to know each other *34*

tidy away sth or tidy sth away *British & Australian* to put things in cupboards and drawers, etc. after you have been using them *21*

tidy up (sth) or tidy (sth) up to make a room or a group of things tidy by putting things in the correct place *5, 13*

tie in with sth if one event ties in with another, it is planned so that both events happen at the same time *33*

tie up sth or tie sth up to put string or rope around something so that it is fastened together *29*

tied up *informal* to be busy so that you are unable to see or speak to anyone else or go anywhere *46*

tip off sb or tip sb off to warn someone secretly about something that will happen so that they can take action or prevent it from happening *67*

tip-off *n* a secret warning or piece of secret information *67*

tone down sth or tone sth down to make a piece of writing, a speech, or a performance less offensive or less critical *44*

top up sb or top sb up to put more drink into someone's glass or cup *60*

top-up *n* more drink poured into a glass or cup *60*

touch down when an aircraft touches down, it lands on the ground *62*

touchdown *n* when an aircraft lands *62*

touch on sth to mention a subject briefly when speaking or writing about something *44, 70*

track down sb/sth or track sb/sth down to find someone or something after searching for them in many different places *35*

trigger off sth or trigger sth off to make something suddenly begin, often a difficult or violent situation *25*

try on sth or try sth on to put on a piece of clothing to find out whether it fits you or whether you like it, especially before buying it *16*

try out sth or try sth out to test something in order to find out if it works or to decide whether you like it *14*

tucked away to be in a quiet or hidden place which not many people see or go to *24*

turn away to move your face so you are not looking at something *21*

turn down sb/sth or turn sb/sth down to refuse an offer or request *31*

turn in sth or turn sth in to give a piece of written work [e.g. essay] to a teacher *42*

turn off (sth) to leave the road you are travelling on and travel along another one *63*

turn off sb or turn sb off (sth) to make someone decide that they are not interested in something *15*

turn off sth or turn sth off to touch a switch so that a machine or a piece of electrical equipment stops working, or to stop the flow or supply of something [e.g. water, electricity] *2*

turn-off *n* a place where you can leave a main road and go onto another road *63*

turn on/upon sb to attack someone or criticise someone very strongly *30*

turn on sb or turn sb on to make someone interested in something *52*

turn out to happen in a particular way or to have a particular result *34*

turnout *n* the number of people who come to watch or take part in an event or activity *33*

turn over (sth) or turn (sth) over to turn a page in a book so that the side which was facing down is now facing up *3, 44*

turnover *n* the total amount of money made by a company or business in a particular period of time *4, 49*

turn to sb to ask someone for help, sympathy or advice *31*

turn to sth to start to do or take something bad [e.g. crime, drugs, drink], usually because you are unhappy *55*

turn (sth) to sth if someone turns to a particular subject, or if they turn their thoughts or attention to it, they begin to think, speak or write about it *35, 70*

turn up if someone or something turns up somewhere, they arrive at that place *1, 2, 5, 13*

turn up sth or turn sth up to increase the amount of something, especially sound or heat, that is produced by a machine [e.g. television, oven] *64*

type in sth or type sth in to put information into a computer using a keyboard *65*

upkeep *n* the cost or process of keeping something, such as a building, in good condition *49*

use up sth or use sth up to finish a supply of something *13, 64*

visit with sb *American* to spend time talking with someone that you know *69*

wait about/around to stay in one place without doing anything while you are waiting for something to happen *18*

wait up to stay awake because you are expecting someone to arrive *58*

Wait up! *American* something you say to tell someone to stop so that you can talk to them or go somewhere with them *69*

wake up (sb) or wake (sb) up to become conscious after sleeping, or to make someone do this *3, 58*

wake up to sth to become aware of a situation or problem *26*

walk into sth to get a job very easily *27*

walk off with sth *informal* to steal something, or to take something without the owner's permission *67*

walk out to leave a performance or meeting before it has ended because you do not like it or because you are angry *33*

warm to sth to become more enthusiastic about an idea *51*

warm up (sth) or warm (sth) up to prepare yourself for a physical activity by doing some gentle exercise *4, 57*

warm up (sth/sb) or warm (sth/sb) up to become warmer, or to make something or someone warmer *61*

warm-up *n* a preparation for physical activity *4, 57*

wash up *American* to clean your hands and face with soap and water *69*

wash up (sth) or wash (sth) up *British & Australian* to clean the plates, pans and other things you have used for cooking and eating a meal *69*

Watch out! something you say to tell someone to be careful so that they can avoid danger or an accident *41*

watch out for sb/sth to be careful to notice someone or something interesting *35*

watch out for sth to be careful to notice something, especially something that might cause you problems *35*

wear down (sth) or wear (sth) down to make someone feel tired and less able to deal with a situation *17*

wear off if a feeling or the effect of something [e.g. anaesthetic, alcohol] wears off, it gradually disappears *26*

wear out (sth) or wear (sth) out use something so much that it becomes weak or damaged and cannot be used any more, or to become weak and damaged in this way *14*

weigh down sb or weigh sb down if you are weighed down with something, you are carrying too much of it *17*

weigh on sb/sth if a problem or responsibility weighs on you, it makes you worried or unhappy *16*

weigh up sth or weigh sth up to think carefully about the advantages and disadvantages involved in a situation before making a decision *37*

while away sth or while sth away to spend time in a relaxed way because you are waiting for something or because you have nothing else to do *22*

wind down to gradually relax after doing something that has made you feel tired or worried *28*

wind down (sth) or wind (sth) down if a business or organisation winds down, or if someone winds it down, the amount of work it does is gradually reduced until it closes completely *49*

wind up to finally be in a particular place, state, or situation, especially without having planned it *55*

wind up doing sth to finally do something, especially without having planned to *55*

wind up sb or wind sb up *informal, British* to tell someone something that is not true in order to make a joke *54*

wipe off to remove writing from something by wiping it with a cloth *42*

work off sth or work sth off to get rid of an unpleasant feeling [e.g. aggression, anger] by doing something energetic *57*

work on sth to spend time working in order to produce or repair something *46*

work out to exercise in order to improve the strength or appearance of your body *57*

work out sth or work sth out to do a calculation to get an answer to a mathematical question *42*

work out sth or work sth out to understand something or to find the answer to something by thinking about it *69*

work through sth or work sth through to deal with a problem or difficulty by talking about it in detail *36*

work towards sth to try hard to achieve something *46*

wrap up (sb) or wrap (sb) up to dress in warm clothes, or to dress someone in warm clothes or cover them with material that protects them from the cold *32*

wrap up sth or wrap sth up to cover something in paper, cloth, or other material, especially in order to give it to someone as a present or in order to protect it *29*

wriggle out of sth *informal* to avoid doing something that other people think you should do, often in a dishonest way *46*

write off sth or write sth off to accept that an amount of money [e.g. debt, investment] has been lost or will never be paid *47*

write off sth or write sth off to damage a vehicle so badly that it cannot be repaired *63*

write-off *n* a vehicle that is too badly damaged to be repaired *63*

write out sth or write sth out to write information on a document [e.g. cheque, prescription] so that it can be used *44*

write up sth or write sth up to write something on paper or on a computer in a complete or final form, often using notes you have made *43*

zoom in if a camera zooms in, it starts to show a clear and detailed picture of something, as if the camera was moving closer to that thing *64*

zoom out if a camera zooms out, it starts to show someone or something in less detail, as if the camera was moving away from that person or thing *64*